FOREWORD

THIS BOOK is the first of several which will be devoted to basic federal income tax law. For some time it has appeared to me that, although there is no scarcity of writing devoted to the federal income tax, there has existed no reasonably current source where the topics usually presented in the standard law school income tax course were set forth in a manner which quickly would enable the reader to see and understand the legal, historical, and policy contexts within which the principal problems of the tax exist. This book attempts to supply this omission in the area of gross income. Subsequent volumes will be devoted to the other areas which make up what I have designated as basic federal income tax law.

In conceiving this project, law school students obviously were in the forefront of my mind. However, efforts have been made to make this volume also useful to practitioners, particularly those who, in the early stages of their research, need an introduction to the general outlines of the area to which their practice has brought them. Moreover, practitioners will find in the notes citations which can "activate" their quest for a comprehensive collection of all relevant authority.

The technique employed in the preparation of this volume is quite simple. The first step was to design a reasonably explicit policy framework, which is described in Chapter I. Next, the gross income structure was divided into two parts, the first designed to trace the configurations of "gross income" as initially defined by the Code, and the second to describe the more important modifications and qualifications imposed by specific statutory provisions. In each part considerable emphasis is given to the administrative, judicial, and legislative history of the particular problem being discussed. Finally, each major problem area has been measured against the first chapter's policy framework.

In this manner the main threads of the texture of rules, policy, and history are traced. As the reader follows the course of these threads, it is hoped he will become aware of the illuminating contrasts which make tax law irresistibly fascinating to many. More specifically, the book is designed to make it possible for the reader to experience not only the statics of today's tax law, but also the dynamics which make yesterday's into tomorrow's, to know both its constancy and evanescence, and to delight in its carefully calculated refinements as well as its improvisations.

I wish to thank the faculty and students of the Ohio State University College of Law who made it possible for me to present a slightly condensed version of Part I of this book as the 1966 Law Forum Lectures. To have received this invitation is an honor which I value very highly. Those who took special steps to make my visit to Columbus a memorable one, Dean Rutledge, Professors Bernstein and Raskind, as well as many others, have my enduring gratitude.

Finally, with an enthusiasm much greater than is usually suggested by concluding remarks such as these, I wish to thank the several secretaries and research assistants who have given indispensable aid in the preparation of this volume.

Joseph T. Sneed

Stanford, California
September 6, 1966

LAW FORUM SERIES

College of Law, Ohio State University

THE
CONFIGURATIONS
OF GROSS INCOME

THE CONFIGURATIONS
OF GROSS INCOME

JOSEPH T. SNEED

Ohio State University Press

Columbus, Ohio

1967

CONTENTS

Contents

THE
CONFIGURATIONS
OF   GROSS   INCOME

I. The Structure

THIS BOOK builds upon a paper which appeared in the *Stanford Law Review* [1] some time ago. In this paper there was a description of many, although by no means all, of the criteria by which we judge the federal income tax. These criteria were divided into two categories—macrocriteria and microcriteria. In the first were placed seven criteria designated in the Stanford paper as Adequacy, Practicality, Equity, Reduced Economic Inequality, Free Market Compatibility, Stability, and Political Order. All others were tossed together in a category of microcriteria. A brief description of the seven macrocriteria will provide the foundation for what I wish to do in this book.

Adequacy refers to the aggregate revenue impact of any particular feature of the federal income tax being examined. The criterion is badly served when the provision either diminishes the collection of, or permits the escape of, substantial amounts of revenue. Practicality obviously refers to the feasibility of a provision. Equity, to which frequent reference is made in this book, is given a quite specific content. It is built on the accretion theory of income, as expressed by Henry Simons, and it requires that those whose incomes are equal under this theory be taxed equally.

1. Sneed, *The Criteria of Federal Income Tax Policy*, 17 STAN. L. REV. 567 (1965).

Reduced Economic Inequality, the fourth of the macro-criteria, reveals its purpose on its face. A feature of the tax which narrows the economic gap between citizens serves this criterion; one which widens it does not. To avoid misunderstanding it should be pointed out that this criterion remains operative so long as universal economic equality does not exist. This does not mean that economic equality is a desirable state of affairs or that the full potential of the federal income tax should be used to achieve such equality. The point is merely that so long as equality does not exist, the criterion of Reduced Economic Inequality has a part to play. Its pointer, directed unwaveringly toward economic equality, can be ignored when other criteria require it, but no distribution of wealth short of perfect equality will cause it to turn aimlessly on its axis.

Free Market Compatibility, which perhaps more accurately could have been captioned "Optimum Resources Allocation," requires that the income tax be designed so as to disturb the workings of the market as little as possible. The criterion rests on the premise, which admittedly is subject to numerous qualifications and limitations, that the optimum allocation of resources is most closely approached through the operation of a free, competitive market. Such a market functions best with a broadly based income tax which counteracts the signals of the market place as infrequently as possible.

Stability, the sixth of the criteria, may be thought of as referring to what has come to be called in the popular press "the new economics." It focuses attention on the contribution, if any, which the aggregate tax structure, or any particular portion thereof, makes to the full utilization of resources in a manner which avoids inflation. De-

4

spite recent qualified successes in curbing the economic cycle, there is much we do not know about the relationships between aggregate income, consumption, savings, and investment upon which the theorems of compensatory finance rest. It is clear, however, that the criterion tells us more about rates and the breadth of the income tax base than about detailed structural problems. As to the solution of these, the criterion contributes little except to suggest repeatedly that the base of the tax not be eroded.

Finally, the Stanford paper set forth Political Order as the seventh criterion. As was done in that paper, it must now be acknowledged that this criterion has no unity. Rather, it provides the caption under which are brought together all those considerations, both universal and parochial, which relate to the political structure within which we live. Because tax law is an indigenous part of the political structure, it is necessary that its consistency with other features of that order be considered even though the undertaking is more intuitive than mathematical.

A partial listing of the many microcriteria, an ordering of the macrocriteria, and a demonstration of the operation of the type of analysis which these criteria facilitate occupied the balance of the Stanford paper. The purpose of this book is to trace the configurations of gross income under the federal income tax and, in doing so, to demonstrate the contribution the criteria analysis of that paper makes to understanding of this part of tax law.

In Part I, the analytical focal point is section 61 of the present Internal Revenue Code. However, concern with the constitutional problems, which ever since *Pollock* v. *Farmers' Loan & Trust Co.*[2] have pervaded this area, will be deferred. The first task, accordingly, will be to trace the

2. 157 U.S. 429 (1895).

sometimes obscure boundary of gross income as encompassed by section 61 and relate such cartography to the criteria just mentioned. Only then will the constitutional problems be examined. This order may appear inverted, but its appropriateness will become clear in due course.

It is obvious that, since the criterion of Equity is founded on a definition of personal income, the immediate task of establishing the frontier of gross income should be guided by the dictates of that criterion. Hence, the adumbration of the reach of section 61 and closely supporting sections will be divided into two main headings which roughly correspond to the two parts of the equation employed by Simons to define personal income. That definition is as follows:

Personal income may be defined as the algebraic sum of (1) the market value of rights exercised in consumption and (2) the change in the value of the store of property rights between the beginning and end of the period in question.[3]

The second part of this definition will be dealt with first under the heading of *Gain in the Form of an Increase in the Value of Property Rights*. Following this is the discussion of "the market value of rights exercised in consumption," the first half of Simons' equation, captioned *Gain in the Form of Consumption*. It should be noted that these headings underscore what Simons, a few lines below his definition of personal income, acknowledged was the *sine qua non* of income, viz., gain.[4] Under this definition income, speaking loosely, consists of consumption plus accumulations.

Following the discussion under these two headings

3. SIMONS, PERSONAL INCOME TAXATION 50 (1938).
4. *Ibid.*

comes an exploration of a somewhat obscure area which I have designated as *Gains from Status*. These increments to wealth, as we shall see, may consist of either or both types of gain described in the first two headings. Then appears a discussion of constitutional problems.

Part II consists of a discussion of some statutory modifications and refinements of the structure of gross income. Not only does this part round out the picture of gross income, it also provides the opportunity to point out that many of the problems and solutions encountered in surveying the structure of gross income reappear when specific qualifying sections are examined. This examination focuses on the exclusion from gross income of gifts, bequests, and inheritances; [5] the treatment of receipts paid under insurance, annuity, or endowment contracts; [6] the circumstances under which alimony is brought within the gross income of the recipient; [7] the scope of the exclusion of compensation for injuries and sickness (including amounts received from accident and health insurance plans) ; [8] the manner in which certain "fringe benefits" are handled; [9] the exclusion of interest on certain governmental obligations; [10] and the treatment of discharge from indebtedness.[11]

5. Int. Rev. Code of 1954, § 102. There also will be discussed under this heading the problems of scholarships and prizes as generated by §§ 117 and 74 of the Code.

6. Int. Rev. Code of 1954, §§ 72 and 101.

7. Int. Rev. Code of 1954, § 71.

8. Int. Rev. Code of 1954, §§ 104, 105, 106, and 107.

9. These include group term insurance, Int. Rev. Code of 1954, § 79; meals and lodging, Int. Rev. Code of 1954, § 119.

10. Int. Rev. Code of 1954, § 103.

11. Int. Rev. Code of 1954, § 108.

PART ONE
A SKETCH OF GROSS INCOME

A. Gain in the Form of an Increase
in the Value of Property Rights

II. Gain or Return of Capital

AS POINTED OUT, the latter part of Simons' definition of income is concerned with the *net* change in the "store of property rights." Thus, within it is an explicit allowance for losses; it is "merely an arithmetic answer and exists only as the end result of appropriate calculations." [1] On the other hand, section 61 of the Code must address itself to the starting point of these calculations rather than their end result. It must be concerned, for the most part, with those values preceded by the plus (+) sign and leave for other Code provisions, such as those relating to deductions and losses, the introduction of many which bear a negative (−) sign. To put the matter differently, an attempt to use Simons' definition of personal income as a definition of gross income would amount to compressing a structure more appropriately spread over a number of different sections into one highly compact section in which gross income and taxable income were synonymous.

Once having recognized this, it is tempting to embrace the view that receipts, undiminished by any allowance of whatever sort, should constitute the meaning of the gross income. Such a view was once advanced by the government but rejected by the Supreme Court in *Doyle* v.

---

1. SIMONS, PERSONAL INCOME TAXATION 51 (1938).

Mitchell Bros. Co.[2] In a common-sense fashion, the Court observed:

In order to determine whether there has been gain or loss, and the amount of the gain, if any, we must withdraw from the gross proceeds an amount sufficient to restore the capital value that existed at the commencement of the period under consideration.[3]

The key idea of gross income then is *gain,* an idea which fixes the scope of gross income somewhere between taxable income, on the one hand, and gross receipts, on the other.[4]

2. 247 U.S. 179 (1918). The Court stated the Government's argument as follows: "Starting from this point [that the entire proceeds from conversion of a capital asset could not be omitted from income in all cases], the learned Solicitor General has submitted an elaborate argument in behalf of the Government, based in part upon theoretical definitions of 'capital,' 'income,' 'profits,' etc., and in part upon expressions quoted from our opinions in Flint v. Stone Tracy Co., 220 U.S. 107, 147 (1910), and Anderson v. Forty-two Broadway Co., 239 U.S. 69, 72 (1915), with the object of showing that a conversion of capital into money always produces income, and that for the purposes of the present case the words 'gross income' are equivalent to 'gross receipts'; the insistence being that the entire proceeds of a conversion of capital assets should be treated as gross income, and that by deducting the mere cost of such assets we arrive at net income." *Id.* at 183–84.

3. *Id.* at 185.

4. Thus, in a merchandising, manufacturing, or mining business, gross income includes only total sales less cost of goods sold. See Treas. Reg. § 1.61–3 (a) (1957). Although Equity plainly requires such a deduction at some point in arriving at taxable income, puzzling issues remain.

What items, for example, properly constitute additions to cost of goods sold? See Rev. Rul. 141, 153–2 C.B. 101, which permits, but does not require, the inclusion of amounts for depreciation or depletion based on cost in computing cost of goods sold. The ruling appears to suggest that ordinary cost accounting principles supply the guidelines. On whether feed and labor expenses of a farmer are proper subtractions from gross receipts to arrive at gross income, see Woodside Acres, Inc. v. Comm'r, 134 F.2d 793 (2d Cir. 1943); McCulley v. Kelm, 112 F. Supp. 832 (D. Minn. 1953); Washington Farms, Inc. v. United States, 116 F. Supp. 142 (M.D. Ga. 1953).

To what extent is it within the power of Congress to define gross income in a manner which, in whole or in part, eliminates the subtraction of cost of goods sold from total sales? See Pedone v. United States, 151 F. Supp. 288 (Ct. Cl. 1957); Comm'r v. Weisman, 197 F.2d 221 (1st Cir. 1952); Lela Sullenger, 11 T.C. 1076 (1948) and the discussion pp. 122–26 *infra.* (*Continued on next page.*)

The Configurations of Gross Income

Whatever doubts may have existed about the importance of the notion of gain were put to rest by the Court in its more recent decision in *Commissioner* v. *Glenshaw Glass Co.*[5] where, in holding that the receipt of exemplary or punitive damages must be reported as gross income, it repeatedly employed the term "gain" in describing the scope of gross income.[6] Thus, it is now certain that gross income, as used by the present Revenue Code, must be approached initially from the standpoint of "clearly realized" gain.

Often, it is assumed that the determination of the exist-

Is the meaning of "gross income" for purposes of § 61 of the 1954 Code to control the meaning of that term when used elsewhere in the Code? See Woodside Acres, Inc. v. Comm'r, 134 F.2d 793 (2d Cir. 1943) (meaning of gross income when used to determine whether a corporation is a personal holding company) ; Uptegrove Lumber Co. v. Comm'r, 204 F.2d 570 (3d Cir. 1953) (meaning of gross income when used to determine the existence of an obligation to file an income tax return). Observe how Int. Rev. Code of 1954, § 542, as amended in 1964, employs the term "adjusted ordinary gross income" in lieu of "gross income" in the present definition of a personal holding company. For a short discussion linking the cases cited in the last two paragraphs with the constitutional issue of the gross income–gross receipts problem, see SURREY & WARREN, FEDERAL INCOME TAXATION 402–4 (1960 ed.) .

5. 348 U.S. 426 (1955) .

6. These relevant passages demonstrate the point. "But Congress applied no limitations as to the source of taxable receipts, nor restrictive labels as to their nature. And the Court has given a liberal construction to this broad phraseology in recognition of the intention of Congress to tax all gains except those specifically exempted. [Citations omitted.] Thus, the fortuitous gain accruing to a lessor by reason of the forfeiture of a lessee's improvements on the rented property was taxed in Helvering v. Bruun, 306 U.S. 461 (1938) [Citations omitted.] Such decisions demonstrate that we cannot but ascribe content to the catchall provision of 22 (a), 'gains or profits and income derived from any source whatever. . . .'

"Here we have instances of undeniable accessions to wealth, clearly realized, and over which the taxpayers have complete dominion." *Id.* at 429, 430, 431. Observe also that in General American Investors Co. v. Comm'r. 348 U.S. 434 (1955) , decided the same day as *Glenshaw,* the Court spoke of gross income as embracing "all gain constitutionally taxable."

For a discussion of the constitutional implications of *Glenshaw Glass Co.,* see Wright, *The Effect of the Source of Realized Receipts upon the Supreme Court's Concept of Taxable Receipts,* 8 STAN. L. REV. 164, 202 (1956) . See pp. 120–21 *infra.*

ence of gain is a simple matter and, at least sometimes, it is. Thus, when the taxpayer receives compensation for personal services in the form of cash or property there is gain to the extent of the cash or the fair market value of the property.[7]

Nonetheless, more frequently than realized, the undertaking is not a simple one. One source of difficulty is the requirement that invested capital be returned before gain may exist. Another is the necessity in many instances to allocate receipts between a return of capital and gain. What follows in this chapter is an examination of the return of capital requirement and the problems arising from this need to apportion receipts.

1. Return of Capital

a. Fundamental Requisites of a Return of Capital

A simple, yet revealing, example of a receipt not considered as gain because it is the return of capital previously invested is repayment by a borrower of the principal of a loan made by a lender-taxpayer. This example illustrates the following three fundamental requisites of a return of

---

7. United States v. Frazell, 335 F.2d 487 (5th Cir. 1964), *cert. denied*, 380 U.S. 961 (1965) (stock partially compensation for services rendered); Mason v. Comm'r, 125 F.2d 540 (6th Cir. 1942) (compensation income equal to fair market value of stock employee required to purchase by contract with cash bonus); Allen v. Comm'r, 107 F.2d 151 (4th Cir. 1939) (attorney's fee paid in stock income to extent of fair market value of stock); Walls v. Comm'r, 60 F.2d 347 (10th Cir. 1932) (interest in the net profits of the operation of a mineral lease taken as legal fee income to extent of fair market value); Lewis Eng'r, Inc., 39 T.C. 482 (1962) (interest in oil and gas lease income to extent of fair market value). Treas. Reg. § 1.61–2 (d)(1) (1957). Often, the issue is whether there is compensation in the form of property or a bargain purchase. Knowles, 24 T.C. Memo. 1965–27, *aff'd* 66–1 USTC ¶ 9245 (3d Cir. 1966). See pp. 101–2 *infra*. The valuation of property received as compensation when the property is subject to restrictions presents problems. See pp. 51–55 *infra*.

capital. First, to constitute a return of capital, there must have been a capital investment by the taxpayer; second, such capital investment must in fact be *returned* in the course of the transaction which yields the receipt; and, finally, the capital investment must not have been returned previously. Put in accounting terms, a receipt which, in whole or in part, constitutes a return of capital must involve both a credit to an existing asset account which had previously a debit balance and a debit to a different such account.

(*1*) *Necessity of Investment*

The first of the three requisites, the necessity of an investment, is not only demonstrated by much of the fundamental structure of the Code,[8] but also by a fairly large group of cases relating to the tax treatment of recoveries of damages for various sorts of business injuries.[9] In an early case involving a recovery by the taxpayer of damages for permanent injury to "its reputation, standing, growth, and prosperity," [10] the court regarded the entire amount recovered as a return of capital. This was done although there was no showing that the taxpayer's good will was an asset into which an identifiable and specific investment by the taxpayer could be traced. In short, the entire recovery was treated as a return of capital even though the tax-

8. Section 1001 defines gain from the sale or other disposition of property as "the excess of the amount realized therefrom over the adjusted basis." The return to the extent of adjusted basis is a return of capital. Section 1012 defines "basis," and § 1011 in turn defines "adjusted basis" as basis "adjusted as provided in section 1016." The latter section deals with adjustments for depreciation, capital improvements, etc.

9. See Note, *Income Taxation and Treble Damage Awards*, 48 Nw. U.L. Rev. 85 (1953). See also Costigar, *Income Taxes on Recoveries from Civil Litigation*, U. So. Cal. 1954 Tax Inst. 559.

10. Farmers' & Merchants' Bank v. Comm'r, 59 F.2d 912 (6th Cir. 1932).

payer did not establish a basis, or investment, in good will equal to the recovery. This view did not long endure. The proper approach was clearly marked out something over a decade later in *Raytheon Production Corp.* v. *Commissioner,*[11] where damages recovered in an antitrust action, although treated as a recovery for destruction of good will, were considered as income to the extent the recovery exceeded the "cost" of the good will.[12] At present the rules are clear. To constitute a non-taxable return of capital, the damages recovered must not be a substitute for lost profits, but must be for injury to tangible or intangible assets and not in excess of the taxpayer's adjusted basis therein.[13] Any excess is taxable gain.[14]

11. 144 F.2d 110 (1st Cir. 1944). There were earlier indications that the approach of Farmers' & Merchants' Bank v. Comm'r, n. 10 *supra* was erroneous. Thus, in H. Liebes & Co. v. Comm'r, 90 F.2d 932 (9th Cir. 1937) the court refused to consider *Farmers' & Merchants' Bank* as controlling because it did not appear in the opinion "whether or not evidence was received to overcome the presumption of correctness accompanying the Commissioner's determination." Such a presumption was relied upon in *H. Liebes & Co.* and the recovery of damages was treated as a recovery of profits and hence fully taxable. Cases of about the same vintage demonstrated a marked willingness to regard recoveries as a return of lost profits rather than capital. *E.g.,* Swastika Oil & Gas Co. v. Comm'r, 123 F.2d 382 (6th Cir. 1941); Martin Bros. Box Co. v. Comm'r, 142 F.2d 457 (6th Cir. 1944), *aff'g without opinion* 1 T.C.M. 999. *But see* Highland Farms Corp., 42 B.T.A. 1314 (1940), where a portion of a damage recovery was treated as a return of capital, the Board determining the extent of the loss of capital on the basis of the decline in the value of properties rather than the extent to which taxpayer's investment in such properties was destroyed.

12. See Harnett, *Torts & Taxes,* 27 N.Y.U.L. REV. 614, 632–34 (1952), for a discussion of the general subject of taxation of tort recoveries and the treatment of the specific problem of good will as a "troublesome factor" in the "return of capital" cases.

13. See Sager Glove Corp. v. Comm'r, 311 F.2d 210 (7th Cir. 1963); M. G. Carter Est. v. Comm'r, 298 F.2d 192 (8th Cir. 1962); Phoenix Coal Co. v. Comm'r, 231 F.2d 420 (2d Cir. 1956); Durkee v. Comm'r, 162 F.2d 184 (6th Cir. 1947); Ralph Freeman, 33 T.C. 323 (1959); Telefilm, Inc., 21 T.C. 688 (1954); Iona Thomson, T.C. Memo. 1965–237; Aluminum & Metal Service, Inc., T.C. Memo, 1965–129, *aff'd,* 66–1 USTC ¶ 9323 (7th Cir. 1966); Levy Collins, Sr., 18 T.C.M. 756 (1959); Michael Berbiglia, 10 T.C.M. 413 (1951). The Sixth Circuit quietly put aside the error of *Farmers' & Merchants' Bank* in *Durkee.*

14. Such gain may be capital, however. Big Four Indus., 40 T.C. 1055

The necessary investment of capital can be made in a number of ways. The paradigm, of course, is the acquisition by purchase with cash of a particular asset. However, an investment may be made by means other than the payment of cash. A promise to pay in the future, for example, when given in exchange for an asset constitutes an investment therein.[15] These two modes of investment coexist in the case of an ordinary loan—the lender invests the amount of the loan in the promise to repay of the borrower, while the latter invests the amount which he promises to repay in the loan proceeds.[16] As a consequence, neither the receipt of the loan proceeds nor their repayment constitutes income to the borrower or lender respectively.

These consequences flow even though the loan may not be based on an agreement explicit in all details.[17] A lawyer, for example, may incur expenses on behalf of his clients which are not deductible business expenses of his

---

(1963) (A). A possible alternative to the treatment of the excess as gain would be to reduce the basis of other assets of the taxpayer to the extent of such excess. This would defer gain until the disposition of the assets. The recovery under this approach would be treated as entirely a return of capital invested in those assets whose basis is reduced. The Tax Court appears to have rejected this method of deferment. Telefilm, Inc., n. 13 *supra*, at 695.

15. Crane v. Comm'r, 331 U.S. 1 (1947).

16. The receipt of the loan proceeds is not income because the value of the receipt is offset by this investment. A somewhat different formulation of the same idea is that the receipt of the loan proceeds is a return of capital, the investment of which occurs when the borrower promises to repay. See SURREY & WARREN, *op. cit.* n. 4 *supra*, at 132. For an interesting case where amounts distributed by a trust were considered as loan proceeds and hence not income, see Estate of Katharine P. Loring, 3 T.C.M. 705 (1944).

17. Margolis v. Comm'r, 339 F.2d 537 (9th Cir. 1964) (reimbursement of certain advances on behalf of trusts not taxable); Ingalls v. Patterson, 158 F. Supp. 627 (N.D. Ala. 1958) (reimbursement of expenses incurred by shareholder which were primary obligation of reimbursing corporation not taxable).

and which when reimbursed will not constitute gross income to him.[18] Or a lessor may incur expenses which are properly attributable to the interest of the lessee which are not includable in gross income when reimbursement by the lessee is received by the lessor.[19] To constitute a return of capital it must be established, however, that the obligation discharged by the taxpayer who has received reimbursement was not his own. When the obligation was that of the taxpayer, the reimbursement represents gain, not a return of capital.[20]

18. Henry F. Cochrane, 23 B.T.A. 202 (1931); Max E. Cohen, T.C. Memo, 1965–136 (dictum).

19. Langdon-Warren Mines v. Reynolds, 52 F. Supp. 512 (D.Minn. 1943); Estate of William F. Markham, 2 T.C.M. 244 (1943).

20. Old Colony Trust Co. v. Comm'r, 279 U.S. 716 (1928); United States v. Boston & Me. R.R., 279 U.S. 732 (1928); Schalk Chem. Co. v. Comm'r, 304 F.2d 48 (9th Cir. 1962); Rev. Rul. 66–41, 1966–8 INT. REV. BULL. 52 (reimbursement of employment agency fee previously paid by taxpayer employee includable in income).
Similarly, gain results when personal expenditures of a taxpayer, such as his living expenses, are reimbursed by another. England v. United States, 345 F.2d 414 (7th Cir. 1965), *cert. denied*, 382 U.S. 986 (incidental moving expenses in connection with job transfer). Willis B. Ferebee, 39 T.C. 801 (1963); Harris W. Bradley, 39 T.C. 652 (1963); Arthur J. Kobacker, 37 T.C. 882 (1962).
A reimbursement of personal expenditures, however, may constitute a return of capital and not gain under some circumstances. One common situation is where the taxpayer, after expending a sum to acquire assets to be used for personal purposes, rescinds the transaction and obtains a refund of the sum previously expended. The original expenditure constitutes the investment of capital, and its return is not subject to tax. Another is where by negotiation with the payee, either before or after the personal expenditure by the taxpayer, an adjustment or rebate of the price previously paid in cash is obtained. *E.g.*, life insurance dividends are not taxable because they represent a return of a portion of the premium. Special Ruling, December 13, 1940, 41–3 CCH Federal Tax Service, ¶ 6124. This must be distinguished from "increments in value" due to advance premiums which may constitute income, Rev. Rul. 65–199, I.R.B. 1965–33, 7.
The return of capital analysis is also proper where the reimbursement of the personal expenditure is by one whose wrongful conduct was the cause of the expenditure. This is clearly demonstrated in Edward H. Clark, 40 B.T.A. 333 (1939), where a recovery by a taxpayer for excess taxes paid because of the faulty advice by tax counsel was considered "compensation for a loss which impaired petitioners capital." *Id.* at 335.

A third means by which an investment can be made is by inclusion of the value of an item in the gross income of the taxpayer. Thus, to acquire a basis in an item, such as a right to fees for personal services,[21] it is necessary that its value be included in income.[22] An inclusion creates a basis to the extent of the value of the right even though no tax becomes payable as a result.[23] The inclusion in income may be regarded as either the equivalent of a receipt of cash in exchange for goods or services and a reinvestment of the cash in the item received, or as an investment, in the form of incurring a "tax cost," actual or potential, to the extent of the inclusion. Either view of the matter can justify the existence of an investment—and hence, basis—to the extent that an item has been included in gross income.

A fourth method by which an investment may be acquired is by legislative grace. In some instances the Code decrees the existence of an investment for one purpose or another even though such in fact does not exist. This type of investment can be described as "constructive investment." An example is percentage depletion in the case of oil and gas production.[24] By continuing percentage depletion after the entire investment has been recovered (that

21. See Mary O'Hara Alsop, 34 T.C. 606, 609–10 (1960), *aff'd*, 290 F.2d 726 (2d Cir. 1961).

22. Palmer Hutcheson, 14 T.C. 14 (1960); John L. Seymour, 14 T.C. 1111 (1950); Charles A. Collin, 1 B.T.A. 305 (1925).

23. Comm'r v. Oxford Paper Co., 194 F.2d 190 (2d Cir. 1952) (by implication); Maurice P. O'Meara, 8 T.C. 622 (1947) (A).

24. Int. Rev. Code of 1954, § 613 (a) and (b) (1). Some of the most illuminating articles on the depletion allowance are: *Symposium*, 33 TEXAS L. REV. 307 (1957); Bruen, *Federal Income Tax Aspects of Oil and Gas Ventures: A Summary for the Investor*, 14 TAX L. REV. 353, 505 (1959); Ray, *Forms of Oil Development Financing*, 14 TUL. L. REV. 395 (1955). An interesting correspondence on the subject can be read in Baker & Griswold, *Percentage Depletion: A Correspondence*, 64 HARV. L. REV. 361 (1951).

is, after the adjusted basis is zero), Congress may be considered to have granted to the taxpayer an additional basis, despite the absence of any new investment, to the extent of such post-zero–basis depletion allowances. Another and much less venerable example of constructive investment exists when the taxpayer obtains a tax credit equal to 7 per cent of his investment in certain types of property.[25] Notwithstanding the Government's contribution to the purchase price, the taxpayer is regarded as having made an unassisted investment. That is, his basis in the credit-generating asset is not diminished by the amount of the credit.

The justification for these examples must be found, if possible, in criteria other than Equity. No macrocriteria gives unqualified support to either, although those of Stability and Practicality can be marshaled in defense of the Code's failure to require a reduction of basis by the amount of the investment credit. That is, aggregate demand may be somewhat increased by the credit undiminished by a basis adjustment, and the elimination of the reduction promotes a simpler technical structure. It is likely, however, that economic growth (a microcriterion under the Stanford paper's analysis) provides the chief support. Percentage depletion's boon must rest, and very uneasily at that, on a mixed bag of criteria, such as national defense, support of the automotive segment of the economy, regional development, political expediency, etc.

A final example of constructive investment exists under the Code provisions which provide that the basis of property acquired from a decedent shall be the fair market

25. Int. Rev. Code of 1954, §§ 38, 46, and 48. Prior to the Revenue Act of 1964, the basis of property which yielded the 7 per cent credit was required to be reduced by the amount of the credit. The 1964 Act eliminated the necessity for this adjustment.

value of the property at the decedent's death.[26] Second to the differential treatment of capital gain, perhaps no other single Code provision exerts a more powerful influence on the Code's technical structure and the behavior of taxpayers than this one. Such a rule does not harmonize with Adequacy, Equity, or Reduced Economic Inequality. Only Practicality can be marshaled convincingly in its support, for few will deny that its operation is more simple than would be any feasible alternative.[27] Contravention of Adequacy is manifested by the significant amounts of gain which escape tax at death and the eternal vigilance which must be practiced by the Government to prevent deferment of realization of gain until death.[28]

26. Int. Rev. Code of 1954, § 1014.

27. In the President's 1963 Tax Message it was proposed to make the investment by those who take from a decedent "real" rather than "constructive" by imposing a tax on the spread between the fair market value of the property at death and its adjusted basis in the hands of the decedent. The provision was subject to several complicating exceptions, however. *President's 1963 Tax Message, Hearings before the House Committee on Ways and Means,* 88th Cong., 1st Sess., pt. 1, 128–37 (1963). Similar exceptions existed under a proposal considered by the House Ways and Means Committee which would have continued in the hands of one who acquired the property from a decedent the adjusted basis of the property in the hands of the decedent.

28. Note that except in the instance of a constructive investment, the investment need not have been made by the taxpayer. Under the Code it is possible for the investment made by another person or entity to be considered as the taxpayer's basis in the property for the purpose of determining the extent to which a receipt constitutes gain or loss. A donee, for example, generally is considered to acquire a basis in the donated property which is the same as that of the donor. Int. Rev. Code of 1954, § 1015; Taft v. Bowers, 478 U.S. 470 (1929). But for the purpose of determining *loss* on a disposition by the donee, his basis will be the fair market value of the gift property at the time of the gift where such value was less than the basis of the property in the hands of the donor at that time. This means that a disposition by a donee for a consideration different from either the donor's basis or the fair market value at the time of the gift can result in neither gain nor loss.

A corporation or partnership also acquires the basis which the transferor shareholder or partner had in property contributed by them to the capital. Int. Rev. Code of 1954, §§ 362 (basis to corporations), 723 (basis to partnerships). Similarly, the basis of assets contributed by a grantor to a trust in the hands of the trustee is the same as the grantor's when the

(2) *The Necessity of a Return: A Problem of Characterization*

As said before, characterization of a receipt as a return of capital requires not only an investment either actual or constructive but also a *return* thereof.

Often, it is necessary to analyze closely a transaction to discover whether a receipt involved any return of capital at all. There are many transactions which, when viewed in their entirety, do not involve any return or transformation of capital, although an investment has been made in a related transaction. A fairly common illustration is when liquidated damages are received by a vendor upon the failure of the vendee to perform an executory contract to buy real estate. Often, such a contract provides for the initial, or other, payments by the vendee to be retained by the vendor as liquidated damages in the event of default by the vendee.[29] Such damages constitute income, and no

---

transfer is by means of gift. The exception in respect to the determination of losses referred to in the last paragraph is also applicable. Int. Rev. Code of 1954, § 1015 (a). As to transfers in trust by bequest or devise and transfers other than by gift, bequest, or devise, see §§ 1014, 1015 (b).

It is also possible that an investment by the taxpayer in one particular piece of property will be treated as his investment in another. For example, if the taxpayer exchanges property held for productive use in a trade or business solely for property of a like kind, the exchange does not result in recognized gain or loss and the basis of the property acquired becomes that of the property exchanged. Int. Rev. Code of 1954, § 1031. Basis acquired and determined in this manner is designated as "substituted basis" by the Code, § 1016. This use of the adjusted basis of the property exchanged as the basis of the property acquired preserves, or "freezes in," the gain or loss in respect to the exchanged property which was not recognized upon the exchange by reason of the specific provisions of the Code. Where the taxpayer receives, in addition to the property of a like kind, cash or property of an unlike kind, the adjustments are somewhat more complicated. See § 1031(d). For a thorough discussion of the predecessor of § 1031, its history and uncertainties of statutory interpretation, see Molloy, *Tax Free Exchanges of Property of Like Kind under Section 112 (b) (1) of the Internal Revenue Code,* 37 VA. L. REV. 555 (1957).

29. See Doyle v. Comm'r, 110 F.2d 157 (2d Cir. 1940) ; Ralph A.

portion is properly attributable to a return of capital.[30] An amount paid to obtain an option to purchase, which sum is to be applied to the purchase price in the event the option is exercised, also is not treated as a return of capital when the option is not exercised.[31]

An even more common situation exists in connection with corporate distributions in redemption of stock. If the distribution is "essentially equivalent to a dividend," [32] it is taxed accordingly [33] and does not constitute a return of capital. On the other hand, a redemption may be treated "as a distribution in part or full payment in exchange for the stock" [34] in which case it does constitute, to the extent of the shareholder's adjusted basis in the stock, a return of capital.[35] The task of distinguishing the redemption which involves a return from a dividend which does not is by no

Boatman, 32 T.C. 1188 (1959); Emily B. Harrison, 7 T.C. 1 (1946); A. M. Johnson, 32 B.T.A. 156 (1935). *Cf.* Briar Homes Corp. v. United States, 245 F. Supp. 646 (D.Md. 1965) (rents received by purchaser between date of contract and closing day held income and not a reduction of cost).

30. The payments constitute income in the year of the forfeiture. Ralph A. Boatman, n. 29 *supra;* Emily B. Harrison, n. 29 *supra.*

31. Virginia Iron Coal & Coke Co. v. Comm'r, 99 F.2d 919 (4th Cir. 1938). Also, it appears the year of taxation may be the year in which the option lapses when the option is not part of a "lease and option to purchase" transaction under which the lessee has both the option as well as the possession and use of the property during the option period. See Hitchin v. Comm'r., 353 F.2d 13 (4th Cir. 1965). A good discussion of this and related areas appears in Voegelin, *Use of Options in Tax Planning,* So. CAL. 1965 TAX INST. 729.

32. Int. Rev. Code of 1954, § 302 (b)(1). See Brodsky and Pincus, *Case of the Reappearing Basis,* 34 TAXES 675 (1956), for a good practical discussion of §§ 302 and 306.

33. That is, the distribution is governed by Int. Rev. Code of 1954, § 301 and is ordinary income to the extent of either current or accumulated (since February 28, 1913) earnings and profits. The statement in the text assumes earnings and profits exceed the distribution.

34. See Int. Rev. Code of 1954, § 302 (a).

35. Where the distribution is essentially equivalent to a dividend, the regulations permit a "proper adjustment" of the basis of the remaining stock. Treas. Reg. § 1.302–2 (c) (1954).

means easy.[36] However, the analytical difference for our purposes is clear. Other examples of the difficulty in determining whether the receipt constitutes a return of previously invested capital could be marshaled;[37] however, these are sufficient to justify turning to the requirement that there has been no *previous* return of the same capital.

(3) *The Requirement of No Previous Return: The "Tax Benefit" Problem*

This third and final requirement appears at first to be no more than an injunction against double counting. It is a truism to assert that capital which has been returned

36. See BITTKER, FEDERAL INCOME TAXATION OF CORPORATIONS AND SHAREHOLDERS 223–34 (1959).

37. For example, do payments made under what purports to be a lease with an option to purchase constitute rent or portions of the purchase price? If the payments represent rent, there is no return of capital embodied in their receipt, and thus they are fully taxable as ordinary income. *E.g.,* Earl L. Lester, 32 T.C. 711 (1959) (payments ordinary income until option is exercised); Estate of Mary G. Gordon, 17 T.C. 427 (1951) (payment prior to exercise of option ordinary income), *aff'd*, 201 F.2d 171 (6th Cir. 1952); Rev. Rul. 57–261, 1957–1 C.B. 262. But if the payments are portions of the purchase price, there is to a certain extent a conversion of the investment in the property into cash and hence a different tax treatment. *E.g.,* Truman Bowen, 12 T.C. 446 (1949) (payments treated as a return of capital because transaction considered a sale from the outset); Lemon v. United States, 115 F. Supp. 573 (W.D. Va. 1953) (all payments made in one year and treated as proceeds of sale of property); Kohinoor Coal Co., 15 T.M.C. 403 (1956) (payments treated as a reduction of basis of property sold even though purchaser defaulted after substantial payments made).

To illustrate the rule that capital must be returned, it is enough here to point out the difference between rent and sales proceeds. A detailed outline of the not altogether satisfactory tests used by the Commissioner and the courts to distinguish the two is unnecessary, and only a few references will be offered: See Rev. Rul. 55–540, 1955–2 C.B. 39; Rev. Rul. 55–541, 1955–2 C.B. 19; Rev. Rul. 60–122, 1960–1 C.B. 56, which sets forth the position of the Commissioner. For the approach of the courts, in addition to the cases cited *supra*, see Haggard v. Comm'r, 241 F.2d 288 (9th Cir. 1957); Breece Veneer and Panel Co. v. Comm'r, 232 F.2d 319 (7th Cir. 1956); Chicago Stoker Corp., 14 T.C. 441 (1950); Judson Mills, 11 T.C. 25 (1948) (A). The classification adopted affects, of course, both the recipient and payor of the funds. Not only is it possible to treat the entire sum involved as either rent or purchase price payments, allocation between rent and payments for an option also may be justified. *Cf.* Kitchen v. Commissioner, n. 31 *supra*.

once cannot be considered as being returned again in the absence of a reinvestment. The difficulty arises, however, because it is not always clear that capital has been returned previously. For example, there may be confusion over whether a prior receipt was properly allocated to a return of capital. If so allocated, then the present receipt may not be properly classified as such a return; but, if not, then treatment as a return of capital may be possible.

More puzzling difficulties than this exist, however. For example, has an investment (such as made by a creditor in extending a loan) been "returned" by means of a deduction (bad debt, for example) which, because of the presence of other deductions which exceed income,[38] yields no tax benefit to the taxpayer. If so, a subsequent repayment by the debtor is taxable income and not a return of capital. A single investment may be recovered only once.[39]

In 1940 the Commissioner ruled that, without regard to whether the deduction resulted in a "tax benefit," a bad debt deduction was the equivalent of an expense of doing business, and any subsequent recovery of the amount so deducted was not to be treated as a return of capital.[40] The

38. Dobson v. Comm'r, 320 U.S. 489 (1943), contains a summary of the Tax Court's position on the "tax benefit" doctrine in respect to bad debts which existed prior to the enactment in 1942 of what is now § 111 of the 1954 Code. See Plumb, *The Tax Benefit Rule Today*, 57 HARV. L. REV. 129 (1943), an exhaustive exposition of the pre-Dobson atmosphere regarding treatment of bad debt recoveries, recovery of taxes and "delinquency amounts," reimbursements, rebate, and cancellation of expenses and interests, recoupment of losses, depreciation, amortization and depletion, bond discount, bond premium. A second article by this author, *The Tax Benefit Rule Tomorrow*, discusses the impact of *Dobson* from the position that it " . . . has created a difficult and undesirable, if not impossible situation with respect to the formula for determining tax benefit." 57 HARV. L. REV. 675 at 685. Also see Tye, *The Tax Benefit Doctrine Re-Examined*, 3 TAX L. REV. 329 (1948).

39. Burnet v. Sanford & Brooks Co., 282 U.S. 359 (1930).

40. G.C.M. 22163, 1940–2 C.B. 76. The ruling also explicitly states that an expense incurred in carrying on a trade or business is not a capital investment. This is the position, of course, of Burnet v. Sanford & Brooks Co., n. 39 *supra*.

effect of this was to treat a bad debt deduction resulting in no tax benefit as a return of capital. Practicality strongly supports this result [41] and Reduced Economic Inequality somewhat less so. Equity, however, provides no inflexible guide. Thus, inclusion in the year of recovery can result in a tax burden greater in amount than any tax reduction which might have been possible in the earlier year. On the other hand, exclusion in the year of recovery can save more taxes than would have a tax-reducing deduction in the year in which the deduction was actually taken. In any event, Congress in 1942 enacted legislation which permits exclusion of recovery on a bad debt where no tax benefit resulted from the deduction.[42] Such a deduction is not a

41. Treating each year as a unit and minimizing the impact on the present year of events of previous years tends to simplify administration and compliance. The tax law has never been able to adhere inflexibly to the "annual accounting" concept.

42. Int. Rev. Code of 1954, § 111 now contains this legislation. This exclusion also covers recoveries of "prior tax (es) ," of "delinquent amounts," § 111a, and of "all other losses, expenditures, and accruals made the basis of deductions from gross income for prior taxable years." Treas. Reg. § 1.111–1 (a) (1956) . The breadth of the regulations appears to reflect the Supreme Court's willingness, revealed in Dobson v. Comm'r, n. 38 *supra,* to tolerate the existence of a tax benefit doctrine without benefit of explicit statutory authority. *But see* Smith v. United States, 248 F. Supp. 873 (D.Md. 1965) (limiting § 111 to instances where loss and recovery are parts of same transaction) . Compare Ridge Realization Corp., 45 T.C. 508 (1966) (§ 111 available to taxpayer corporation even though deduction taken by predecessor corporation from which taxpayer acquired claim in a reorganization) . In addition, there may exist a general "tax benefit" doctrine of somewhat uncertain scope which rests entirely on case law. *Cf.* Quincy Mining Co. v. United States, 156 F. Supp. 913 (Ct. Cl. 1957) (costs incurred in connection with disposing of copper-bearing sands, which yielded no tax benefit when deducted, permitted to be used against sales of copper resulting from processing such sands many years later) ; Perry v. United States, 160 F. Supp. 270 (Ct. Cl. 1958) (tax saving resulting from charitable contribution required to be restored to taxes payable in year contribution returned to taxpayer by charity) . Both cases represent applications of the doctrine that are difficult to put within the framework of the statute or regulations. The Service refuses to follow *Perry,* Rev. Rul. 59–141, 1959–1 C.B. 17. *Quincy Mining* perhaps is erroneous in considering ordinary and necessary expenses as capital investments which must be returned tax free.

return of capital; the recovery is the first return of the creditor's investment.

b. Problem of Allocation of Receipts between Return of Capital and Gain

Turning from these fundamental elements of a return of capital, one encounters the problem of allocating receipts between return of capital and gain. The simple example of repayment of the principal of a loan, with which this discussion of return of capital began, provides the means by which the allocation problem may be approached. While repayment of the principal is to the creditor a return of capital,[43] the contemporaneous receipt of interest by him is gain and thus income.[44] The two must be distinguished, and this requires characterization and frequently apportionment of the receipt.

As might be expected, the identification of a receipt as either principal or interest is frequently difficult and, in fact, is accomplished by means of a number of special rules which find their justification in the criteria of Practicality, Adequacy, and Equity. A fairly simple illustration of such rules relates to the power of the borrower and lender to allocate by agreement payments made by the borrower between interest and principal. Where both agree that all payments are to be applied to principal until the amount advanced is recovered and the lender is not required by the accounting method he employs periodically to accrue

43. An early ruling, I.T. 1684, II–1 C.B. 60 (1923), illustrates the point that if more than the principal is returned, there is gain. Where a cash-basis taxpayer deposits a certain sum pursuant to an investment instrument whereby after a term of years he receives twice as much as deposited, the excess of the amount received over the amount deposited is income in the year received.

44. Int. Rev. Code of 1954, § 61 (4).

interest,[45] such an agreement is controlling, and interest, hence gain, is not reportable until the entire amount of capital advanced has been recovered.[46] Where no such agreement exists, the debtor has the power to designate the nature of his payment; [47] should he fail to do so, the power of designation rests with the creditor; [48] and, in the absence of designation by either, payments will be applied first to interest.[49] Somewhat more complex rules relate to securities on which interest is in arrears [50] and securities either issued or purchased at a discount.[51]

45. That is, the lender is a cash-basis taxpayer.

46. Ishael S. O'Dell, 26 T.C. 592 (1956); Huntington-Redondo Co., 36 B.T.A. 116 (1936); Rev. Rul. 63–57, 1963–1 C.B. 103.

47. Lincoln Storage Warehouses, 13 T.C. 33, 39 (1949).

48. Clay B. Brown, 37 T.C. 461, 489 (1961), *aff'd*, 380 U.S. 563 (1965); Chicago & No. West. Ry., 29 T.C. 989, 996 (1958).

49. Estate of Daniel Buckley, 37 T.C. 664, 670 (1962). These rules are drawn from state law sources so that an alteration of such law probably would alter the rules. See Peterson v. United States, 344 F.2d 419 (5th Cir. 1965). An exception to the rule allocating payments to interest in the absence of an agreement between debtor and creditor exists where the debtor's assets are less than his liabilities. In such a case all payments are applied to principal. G.C.M. 2861, VII–1 C.B. 255 (1928). But even where insolvent, a designation by the debtor that a payment is interest controls. Herbert Payson, Jr., 18 T.C.M. 686 (1959). "Guaranteed interest" paid by a guarantor after the obligor has no assets for payment of principal or interest is considered interest. Rev. Rul. 54–563, 1954–2 C.B. 50.

50. Amounts received by the purchaser subsequent to his acquisition in respect to interest which came due prior to such acquisition are treated as a return of capital until such receipts exceed the amount of such past-due interest at the time of purchase or the amount of capital invested therein, whichever is smaller. Also, payments on the principal of such obligations constitute a return of capital to the extent of the capital invested therein. Thereafter, all sums received from the debtor are gain and must be further allocated between interest which has accrued since the date of purchase and capital gain.
See United States v. Langston, 308 F.2d 729 (5th Cir. 1962); Jaglom v. Comm'r, 303 F.2d 847 (2d Cir. 1962); Pierce Corp. v. Comm'r, 120 F.2d 206 (5th Cir. 1941); Allen Tobey, 26 T.C. 610 (1956); Warner A. Shattuck, 25 T.C. 416 (1955); Adrian & James, Inc., 4 T.C. 708, 715 (1945); Holton & Co., 44 B.T.A. 202 (1941); Erskine Hewitt, 30 B.T.A. 962 (1934); Treas. Reg. § 1.61–7 (c).

51. When securities are either issued or purchased at a discount, an

Allocation problems also exist in contracts for the sale of land. It would be inappropriate to set forth here a recital of the various rules which have developed in this area for determining what portion, if any, of each payment made by the purchaser is properly allocable to the return of capital, to gain from the sale or exchange, and to interest or discount income. These rules have been shaped by the method of tax accounting used by the recipient of the payments,[52] the form by which the obligations of the purchaser were evidenced,[53] whether the recipient was the seller of the land or an investor in such contracts,[54] whether the contracts expressly provided for interest,[55] and

---

allocation between the return of capital, interest, and capital gain components is necessary. Thus, a municipal bond, for example, having a par value of $100, but issued at $97, would yield upon redemption gain of $3 which would be properly classified as interest exempt from taxation. Int. Rev. Code of 1954, § 103. When such a bond is issued at par but purchased by an investor at $97, the gain of $3 upon redemption is, however, not tax exempt interest but capital gain. The examples assume the holder of the bond at redemption is neither a dealer nor a life insurance or mutual insurance company. The rules are set forth in Rev. Rul. 60–210, 1960–1 C.B. 38, as modified by Rev. Rul. 60–376, 1960–2 C.B. 38, which rely upon the earlier rulings in G.C.M. 10452, XI–1 C.B. 18 (1932) and I.T. 2629, XI–1 C.B. 20 (1932) as indicated; "issue" discount is treated as interest and "market" discount otherwise.

52. That is, whether the cash or accrual method is used.

53. There is a group of cases involving cash-basis vendors who sell by way of land contracts unaccompanied by promissory notes or other evidence of indebtedness or mortgage which permit all payments to be applied as a return of capital until the entire investment has been recovered. Nina J. Ennis, 17 T.C. 465 (1951); Harold W. Johnson, 14 T.C. 560 (1950). The rule of these cases will be affected by the recently enacted § 483 of the 1954 Code. See n. 57 *infra.*

54. See Phillips v. Frank, 295 F.2d 629 (9th Cir. 1961), where this distinction was relied upon to permit an investor to allocate the entire amount received to a return of capital when the amounts received during the period in question and all previous payments did not equal the amount invested in such contract.

55. At least, prior to the enactment of § 483 of the 1954 Code, a contractual provision for interest often precluded an additional allocation to interest by the Commissioner.

the certainty of performance by the purchaser.[56] In addition, the Code has been amended recently to provide that "any payment on account of a sale or exchange of property which constitutes part or all of the sales price" must be apportioned between "unstated interest" and all other amounts in a manner which will preclude both the deferral of interest income until the entire capital invested has been recovered and its conversion into capital gain.[57] The influence of this amendment on the rules just mentioned

56. The Tax Court recently put the matter this way: "Where a taxpayer acquires at a discount contractual obligations calling for periodic payments of parts of the face amount of principal due, where the taxpayer's cost of such obligations is definitely ascertainable, and where there is no 'doubt whether the contract[s] [will] be completely carried out' [citing Hatch v. Comm'r, 190 F.2d 254, 257 (2d Cir. 1951)], it is proper to allocate such payments, part to be considered as a return of cost and part to be considered as a return of discount income; but, conversely, where it is shown that the amount of realizable discount gain is uncertain or that there is 'doubt whether the contract [will] be completely carried out,' the payments should be considered as a return of cost until the full amount thereof has been recovered, and no allocation should be made as between such cost and discount income." Morton Liftin, 36 T.C. 909, 911 (1961).

Thus, an investor in real estate contracts which were the equivalent of second mortgages who reports his income on a cash basis has been permitted to treat each payment received as a return of capital until his investment has been recovered where such contracts were purchased at a discount and were highly speculative in character. Phillips v. Frank, n. 54 *supra*. On the other hand, an allocation between gain in the form of interest or discount income and a return of capital in respect of each payment made by the purchaser has been required where the obligations of the purchaser had an ascertainable fair market value at the time of the sale and there exists little doubt about the performance of the purchaser. Darby Inv. Co. v. Comm'r, 315 F.2d 551 (6th Cir. 1963) (taxpayer was investor); Shafpa Realty Corp., 8 B.T.A. 283 (1927) (taxpayer was vendor); Victor B. Gilbert, 6 T.C. 10 (1946) (taxpayer was vendor); A. B. Culbertson, 14 T.C. 1421 (1950) (taxpayer was vendor); Joseph J. Weiss, T.C. Memo. 1965–20.

57. Int. Rev. Code of 1954, § 483, added by the Revenue Act of 1964. The amount of interest in respect to each payment is an amount which bears the same ratio to such payment as the "total unstated interest bears to the total of the payments to which this section applies which are due under contract." § 483 (a). "Unstated interest" is the difference between the sum of the payments due under the contract and the sum of the present values of such payments and the present values of any interest payments due under the contract. § 483 (b). If the contract provides for interest at the rate of 4 per cent per annum, § 483 can be avoided. Treas. Reg. § 1.483–1 (d)(2).

is quite likely to be substantial.[58] Finally, mention must be made of section 453 of the Code, which permits an allocation of the gain from the sale of realty to each instalment payment made when certain stated conditions are met.[59]

The problems of taxation of annuity payments, about which more will be said later, also present, in essence, allocation issues. It will be recalled that, prior to the enactment in 1934 of the 3 per cent rule,[60] all amounts received by annuitants were excluded from gross income until the entire investment of capital was recovered.[61] Under present rules, however, the portion of each annuity payment excluded from gross income as a return of capital is fixed by means of an "exclusion ratio." [62] This ratio is that which the "investment in the contract" bears to the "expected return under the contract." The technique adopted with respect to payment by insurance proceeds at a date later than death, which makes post-death interest a

58. To be more specific, is it possible for a cash-basis taxpayer to insist that a land contract unaccompanied by notes or other evidences of indebtedness should not be considered an "amount realized" to the extent of its fair market value when the "present value" of such contract must be determined under regulations to ascertain the amount of "unstated interest"? In short, will *Ennis* and *Johnston, supra* n. 53, continue to stand as authorities which permit the deferral of all gain, other than unstated interest under § 483, until the capital investment is recovered?

59. Primarily, these consist of an election by the taxpayer and payments in the year of sale which do not exceed 30 per cent of the selling price.

60. Section 22 (b)(2) of the 1939 Code, which provided that each payment in respect of an annuity constituted income, and hence not a return of capital, to the extent of 3 per cent of the consideration paid for the annuity contract. On the constitutionality of this rule, see Egtvedt v. United States, 112 Ct. Cl. 80 ('1948). Also see the discussion of apportionment of the aggregate investment to that portion of the property sold, pp. 34–36 *infra*.

61. *Cf. Hearings before the House Ways and Means Committee*, 73d Cong., 2d Sess. 554 (1934). *But see* Guaranty Trust Co. of New York, 14 B.T.A. 20 (1929); Florence L. Klein, 6 B.T.A. 617 (1927); MAGILL, TAXABLE INCOME 428 (rev. ed. 1945).

62. Int. Rev. Code of 1954, § 72 (b).

part of gross income in some instances,[63] also illustrates a solution to a particular allocation problem, as well as another example of a "constructive investment."

In a few instances, the entire amount of a receipt may be allocated to a return of capital because of extreme difficulty in fixing the *amount* of the investment in the item exchanged for the receipt. The situation is best illustrated by the facts of an old case, *Strother* v. *Commissioner*,[64] where the issue was the proper tax treatment of a sum paid to the taxpayer as damages for the unlawful removal of coal from his land. If the amount of coal removed were known, it would be a simple matter to compute any gain or loss by comparing the amount received as damages with the amount invested in the quantity of coal removed. Where, however, the quantity of coal removed is not known, it is impossible to determine the extent to which the capital of the taxpayer was consumed by the wrongful act. *Strother* solved the problem by considering the entire amount as a return of capital.[65]

Another graphic example is found in *Inaja Land Co., Ltd.*[66] Here, a sum paid for conveyance by the taxpayer of a right of way and certain easements to divert foreign waters into a river which flowed through the taxpayer's land, as well as for damages to this land, was considered a

63. Int. Rev. Code of 1954, § 101 (d).

64. 55 F.2d 626 (4th Cir. 1932).

65. It is interesting to observe that Magill suggested that "the relative impossibility of apportioning the capital investment to an unknown number of tons of ore hidden in the ground, plus the likelihood of new discoveries or developments, render it reasonable to treat as net income the gross proceeds of ore sold, less only the mining and selling costs." TAXABLE INCOME, 347 (rev. ed. 1945). This observation was made in an effort to reconcile Doyle v. Mitchell Bros. Co., 247 U.S. 179 (1918) and Stratton's Independence, Ltd. v. Howbert, 231 U.S. 399 (1913).

66. 9 T.C. 727 (1947).

return of capital. The taxpayer's basis in the entire tract was reduced by the amount of the receipt.

Moreover, *Strother* and *Inaja Land Co., Ltd.* do not stand alone; [67] but the principle is a limited one. Only when apportionment is "wholly impracticable or impossible" [68] is the principle available. Thus, the unrecovered cost of the entire property must be, in the words of the Regulations, "equitably apportioned among the several parts." [69] Therefore, the cost of a larger tract of land, for

67. United Mercantile Agencies, Inc., 23 T.C. 1105 (1955) (amount realized on claims purchased as part of a mixed aggregate from the liquidators of four insolvent banks applied to cost before profit reported because "apportionment would be wholly impracticable."); Webster Atwell 17 T.C. 1374 (1952) (cost of a corporation's overdue note not apportionable between twenty identical notes issued to replace it). Where the issue is the availability of a loss deduction, an inability to apportion accurately may result in disallowance of the loss. Pierce v. United States, 49 F. Supp. 324 (Ct. Cl. 1943) (sale of declaration of interests in the proceeds of dissolution of a security company which, when acquired, were locked to bank shares resulted in no loss where cost not apportionable between bank shares and security company interest). *Cf.* Comm'r v. Hagerman, 102 F.2d 281 (3d Cir. 1939); de Cappet v. Helvering, 108 F.2d 787 (2d Cir. 1940); Wise v. Comm'r, 109 F.2d 614 (3d Cir. 1940). In considering Inaja Land Company, Ltd., n. 66 *supra*, it must be remembered that the granting of an easement may not constitute a sale of land. See Rev. Rul. 54–575, 1954–2 C.B. 145; G.C.M. 23162, 1942–1 C.B. 106; I.T. 2621, XI-1 C.B. 67 (1932). In this event the consideration received for granting the easement is applied against the basis of the property and treated as a return of capital to the extent it does not exceed the basis. Although this route to the return-of-capital result is technically distinguishable from the impracticality-of-apportionment route, the former may be but a legalistic way of dealing with the apportionment problem.

68. Inaja Land Company, Ltd., 9 T.C. 727, 735 (1947).

69. Treas. Reg. § 1.61–6 (a) (1957). "Equitable apportionment" may be on the basis of assessed values, J. S. Cullinan, 5 B.T.A. 996 (1927); market values at the time of acquisition, Strauss v. Comm'r, 168 F.2d 441 (2d Cir. 1948) (dictum); the sales prices of the various portions of the larger property, Robert W. Ewing, 17 T.C.M. 626 (1958); book values of the seller, *cf.* Farmers Cotton Oil Co., 27 B.T.A. 105 (1932); or any other practicable basis, Strauss v. Comm'r, 168 F.2d 441 (2d Cir. 1948).
"Equitable apportionment," at least as applied to sales of portions of a larger tract of land, does not mean "ratable apportionment." I.T. 1843, II-2 C.B. 72 (1923). Thus, allocation on an acreage basis will not suffice where some portions of the larger tract are more valuable than others.

example, must be allocated to each portion thereof which is sold,[70] even though a subsequent collapse of the market may cause the taxpayer to receive a gross return less than the cost of the larger tract.

These few examples of the rules for apportioning receipts between those constituting a return of capital and various types of gain illustrate quite clearly that the task is seriously complicated by the existence under the Code of classifications of gain to which is extended differential tax treatment. The necessity to distinguish gain from the sale or exchange of a capital asset from interest income, or tax-exempt interest from capital gain and ordinary income, enhances substantially the complexity of the relevant rules. Undifferentiated treatment for all types of gain, however, would not eliminate allocation problems. Thus, when receipts are spread over different taxable periods, the problem remains whether to (1) treat them as a return of capital until the entire investment has been recovered, (2) apportion to each receipt a proper share of the gain, or (3) require that all receipts be treated as gain until the estimated gain has been subjected to tax, with all subsequent receipts treated as return of capital. Even though the last alternative has never been seriously considered, it remains true that neither of the first two approaches is suitable for all situations. As a consequence, multiple allocation rules will continue to exist.

Recognition of the permanence of the problems of allocation and the variability of solutions suggest some general observations. The first is that almost all allocation rules are devised so as to assure to the taxpayer a reasonable probability that his capital investment will be recovered free of tax. The principal battleground on which

70. Nathan Blum, 5 T.C. 702 (1945).

taxpayers and the Government struggle is whether the taxpayer is to be afforded the maximum assurance that capital will be returned tax-free. To achieve such assurance, as well as a deferral of tax liability, taxpayers repeatedly insist that all receipts be allocated to a return of capital until the entire investment is recovered tax-free, while the Government insists that gain must be allocated in a manner which will assure that some portion of it will be subject to tax prior to a complete return of capital. The tide of this battle probably favors the Government.

III. Fixing the Value and Consequences of Receipts Other than Returns of Capital

1. The Scope of the Chapter

THE DISCUSSION of the return-of-capital idea in the previous chapter involved situations in which the value of what had been received was not usually an issue. Once it was recognized that there was a return of capital, gain, if any, was simply the difference between the amount of the receipt and the portion treated as a return of capital. In this chapter attention shifts to the problems of fixing the value of what has been received.

The necessity of valuing what has been received is recognized in the Code when it provides that "gain from the sale or other disposition of property" shall be the excess of the "amount realized" over the adjusted basis of the property and that the amount realized "shall be the sum of any money received plus the fair market value of the property (other than money) received." [1] Presumably, "gains derived from dealings in property" within the meaning of section 61, to the extent not covered by the language of section 1001,[2] are computed in a similar fashion. Hence, it

---

1. Int. Rev. Code of 1954, §§ 1001 (a) and (b). See Greerbaum, *The Basis of Property Shall Be the Cost of Such Property: How is Cost Defined?*, 3 TAX L. REV. 357 (1948).

2. For a discussion of the scope of § 61 as it relates to "dealings in property" and § 1001, which pertains to gains and losses from sales or other dispositions, see BITTKER, FEDERAL INCOME ESTATE AND GIFT TAXATION, 366–71 (1961).

is imperative to ascertain the "amount realized." In addition, in transactions not involving sales, exchanges, dispositions, or dealings in property, it is frequently necessary to undertake the valuation of what has been received to determine the existence and scope of "realized gain."

These tasks are not easy. Generally speaking, they are made difficult in three ways. First, because there exists no—or at best only a limited—market within which the property received is traded. Second, the existence of contingencies may render the future yield of property sufficiently conjectural to make its market value quite uncertain. Finally, the receipt may be accompanied by either a set of restrictions on its use or the assumption of duties (conditional and unconditional) by the recipient, which may eliminate or reduce to some extent the "net" value of the receipt. The consequences of these difficulties can be varied. Thus, they can result in either (1) the *elimination* of gain at any time; (2) *postponement* of the gain until the marketing difficulties, contingencies, restrictions, assumption of duties, etc., are resolved or eliminated; (3) *realization* of present gain or loss with the receipt being valued in a way to account for the marketing difficulties, contingencies, restrictions, assumption of duties, etc.; or (4) *realization* of present gain or loss with the value of the receipt being unaffected by any complicating factors.

What follows in this chapter is an examination of the three types of difficulties and their consequences in various settings. However, no effort will be made to discuss the mathematical, or other frequently used, valuation techniques. The present concern is more with the legal effects of uncertainty about value than with valuation methods as usually understood. Because of this, certain areas not usually considered as presenting valuation problems—for example, the "claim of right" doctrine—are grouped here with topics more commonly associated with those problems. There is, however, a common thread woven in the texture of each topic discussed, viz., *the effect on the existence and amount of gain in the taxable period in which the receipt occurs of various marketing difficulties, contingencies, restrictions, etc., which pertain to the receipt.* By following this common thread, the focus on the criterion of Equity is maintained.

2. *Consequences of a Limited Market*

To trace the consequences of a limited market within which the property received is traded, it is necessary to turn first to the regulations. There appears a prudent but not completely accurate observation: "The fair market value of property is a question of fact, but only in rare and extraordinary cases will property be considered to have no fair market value." [3] Whatever the correctness of this statement, it has been held that immediate gain or loss is precluded when under the facts the receipt has no ascertainable fair market value.[4] It is frequently said that the term "fair market value" means the "price at which the property would change hands between a willing buyer and a willing seller, neither being under any compulsion to

3. Treas. Reg. § 1.1001–1(a) (1957).

4. Helvering v. Tex-Penn Oil Co., 300 U.S. 481, 499 (1937). The relevant passage is as follows: "The Court is also of opinion that the judgments must be affirmed upon the ground that in the peculiar circumstances of this case, the shares of Transcontinental stock, regard being had to their speculative quality and to terms of restrictive agreement making a sale thereof impossible, did not have a fair market value capable of being ascertained with reasonable certainty, when they were acquired by the taxpayers." Comm'r. v. Marshman, 279 F.2d 27, 33 (6th Cir. 1960); Schuh Trading Co. v. Comm'r, 95 F.2d 404, 412 (7th Cir. 1938); Champlin v. Comm'r, 71 F.2d 23, 29 (10th Cir. 1934); George J. Lentz, 28 T.C. 1157 (1957); Harold H. Kuchman, 18 T.C. 154 (1952).

buy or sell." [5] This definition is at best ambiguous with respect to the scope of trading between buyers and sellers of substantially similar properties necessary to establish a "fair market value." It is apparent, however, that ascertainability of such value becomes increasingly difficult as the scope of this trading diminishes. Thus, valuation of stocks listed upon a stock exchange in the absence of special circumstances is a relatively simple task; [6] but fixing the value of contracts where only a few scattered sales of such interests have been made in the past is more difficult.[7]

Notwithstanding this difficulty, the existence of actual sales of similar property is not necessary to ascertain fair market value.[8] Other factors may be considered, such as, in the case of infrequently traded stock, nature and history of business, economic outlook of business and the industry of which it is a part, financial structure of business, and earning capacity of company.[9] A wide-ranging inquiry is

5. *Cf.* Helvering v. Walbridge, 70 F.2d 683 (2d Cir. 1934) . Treas. Reg. § 20.2031–1 (b) states this definition for use in valuing property for estate tax purposes.

6. Usually, this can be done by determining the mean between the highest and lowest selling price on the valuation date. *Cf.* Treas. Reg. § 20.2031–2 (a) , which states this rule for estate tax purposes.

7. *Cf.* Gersten v. Comm'r, 267 F.2d 195 (9th Cir. 1959) (possible to find an ascertainable fair market value where only six casual sales of similar property at an undetermined price) .

8. Gersten v. Comm'r, n. 7 *supra;* Doric Apartment Co. v. Comm'r, 94 F.2d 895 (6th Cir. 1938) . Compare these cases with the following observations by L. Hand in Helvering v. Walbridge, 70 F.2d 683, 684 (2d Cir. 1934) : "Perhaps there need not be a 'market' to establish a 'market value,' but there must be some assurance that the value is what a 'market' would establish; and a 'market' itself presupposes enough competition between buyers and sellers to prevent the exigencies of an individual from being exploited. It may well imply that the goods have several buyers so that a necessitous seller shall not be confined to one; and that there are several possible sellers of the same goods or their substantial equivalent, so that a hard-pressed buyer shall not have to accept the first offer."

9. See Rev. Rul. 59–60, 1959–1 C.B. 237. The general approach, methods, and factors outlined in the above ruling for valuing closely-held

also appropriate with respect to other properties for which comparable sales are not available; [10] and, at least under some circumstances, even "a rough and inaccurate guess" may be sufficient to establish the presence of a "fair market value." [11] In any event, the taxpayer must show that the value fixed by the Government is incorrect.[12]

Often trading is infrequent because there exists only a very small group of buyers to whom the property can be sold. Indeed, in some instances the possible market may be limited to one potential buyer. A fairly common instance is corporate stock which either is subject to an enforceable agreement with another to buy at a fixed price at any time the owner desires to sell, or which vests in the other party a binding option to purchase at a fixed price.[13] The price fixed by these agreements determines the value of the stock for most purposes.[14]

---

corporate stocks for estate and gift tax purposes are equally applicable for income and other tax purposes. Rev. Rul. 65–192, 1965–2 C.B. 259.

10. It has been said that where the search is for value all evidence is admissible which has "any bearing on the matter." Whitlow v. Comm'r, 82 F.2d 569, 571 (8th Cir. 1936). Events subsequent to the valuation date are not deemed irrelevant when their tendency is to confirm judgments previously formed on the basis of other facts. *Cf.* Buena Vista Land & Dev. Co., 13 B.T.A. 895 (1928), *rev'd*, 41 F.2d 131 (9th Cir. 1930).

11. Warren v. United States, 171 F. Supp. 846 (Ct. Cl. 1959).

12. Helvering v. Taylor, 293 U.S. 507, 515 (1935).

13. The effect of such restrictions arises more frequently in valuation matters under the estate and gift taxes than under the income tax. Most of the case law relating to the effects of such restrictions involves these taxes. However, the consequences of these restrictions upon valuation under the income tax appear substantially identical to those under the two transfer taxes.

14. Helvering v. Salvage, 297 U.S. 106, 109 (1936) (option held by former owner of stock to repurchase at a fixed price established value for income tax purposes). On the effect of binding options to buy exercisable during the life, and subsequent to the death, of the shareholder on the estate tax valuation of shares, see Brodrick v. Gore, 224 F.2d 892 (10th Cir. 1955) (option to buy at fixed price during life of partner should he desire to sell and obligation to sell and buy at same price after his death fixed

Limitation on the number of potential buyers also may exist because of the nature of the property involved. An interesting example exists in the recent Supreme Court decision in *United States* v. *Davis*.[15] In a divorce settlement the wife agreed to a particular property settlement "in full settlement and satisfaction of any and all claims and rights against the husband whatsoever (including but not by way of limitation, dower and all rights under the laws of testacy and intestacy) . . . ."[16] Only one buyer, the husband, could "purchase" the rights surrendered by the wife; and, following his acquisition, they no longer were

---

estate tax value) ; May v. McGowan, 194 F.2d 396 (2d Cir. 1952) (option to buy at fixed price during life should shareholder desire to sell and option exercisable by purchaser at same price after shareholder's death fixed estate tax values) . Other cases holding similarly are Lomb v. Sugden, 82 F.2d 166 (2d Cir. 1936) ; Wilson v. Bowers, 57 F.2d 682 (2d Cir. 1932) ; Estate of Orville B. Littick, 31 T.C. 181 (1958) (A). The gift tax values possibly may not be fixed by agreements such as described in the text. Rev. Rul. 59–60, 1959–1 C.B. 237, 243–44, describes the effect of restrictive agreements as follows: "Frequently, in the valuation of closely held stock for estate and gift tax purposes, it will be found that the stock is subject to an agreement restricting its sale or transfer. Where shares of stock were acquired by a decedent subject to an option reserved by the issuing corporation to repurchase at a certain price, the option price is usually accepted as the fair market value for estate tax purposes." See Rev. Rul. 54–76, 1954–1 C.B. 194. However, in such case the option price is not determinative of fair market value for gift tax purposes. Where the option, or buy and sell agreement, is the result of voluntary action of the stockholders and is binding during the life, as well as at the death, of the stockholders, such agreement may or may not, depending upon the circumstances of each case, fix the value for estate tax purposes. However, such an agreement is a factor to be considered, with other relevant factors, in determining fair market value. Where the stockholder is forced to dispose of his shares during life and the option is to become effective only upon his death, the fair market value is not limited to the option price. It is always necessary to consider the relationship of the parties, the relative number of shares held by the decedent, and other material facts, to determine whether the agreement represents a bona fide business arrangement or is a device to pass the decedent's shares to the natural objects of his bounty for less than an adequate and full consideration in money or money's worth.

15. 370 U.S. 65 (1962) .

16. A property settlement involving a division of community property may not result in a taxable transaction. Clifford H. Wren, 24 T.C.M. (1965) .

subject to disposition. Despite the unusual character of the property received by the husband, the Court held that the "amount realized" by him was the fair market value of the property which he gave in exchange.[17] The lesson of *Davis* appears to be that in an arms-length transaction the value of property received has an ascertainable fair market value when the property surrendered in exchange has such a value. In this manner, the limited market within which the received property is traded is made inconsequential. It remains to be seen whether *Davis* goes beyond its facts and precludes immediate gain or loss only when neither the property received nor the property exchanged has an ascertainable fair market value.

3. Consequences of Uncertainty about Future Income Yield

Should *Davis* not reach so far, it can be said that sometimes uncertainty about the future income yield of received property postpones gain or loss. An example is *Burnet* v. *Logan*.[18] The amount realized from the sale of corporate stock, it will be recalled, was not ascertainable presently because it consisted, in part, of a promise to pay sixty cents per ton of iron to be taken from a particular mine, in respect of which certain rights were owned by the corporation whose stock was the subject matter of the sale. Because the "future money payments [were] wholly contingent upon facts and circumstances not possible to foretell with anything like fair certainty,"[19] the Court deter-

17. *Id.* at 73. On the other hand, the court appeared to recognize that the surrender of inchoate marital rights by the wife in exchange for a present interest in property did not constitute "a taxable event." See pp. 66–68 *infra*.

18. 283 U.S. 404 (1931).

19. *Id.* at 413.

mined that all payments should be considered a return of capital until the investment in the property sold had been recovered. The case underscores the relationship between valuation uncertainties and the previously discussed problem of allocating receipts between gain and a return of capital. Where the uncertainity about future productivity does not impair seriously the probability of full recovery of invested capital, the appeal of *Burnet* v. *Logan* is much reduced.[20]

Moreover, even though the case has been followed on numerous occasions,[21] at present it has a limited and somewhat uncertain scope without regard to the scope of *Davis*. The Service declared in a Revenue Ruling[22] that the case did not decide that "contracts for indefinite payments generally have no ascertainable value." In addition, the Serv-

20. Bruce v. United States, 66–1 USTC ¶ 9276 (S.D. Tex. 1966) (refusal to apply *Burnet v. Logan* to oil and gas royalty contract where taxpayer had already recovered one-half of basis in five years) .

21. Westover v. Smith, 173 F.2d 99 (9th Cir. 1949) (contract to make royalty payments in respect of machinery manufactured pursuant to certain patents held not to have an ascertainable value in a corporate liquidation case) ; Comm'r v. Carter, 170 F.2d 911 (2d Cir. 1948) (oil brokerage contracts had no ascertainable fair market value by reason of stipulation in a corporate liquidation case) ; Comm'r v. Edwards Drilling Co., 95 F.2d 719 (5th Cir. 1938) (right to payment out of oil produced from wells drilled by taxpayer for others need not be included in income in year of drilling because of "hazards and uncertainties attending the recovery") ; Estate of Raymond T. Marshall, 20 T.C. 979 (1953) (exchange of stock for certificates entitling taxpayer to dividends in respect of exchange stock for 10 years) ; Thomas J. Brant, 13 T.C. 712 (1949) (prospect of future payments by Mexican Government uncertain) . See also nn. 53 and 56, chap. ii, *supra,* for other examples applying the *Burnet v. Logan* principle of permitting the returns for an investment to be applied first to basis and then to gain.

The problem of contingencies which make receipt in the future uncertain also arises when the taxpayer is on the accrual basis of accounting. Thus, even though such a taxpayer must accrue an item in the year in which he acquires "a fixed and unconditional right" to receive it, contingencies which render its collection improbable justify non-accrual until the contingencies are eliminated. See Commercial Solvents Corp., 42 T.C. 455, 471 (1964) (A). The principles discussed in the text, however, are generally applicable and are not based on accounting method rules.

22. Rev. Rul. 58–402, 1958–2 C.B. 15.

46

ice asserted that it would "continue to require valuation of contracts and claims to receive indefinite amounts of income, such as those aquired with respect to stock in liquidation of a corporation, except in rare and extraordinary cases." [23] The consequence of requiring valuation is the presence of immediate gain or loss together with the possibility of future gain or loss. [24] Thus, it must be emphasized that the burden a taxpayer must bear to establish that property received in exchange has no ascertainable fair market value is very heavy. [25]

23. *Ibid.*

24. The present gain or loss is determined by the difference between the ascertained fair market value of the claims and the adjusted basis of the property exchanged therefor. The receipts in respect of such claims are then allocated between return of capital and various classifications of gains. Thus, an interest in rentals to be paid pursuant to contract to distribute the motion picture "Gone With the Wind" received in exchange for corporate stock upon the liquidation of the corporation was determined to have an ascertainable fair market value. Grill v. United States, 303 F.2d 922 (Ct. Cl. 1962) . Gain or loss in the year of liquidation was the result.

Future rental payments received in later years were then allocated between gain and return of capital. For similar results see Chamberlin v. Comm'r, 286 F.2d 850 (7th Cir. 1961) ; Gersten v. Comm'r, 267 F.2d 195 (9th Cir. 1959) ; Osenbach v. Comm'r, 198 F.2d 235 (4th Cir. 1952) . See also the discussion of allocation problems, pp. 29–37 *supra.* A taxpayer in the *Grill* situation might argue that the amount to be realized ultimately from the acquired claims is sufficiently uncertain to justify an allocation of all receipts to a return of capital until the investment is returned—even though the claim was determined to have an ascertainable fair market value at the time of receipt. The basis of the claim is, of course, the fair market value at the time of acquisition. The investment consisted of inclusion in gross income. See p. 21 *supra.*

25. Numerous contingencies, however, can exist which, because of the potential effect on the amount that may be received in the future, will either preclude the ascertainability of fair market value or serve to depress that value. Thus, the yield of the property acquired may depend on the earnings of the property exchanged, see R. T. Marshall, 20 T.C. 979 (1953) ; the possibility of future sales being made by the buyer, *cf.* Jay A. Williams, 28 T.C. 1000 (1957) ; the elimination of conflicting claims to the property acquired, Champlin Ref. Co. v. Comm'r, 123 F.2d 202 (10th Cir. 1941) , Minal E. Young, 6 B.T.A. 472; or doubts as to the financial ability of the obligor to perform, Jay A. Williams, 28 T.C. 1000 (1957) ; R. M. Rogers, 7 B.T.A. 711 (1927) .

In several recent cases, doubts as to the obligor's financial ability prevented a finding of ascertainable fair market value with respect to notes

However, a taxpayer who reports his income on the cash basis is able with some frequency to assert successfully that where the receipt consists of non-negotiable notes, contract rights, and open account claims, no gain results until payments thereunder exceed the adjusted basis of any property given up.[26] The contention occasionally fails,[27] and serious questions exist as to whether the method of accounting should have such an effect.[28] Even if the receipt because of its form cannot be considered the equivalent of cash, it does appear to be a form of property which may possess an ascertainable fair market value. Where this is

---

secured by second mortgages. Willhoit v. Comm'r, 308 F.2d 259 (9th Cir. 1963) (no allocation to discount income until capital recovered); Miller v. United States, 235 F.2d 553 (6th Cir. 1956) (notes received in liquidation have no fair market value). For an earlier case see Nichols v. Comm'r, 44 F.2d 157 (3d Cir. 1930). Fair market value is often found to exist, however. *E.g.*, Doric Apartments Co. v. Comm'r, 94 F.2d 895 (6th Cir. 1938); 688 East Ave. v. United States, 4 AFTR 2d 5601 (S.D.N.Y. 1959), 59–2 USTC ¶ 9704; Ernest P. Flint 12 B.T.A. 20 (1928). And, in any event, the determination of the Commissioner is entitled to a presumption of correctness, United States v. Anderson, 269 U.S. 422 (1925), although the opinions of experts, collection history, extent of the first mortgage, and location of property subject to the mortgages and previous sales, if any, of such notes may influence the issue.

It should be added that doubts as to the financial ability of the obligor to perform may also affect the manner of allocating payments by the obligor between a return of capital and gain. See pp. 31–32 *supra*. Such doubts also prevent the accrual of income. See, *e.g.*, Commercial Solvents Corp., n. 21 *supra*.

26. See p. 31 and nn. 52 and 53, Chapter II, *supra. Cf.* Nitterhouse v. United States, 207 F.2d 618 (3d Cir. 1953), where claim against Government arising from condemnation of taxpayer's land was said not to be "property" within meaning of Int. Rev. Code of 1954, § 1001.

27. Cowden v. Comm'r., 289 F.2d 20, 24 (5th Cir. 1961). The court announced this doctrine: "We are convinced that if a promise to pay of a solvent obligor is unconditioned and assignable, not subject to set-offs, and is of a kind that is frequently transferred to lenders or investors at a discount not substantially greater than the generally prevailing premium for the use of money, such promise is the equivalent of cash and taxable in like manner as cash would have been taxable had it been received by the taxpayer rather than the obligation."

28. SEE SURREY & WARREN, FEDERAL INCOME TAXATION 653–55 (1960 ed.).

the case, present gain or loss should be determined, and, as in other cases, future receipts should be apportioned between return of capital and various types of gain.

4. Consequences of Burdens, Restrictions, or Adverse Claims

The consequences of the existence of limited markets and income-yield uncertainties are more easily understood than those which result when the value of the receipt is made conjectural by the presence of burdens, restrictions, or adverse claims which accompany receipts otherwise susceptible to easy valuation. To these increased complexities attention should now be turned. Initially, concern will be with receipts accompanied by the burden of obligations undertaken by the recipient; thereafter, with restrictions on the use of receipts; and, finally, with adverse claims.

a. Receipts Accompanied by the Burden of Obligations Undertaken by the Recipient

A loan, as already pointed out, involves an undertaking by the borrower to repay, which constitutes an investment and precludes treatment of the receipts as income. However, this is not the result in all the instances in which a receipt is accompanied by the creation or assumption of express or implied obligations. Thus, a receipt during the present taxable period in payment for personal services, which the recipient undertakes to render in a future taxable period, constitutes taxable gain to the full extent of the amount paid in the period of receipt.[29] Similarly, advance receipts in exchange for inventory items to be deliv-

29. Lavery v. Comm'r, 158 F.2d 859 (7th Cir. 1946); Jacobs v. Hoey, 136 F.2d 954 (2d Cir. 1943); E. Morris Cox, 43 T.C. 448 (1965). *Cf.* Bouchard v. Comm'r, 229 F.2d 703 (7th Cir. 1956); Holbrook v. United States, 194 F. Supp. 252 (D. Ore. 1961).

ered in a subsequent taxable period,[30] or future occupancy of premises owned and being rented by the recipient, constitute income when received.[31]

In these cases the undertaking of the recipient given in exchange for the cash is, unlike the promise to repay the amount borrowed, not an investment of capital but rather a commitment to render income-producing services in the future. While the borrower's tax accounts are unaffected by either the receipt of the loan proceeds or the repayment of the principal, an advance payment for income-producing services to be rendered in the future *must* result in income either at the time of receipt, the time of performance, or both. The only issue is which is the most appropriate. That the Government prefers the earliest point in time is no occasion for surprise.

Adequacy and Practicality point unwaveringly in this direction because tax collection is more likely and less troublesome if it follows closely on the heels of cash receipts. Perhaps Equity and Free Market Compatibility would be better served by a deferral of the income until the time for performance of the services. This follows because it is possible to assert that, although an advance payment for income-producing services to be rendered in the future is unlike a loan, the resemblance is sufficient to suggest balancing of the value of the receipt against the present value of the obligation to perform in the future in determining the extent of the gain in the year of receipt. Under this view, gain, if any, would be substantially less

30. Fifth & York Co. v. United States, 234 F. Supp. 421 (D. Ky. 1964); Chester Farrara, 44 T.C. 189 (1965); Malloy & Co., 33 B.T.A. 1130 (1936) (NA); Whiting Lumber Co., 21 B.T.A. 721 (1930) (A).

31. Hyde Park Realty v. Comm'r, 211 F.2d 462 (2d Cir. 1954); Gelkin Corp. v. Comm'r, 176 F.2d 141 (6th Cir. 1949); Rev. Rul. 65-141, 1965-1 C.B. 210.

than the value of the receipt; and the difference between the amount of the receipt and this gain would be taken into income in the year of performance.[32] Obviously, the valuation of the obligation would present practical difficulties; however, the theoretically next-best solution—that is, the use of reserves for estimated expenses—would avoid most of these and permit a more accurate reflection of economic gain than does existing practice. Present case law offers little promise of reaching this result, however.

b. Receipts Accompanied by Restrictions on Use

Restrictions on the use to which the funds may be put by the recipient also can make the extent of gain uncertain. An example of such a restriction which precludes the existence of *any* gain is the receipt of funds by an agent charged with the duty of disposing of the funds in a particular way.[33] No income, it is said, accrues to one who acts as a "conduit." [34] Similarly, receipt by a trustee for a particular purpose yields no taxable gain.[35] Receipts, however,

32. This treatment, of course, does not account for the economic benefit to the recipient arising from the use of the funds prior to his performance without an obligation to pay interest. The interest-free loan problem is discussed at pp. 84–88 *infra*.

33. *Cf.* The Seven-Up Co., 14 T.C. 965 (1950) (A) (amounts received by manufacturer of 7-Up extract to be used for national advertising not income because manufacturer administered fund as an agent) ; Max E. Cohen, 24 T.C.M. 136 (1965) (advances paid by principal client to lawyer to finance costs of litigation, other than lawyer's services, not income) ; Rev. Rul. 65–282, 1965–2 C.B. 21 (fees received by attorney as agent for legal aid society not income) ; Rev. Rul. 58–220, 1958–1 C.B. 26 (fees received by doctor as agent for hospital not income to doctor).

34. *Cf.* Lashell's Estate v. Comm'r, 208 F.2d 430, 435 (6th Cir. 1953) ; *Amounts Paid As Illegal Kickbacks Are Excludable from Income,* 75 HARV. L. REV. 1441 (1962).

35. In the ordinary family trust the result is so plain that litigation is pointless. There is, however, a group of cases where the issue whether the receipts are impressed with a trust sufficient to preclude gain has been frequently litigated. These cases involve cemetery corporations, operated for profit, which allocate a portion of the proceeds from the sale of lots to

accompanied by a contractual obligation requiring their use in a particular manner may not eliminate gain.[36] A distinction is drawn between restrictions which limit the recipient's property interests in the receipt and those which do not. In *Krim-Ko Corporation,*[37] for example, the Tax Court held that funds burdened with the duty of furnishing advertising material and services constituted income and, in doing so, observed that the taxpayer "treated them [the receipts] as its property by commingling them with its other assets." [38]

Moreover, there are a few instances where, although the burden undertaken by the recipient does not deprive him of full ownership of the receipt, it is considered as sufficient to justify exclusion of the receipt from gross income. A fairly common example is a deposit by a lessee with his lessor to secure performance by the lessee of certain covenants of the lessee with the understanding that the lessor has the use of the funds during the lease and that the sum not used to compensate the lessor is to be applied to the

---

perpetual maintenance funds. Where state law, or the appropriate by-laws and contracts, or both, require a portion of such proceeds when received be put into an irrevocable trust for perpetual care and maintenance, such portion is excluded from gross income of the corporation. Metairie Cemetery Ass'n v. United States, 282 F.2d 225 (5th Cir. 1960) ; Comm'r v. Cedar Park Cemetery Ass'n, 183 F.2d 553 (7th Cir. 1950) ; Rev. Rul. 58–190, 1958–1 C.B. 15.

36. *E.g.,* United States v. Woodall, 255 F.2d 370 (10th Cir. 1958) (reimbursement to defray moving expenses incurred in accepting new employment income) ; Lykes Bros. S. S. Co., Inc. v. Comm'r, 126 F.2d 725 (5th Cir. 1942) (profits required by term of contract to be used for specified purposes constitute income) ; Boyle, Flagg & Seaman, Inc., 25 T.C. 43 (1955) (premiums on automobile insurance received by taxpayer under arrangement whereby a portion thereof was to be turned over to the dealers remitting the premiums included in income without diminution for the portion paid to dealers) .

37. 16 T.C. 31 (1951) .

38. *Id.* at 40.

rent due for the last period of the lease.[39] The lessor is treated as a borrower of the deposit, not as the recipient of advance rentals.[40] The previously mentioned distinction between loan proceeds and advance receipts in payment for income-producing activities appears again.[41]

It is not surprising in view of these refined distinctions to encounter cases where it is difficult to determine whether the recipient holds funds as (1) an agent or trustee, (2) a borrower, or (3) one who had performed, or is under obligation to perform, income-earning tasks. *Mutual Telephone Co. v. United States*[42] constitutes an example. Sums received by a telephone company by reason of an additional charge designed to discourage new installations of telephones during wartime were required by the public authorities to be held in such a way as to permit immediate compliance with their orders for disposition of such sums. In compliance with this directive, the company "intermingled with other moneys in the general treasury" the additional charges, but "kept on hand at all times sufficient cash or marketable securities" to obey any order the public authorities might make.[43] Despite the fact that none of the above three categories precisely fits this situation, the court had little difficulty in finding sufficient

39. *E.g.*, Clinton Hotel Realty Corp. v. Comm'r, 128 F.2d 968 (5th Cir. 1942); Warren Serv. Corp. v. Comm'r, 110 F.2d 723 (2d Cir. 1940); John Mantel, 17 T.C. 1143 (1952) (A).

40. In Clinton Hotel Realty Corp., n. 39 *supra*, at 969 the court put it this way: "In the latter situation, though the money is rightfully received, and if the parties so intend may be freely used, yet because of the acknowledged liability to account for it, there is no gain; just as in borrowing there is none." When the sums are received as advance rentals they constitute gross income. *E.g.*, Gilken Corp. v. Comm'r, 176 F.2d 141 (6th Cir. 1949).

41. See pp. 19–20 *supra*.

42. 204 F.2d 160 (9th Cir. 1953).

43. *Id.* at 161.

"restrictions" on the use of the funds to eliminate them from the company's gross income.

Restrictions on the use of receipts do not always require an "all or nothing" result. Particularly is this true when the receipt consists of property other than cash. In many situations the restrictions merely depress the fair market value of the receipt and thus reduce the amount included rather than eliminate the item from gross income altogether. An employee, for example, who is given property as compensation which is subject to certain restrictions on its disposition may be required to include in his income an amount equal to the fair market value of the property determined after properly weighing the effects of the restrictions.[44]

However, it is not surprising that the Government often insists that restrictions on the use of property justify a postponement of all gain until their removal when such a course means additional revenue. The present regulations pertaining to non-restricted stock options illustrate the point nicely.[45] These provide that an employee granted such an option may realize compensation income at the time he exercises the option, but that if the stock "is subject to a restriction which has a significant effect on its

44. United States v. Drescher, 179 F.2d 863 (2d Cir. 1950) (retirement annuity contracts purchased by employer for employee may have a value less than premium paid because privilege of accelerating annuity payments impaired by employer's retention of possession of contracts). The plan involved in *Drescher* was a non-qualified plan. See Int. Rev. Code of 1954, §§ 402 (b) and 403 (c), for method of taxability to employee of employer contributions to non-qualified plans. Where employee's rights are non-forfeitable the amount of the contribution is taxable to the employee. Another interesting example of restrictions on use depressing the fair market value of property is found in Jacob J. Cooley, 33 T.C. 223 (1959), *aff'd per curiam,* 283 F.2d 945 (2d Cir. 1960). It was there held that property acquired at a price less than that prevailing in the market in which the taxpayer normally sells, but restricted in use to being donated to charity, has a "fair market value" for the purpose of computing the charitable deduction equal to its cost and not the value at which the taxpayer could have sold it had there been no restriction.

45. Treas. Reg. § 1.421–6 (1959).

value," realization is deferred until the "restriction lapses or at the time the property is sold or exchanged, in an arm's length transaction, whichever occurs earlier." [46] Without going into detail, the consequence of this is frequently to increase the ordinary income, and diminish the capital gain element in the employee's gain.[47]

c. Receipts Accompanied by Adverse Claims

Turning to receipts accompanied by adverse claims, it is obvious that the precise extent to which the wealth of a taxpayer has been increased by such a receipt is conjec-

46. Treas. Reg. § 1.421–6 (d)(2)(i) (1960), as amended by T.D. 6540, 1961–1 C.B. 161, T.D. 6696, 1963–2 C.B. 23. The Tax Court also takes the position that restrictions having a substantial effect on the market value of the stock preclude the realization of compensation income at the time the option is exercised. *Cf.* Harold H. Kuchman, 18 T.C. 154 (1952) (A). However, the Tax Court does not agree that lapse of the restriction will result in realization. Robert Lehman, 17 T.C. 652 (1951) (NA). *But cf.* Jack I. Le Vant, 45 T.C. 185 (1965), where certain other aspects of regulation § 1.421–6 (d) were approved and relied upon.

47. Were the stock valued at the time the option is exercised by taking into account the depressing influence of restrictions, the spread between the option price and value so determined would be reduced or eliminated entirely. Since this spread would constitute the amount of compensation income, its reduction would reduce ordinary income and make possible the treatment of any difference between such value at the time of exercise of the option and the amount realized upon disposition of the stock as capital gain or loss. By deferring the realization and measurement of compensation income until the restrictions are removed, a larger portion of the spread between the option price and selling price (assuming for this purpose that the latter exceeds the value of the stock at the time the restrictions are removed) would be taxed as ordinary income. The regulations restrict the amount of compensation income to the lesser of the spread between the option price and the fair market value of the property when acquired (computed without regard to any restrictions) and that between the option price and its value at the time the restrictions are removed when this occurs prior to any sale or exchange in an arm's-length transaction. Treas. Reg. § 1.421–6 (d)(2)(i) (1960) as amended by T.D. 6540, 1961–1 C.B. 161, and T.D. 6696, 1963–2 C.B. 23. See Jack I. LeVant, n. 46 *supra*, applying this regulation. An older case, Robert Lehman, 17 T.C. 652 (1951) (NA), on the other hand, maximizes the capital gain element by, first, refusing to find a realization of compensation income at the time of the removal of the restrictions and, second, permitting the entire spread between the option price and sales price to be considered as capital gain. These observations, of course, are not applicable to "qualified stock options," "employee stock purchase plans," or "restricted stock options" as described in Int. Rev. Code of 1954, §§ 422, 423, 424, and 425.

tural. While possession is better (even when the possessor's claim of ownership is hotly disputed by another) than permitting the funds to remain in the hands of the adverse claimant, it is clear that the possessor's wealth has not been increased to the full extent of the sum in dispute. This sum is taken *cum onere.*

Nonetheless, it was settled long ago that an adverse claim would neither eliminate nor defer realization of gain to the full extent of the sum received where such sum was otherwise taxable. In *North American Oil Consolidated* v. *Burnet,*[48] a case in which receipts were accompanied by adverse claims known to the taxpayer, Mr. Justice Brandeis said: "If a taxpayer receives earnings under a claim of right and without restrictions as to its disposition, he has received income which he is required to return, even though he may still be adjudged liable to restore its equivalent." [49]

This result—while not nicely adjusted to the dictates of Equity, since a dollar of uncontested income is worth more than the same amount subject to adverse claims— does conform to Practicality because it reduces the time lag between receipt and reporting. In addition, it gives to each taxable period a degree of finality and completeness

48. 286 U.S. 417 (1932).

49. *Id.* at 424. Thus, the taxpayer who received sums in 1917 representing revenues from operation during 1916 of oil properties accompanied by an adverse claim thereto was required to report the sums in its return for 1917, not 1916 (since there was no "constructive receipt" in the earlier year), and was prevented from withholding inclusion until 1922, the year in which the dispute was finally settled in favor of the taxpayer. Had the 1922 settlement been adverse to taxpayer, the 1917 inclusion would still have been appropriate, but the taxpayer would become entitled to a 1922 deduction under § 165 (a) in amounts of the sums required to be returned. See Rev. Rul. 65–254, 1965–2 C.B. 50 (return of embezzled funds).

For a discussion of lack-of-receipt question, see Note, *The Effect of Escrow Arrangements on Federal Income Tax Liability,* 59 Harv. L. Rev. 1292 (1946).

that facilitates the reporting of income on a periodic basis. Even though all other macrocriteria, with the possible exception of Adequacy,[50] played no part in the development of the "claim of right" doctrine, Practicality is sufficiently strong to require little or no assistance.

These justifications carry the docrine beyond the type of fact situation involved in *North American Oil Consolidated*. Thus, inclusion in the year of receipt is required even when the taxpayer, having no knowledge of an adverse claim at the time of receipt, willingly surrenders the sum in a later period when the claim becomes known.[51] Furthermore, some of the situations previously described involving receipts accompanied by restrictions on use provide an opportunity to the Government to assert the "claim of right" doctrine as a basis for inclusion of the receipt notwithstanding the restrictions.[52]

50. By tending to assure the existence of funds with which to pay the tax and in the absence of intervening circumstances—such as death, liquidation, or bankruptcy, which might serve to frustrate the collection task—the doctrine advances the ends of the criterion of Adequacy, Treasury style.

51. Such a situation occurred in Greenwald v. United States, 102 Ct. Cl. 272, 57 F. Supp. 569 (1944), and the Court of Claims refused to apply the "claim of right" doctrine and permitted exclusion in the year of receipt by means of a timely refund filed after the discovery by the adverse claim and repayment of the funds. This so-called mistake-of-fact approach was rejected by the Supreme Court in United States v. Lewis, 340 U.S. 590 (1951). *Accord,* Comm'r v. Gaddy, 344 F.2d 460 (5th Cir. 1965). The Code, however, does permit under certain circumstances the near economic equivalent of exclusion from the year of receipt by permitting a reduction in the tax due in the year of the return of the item by the "decrease in tax . . . for the prior taxable year . . . which would result solely from the exclusion of such item . . . from the gross income for such prior taxable year. . . ." Int. Rev. Code of 1954, § 1341. A correlative provision for the claimant whose efforts are successful appears in § 1342.

52. See Lashell's Estate v. Comm'r, 208 F.2d 430, 435 (6th Cir. 1953); Mutual Tel. Co. v. United States, 204 F.2d 160, 161, (9th Cir. 1953); Clinton Hotel Realty Corp. v. Comm'r, 128 F.2d 968, 969 (5th Cir. 1942); The Seven-Up Co., 14 T.C. 965, 976 (1950) (A). See also Webster, *The Claim of Right Doctrine: 1954 Version,* 10 TAX L. REV. 381 (1955).

North American Oil Consolidated contributed, however, to what proved to be a somewhat short-lived *exclusion* from gross income. In *Commissioner* v. *Wilcox* [53] the
Supreme Court built upon the "claim of right" language
quoted above and stated "that a taxable gain is conditioned upon (1) the presence of a claim of right to the
alleged gain and (2) the absence of a definite, unconditional obligation to repay or return that which would
otherwise constitute gain." [54] Where no "bona fide legal or
equitable claim" to the receipt exists, it does not constitute
gross income. Therefore, the proceeds of embezzlement
were not taxable. The extent to which this reasoning
served to exclude receipts from other illegal activities was
unclear.[55]

This lack of clarity was not dissipated by the Supreme
Court's decision six years later in *Rutkin* v. *United
States*,[56] where it was held that the proceeds of extortion
constituted taxable income. No effort was made to harmonize this result with the use of the "claim of right" analysis
employed in *Wilcox*. Instead, the Court emphasized that
the extortioner taxpayer had such control over the fruits
of the crime as to permit him to derive "readily realizable
economic value from it." [57]

53. 327 U.S. 404 (1946).

54. *Id.* at 408.

55. *E.g.*, Akers v. Scofield, 167 F.2d 718 (5th Cir. 1948) (swindler was
held to have income in view of his acquisition of title to the money, his
intention to claim the money as his at all times, and the failure of the
victim to attempt to rescind the transaction); United States v. Iozia, 104 F.
Supp. 846 (S.D.N.Y. 1952) (proceeds from sale of stolen goods held income
because held under a claim of right even if a duty to account to victim as
trustee *ex malificio*).

56. 343 U.S. 130 (1952).

57. *Id.* at 137. Although it is difficult to perceive why this analysis did
not justify overruling *Wilcox*, as Mr. Justice Black argued in his dissent,

Finally, the Court in *James* v. *United States* [58] put *Wilcox* to rest and declared embezzlement proceeds taxable income. The *Rutkin* emphasis on the type of control to permit the derivation of "readily realizable economic value" was repeated together with the argument that the unlawful should not be treated more favorably than the lawful. And, of more direct interest for the purposes at hand, the Court refused either to ignore or to render inapplicable the "claim of right" doctrine; instead, it was recast to accommodate its new position. [59] This formulation permits exclusion from income only where the receipt is accompanied by "consensual recognition, express or implied, of an obligation to repay." As recast, the doctrine reads as follows: "When a taxpayer acquires earnings,

---

that case was left standing but limited to its facts. Naturally, uncertainty continued. *E.g.*, Kann v. Comm'r, 210 F.2d 247 (3d Cir. 1953) (officer-stockholders unsuccessful in attempting to avoid taxation by appearing as embezzlers of corporate funds because, *inter alia*, they had not been prosecuted for embezzlement and no adequate proof that the act was not condoned); J. J. Dix, Inc. v. Comm'r, 223 F.2d 436 (2d Cir. 1955) (corporate officer permitted to exclude receipts on ground that they were fruit of embezzlement); Davis v. United States, 226 F.2d 331 (6th Cir. 1955) (taxpayer could not embezzle from his wholly owned corporation); Marienfeld v. United States, 214 F.2d 632 (8th Cir. 1954) (taxpayer held taxable on illegal receipts on grounds that his "possession, dominion over, opportunity for use of, and freedom to dispose of the funds" more resembles *Rutkin* than *Wilcox*). For law review material relating to this era, see Keesling, *Illegal Transactions and the Income Tax*, 5 U.C.L.A. L. Rev. 26 (1958); Note, *Embezzlement and Income under the Internal Revenue Code*, 30 Ind. L.J. 487 (1955); Note, *Taxation of Misappropriated Property: The Decline and Incomplete Fall of Wilcox*, 62 Yale L.J. 662 (1953).

58. 366 U.S. 213 (1961). For a comprehensive discussion of the *James* decision from a number of different aspects see Libin & Haydon, *Embezzled Funds as Taxable Income: A Study in Judicial Footwork*, 61 Mich. L. Rev. 425 (1963).

59. *Id.* at 216, n. 7, the Government's contention that the doctrine dealt with *when* an item is income, not *whether* it is income, expressly was not passed on. The footnote continued: "The use to which we put the claim of right test here is only to demonstrate that, whatever its validity as a test of whether certain receipts constitute income, it calls for no distinction between *Wilcox* and *Rutkin*."

lawfully or unlawfully, without the consensual recognition, express or implied, of an obligation to repay and without restriction as to their disposition, he has received income which he is required to return, even though it may still be claimed that he is not entitled to retain the money, and even though he may still be adjudged liable to restore its equivalent." Wrongful appropriations, notwithstanding the existence of the adverse claims of rightful owners, constitute "accessions to wealth" to the full extent of the receipt, while loans and other receipts accompanied by the proper consensual recognition of a duty to repay do not.[60] Once again, no effort is made to measure precisely the value-depressing effect of extrinsic circumstances accompanying a receipt and, after vacillation, the "all" rather than the "nothing" approach has been settled upon.

Analysis in terms of the criteria used herein suggests that the decision in *James* is proper unless great importance is attached to excluding the Federal Government from prosecution of local crimes, such as theft, robbery, and embezzlement. This exclusion would protect the wrongdoer from what Mr. Justice Black designated as "double punishment" which he regards as not unlike "double jeopardy." [61] Whether one regards this objective

60. The embezzler cannot avoid inclusion by arguing that since he intended to make a restitution of the embezzled funds, the funds should be treated as a loan. There is no "consensual" recognition of an obligation to repay in this situation. Donald R. Robinson, T.C. Memo. 1966–5.

61. Mr. Justice Black observed in his dissent: "This graphically illustrates one of the great dangers of opening up the federal tax statute, or any others, for use by federal prosecutors against defendants who not only can be but are tried for their crimes in local state courts and punished there. If the people of this country are to be subjected to constitutional command against double jeopardy, it seems to us it would be far wiser for this Court to wait and let Congress attempt to do it." 366 U.S. 213, 230 (1961).

Another constitutional problem which can arise in connection with the problem of taxing illegally acquired gain is the extent to which the fifth

as within the scope of Political Order, or more appropriately reflective of a microcriterion fashioned to describe a concern with fairness to those accused of crimes, it is true that it must provide most of the justification for a preference for *Wilcox* over *James*.

Practicality supports *James* by suggesting that no attempt be made to balance the value of the receipt against the value of the claim of the victim to determine the precise extent to which the wrongdoer has been enriched. In addition, it condemns the illusive distinction between *Rutkin* and *Wilcox*.[62]

Equity is somewhat less adamant. If the embezzler is compared with the honest taxpayer who acquires a receipt accompanied by a known adverse claim, Equity cannot justify complete inclusion in the case of the honest taxpayer and total exclusion in the instance of the dishonest.[63]

---

amendment's proscription against self-incrimination may limit the congressional taxing power when it seeks to ascertain the source of the income. See, for example, McFee, *The Fifth Amendment and the Federal Gambling Tax,* 5 DUKE L.J. 86 (1956); Chenoweth, *A Judicial Balance Sheet for the Federal Gambling Tax,* 53 Nw. U.L. REV. 457 (1958).

62. This leaves the possibility that in *James* the Court could have eliminated *Rutkin* and returned to *Wilcox* and thus removed from income the "sporadic loot of an embezzler, an extortioner or a robber." Rutkin v. United States, 343 U.S. 130, 141 (1952) (Black, J., dissenting). Practical problems would remain however, because it then would become necessary to distinguish between "sporadic loot" and the earnings of an illegal business, trade or profession for which there is little or no case for exclusion. See United States v. Sullivan, 274 U.S. 259 (1927). Exclusion of all receipts from illegal sources, even where such source rose to the "dignity" of an illegal business would collide harshly with the criterion of Equity. This would not be an easy task. See Keesling, *Illegal Transactions and the Income Tax,* 5 U.C.L.A. L. REV. 26, 33, n. 37 (1958).

63. In *Rutkin* the Court put it this way: "There is no adequate reason why assailable unlawful gains should be treated differently in this respect from assailable lawful gains." 343 U.S. 130, 137 (1952). In *James* the Court said: "When a law-abiding taxpayer mistakenly receives income in one year, which receipt is assailed and found to be invalid in a subsequent year, the taxpayer must nonetheless report the amount as 'gross income' in the year received. . . . We do not believe that Congress intended to treat a

Nonetheless, when the honest and dishonest receive an equal amount, it is unlikely each experiences an equal change "in the store of property rights." Treating them alike by requiring complete inclusion by both may frequently closely approximate Equity; but it remains an approximation and not a refined application of the standard. Few areas better illustrate that the determination of the existence of gain often is a task more judgmental than arithmetical in nature.

---

law-breaking taxpayer differently." 363 U.S. 213, 219–20 (1961). See also Note, *Taxation of Misappropriated Property: The Decline and Incomplete Fall of Wilcox*, 62 YALE L.J. 662, 667 (1953).

IV. Realization and Non-recognition

THE PRECEDING CHAPTERS have made plain that economic gain and taxable gain frequently are not coterminous. Sometimes economic gain exceeds taxable income,[1] while at other times the reverse is true.[2] However, nowhere is this disparity more apparent than when the meaning of "realization" and its relationship to "non-recognition" of gain or loss is examined.

It has always been true that the mere appreciation in value of property does not constitute taxable gain.[3] It is also presently true that the gift, or transfer at death, of appreciated property does not constitute taxable gain to the transferor.[4] In these situations, as well as in many others, the reason often given for the absence of taxable gain is that the gain has not been realized.

1. For example, where the contingencies affecting the amount to be received result in a postponement of gain until the recovery of basis.

2. For example, where receipts are subject to accompanying obligations or restrictions which do not preclude inclusion of the full amount in income.

3. Baldwin Locomotive Works v. McCoach, 221 Fed. 59 (3d Cir. 1915); Sprunt & Son, Inc., 24 B.T.A. 599 (1931) (A); T.B.M. 42, 1 C.B. 273 (1919); T.B.M. 41, 1 C.B. 292 (1919).

4. On the reversion of beneficial enjoyment to a grantor of property on the termination of a prior interest, see Perry v. United States, 160 F. Supp. 270 (Ct. Cl, 1958) (dissenting opinion). *But cf.* Helvering v. Bruun, 309 U.S. 461 (1940). See also Griswold, *Charitable Gifts of Income and the I.R.C.,* 65 HARV. L. REV. 84 (1951); Bittker, *Charitable Gifts of Income and the I.R.C.: Another View,* 65 HARV. L. REV. 1375 (1952); Note, *Gratuitous Disposition of Property on Realization of Income,* 62 HARV. L. REV. 1181 (1949); Rice, *Judicial Trends on Gratuitous Assignments to Avoid Estate Tax,* 64 YALE L.J. 991 (1953).

The necessity for "realization" as a condition to taxable gain is reflected in, and imposed by, the language of section 61 (a) of the Code, which speaks of "income from whatever source derived," "Gross income derived from business," and "Gains derived from dealings in property." [5] At one time, realization was thought to be a constitutional requirement as well. While a comprehensive discussion of the constitutional aspects of gross income is deferred until Chapter VII, an understanding of "realization" requires a brief look at some of the cases in which constitutional issues were involved.

In *Eisner* v. *Macomber* [6] the Supreme Court, in determining that it was unconstitutional to tax as income a stock dividend of common declared in respect of common, uttered what Surrey has called "fateful words": [7]

Here we have the essential matter: not a gain accruing to capital, not a growth or increment of value *in* the investment; but a gain, a profit, something of exchangeable value *proceeding from* the property, *severed from* the capital however invested or employed, and *coming in,* being *derived,* that is, *received* or *drawn by* the recipient (the taxpayer) for his *separate* use, benefit and disposal;—that is income derived from property. Nothing else answers the description.

Income must be severed from capital and does not exist when a "stockholder has received nothing out of the company's assets for his separate use and benefit." [8]

5. SURREY & WARREN, FEDERAL INCOME TAXATION 608 (1960 ed.) ; Griswold, *In Brief Reply,* 65 HARV. L. REV. 1389 (1952) said: "For better or for worse, we are operating under a tax system which regards realization as of some importance. Even though this may not necessarily be a constitutional requirement, it is a practical conclusion. Without 'realization' of some sort, we do not take income into account."

6. 252 U.S. 189 (1920).

7. Surrey, *The Supreme Court and the Federal Income Tax: Some Implications of the Recent Discussions,* 35 ILL. L. REV. 779 (1941).

8. 252 U.S. 189, 211 (1920).

Despite this language, the Court thereafter commenced a long process of transforming realization from an inflexible constitutional mandate to a statutory requirement largely based on administrative convenience. The manner in which this was done has been described many times.[9] In *Marr* v. *United States* [10] the Court approved the argument that in a corporate reorganization, involving the exchange of common and preferred stock of a Delaware corporation for common and preferred of a New Jersey corporation, the "gain in value resulting from profits" is taxable to the shareholder "when it is represented by an essentially different interest in the same business enterprise or property. . . ." [11] *Eisner* v. *Macomber* was distinguished as one in which, following the distribution, the taxpayer had "the same proportional interest of the same kind in essentially the same corporation." [12] Although, as Magill pointed out,[13] a layman or economist would not appreciate this distinction, it was enough for the Court.

Fifteen years later, the Court held that a lessor had gain upon termination of a lease under which the lessee had erected a building which reverted to the lessor. This decision, *Helvering* v. *Bruun*,[14] interpreted the emphasis upon severance in *Eisner* v. *Macomber* as "expressions . . . used to clarify the distinction between an ordinary dividend and a stock dividend. . . ." The principle of realization

9. See, MAGILL, TAXABLE INCOME 24–80 (1945); Surrey, n. 7 *supra*. For a previous brief description by the author, see Sneed, *A Defense of the Tax Court's Result in Prunier and Casale,* 43 CORNELL L.Q. 339, 347–53 (1958).

10. 268 U.S. 536 (1925).

11. *Id.* at 540. See also Hall, *Exchange of Securities in Corporate Reorganization as Income,* 20 ILL. L. REV. 601 (1926).

12. *Id.* at 542.

13. MAGILL, TAXABLE INCOME 79 (1945).

14. 309 U.S. 461 (1940).

which permits the finding of gain even though the building was not removable was then stated as follows:

> Gain may occur as a result of exchange of property, payment of taxpayer's indebtedness, relief from liability, or other profit realized from the completion of a transaction. The fact that gain is a portion of the value of property received by the taxpayer in the transaction does not negative its realization.[15]

With gathering momentum, the Court in the next term characterized the requirement of realization as one "founded on administrative convenience." The occasion was *Helvering* v. *Horst*,[16] in which it was held that a donor of a negotiable interest coupon realized income where the donee received payment thereon in the same year in which the transfer was made. Realization is a taxable event which occurs "when the last step is taken by which he [the taxpayer] obtains the fruition of the economic gain." [17] It merely requires the postponement of the taxation of economic gain until the "final event of enjoyment." [18]

The Court has not drifted from *Brunn* and *Horst*. In *Commissioner* v. *Glenshaw Glass Co.*[19] the Court described *Eisner* v. *Macomber* as holding that the distribution of the stock dividend was not a "taxable event," a term obviously more suitable than "realization" for centering attention

---

15. *Id.* at 469. The result in Helvering v. Bruun was altered by Congress in 1942. Int. Rev. Code of 1954, § 109.

16. 311 U.S. 112. See Surrey, *The Supreme Court and the Federal Income Tax: Some Implications of the Recent Decisions*, 35 ILL. L. REV. 779, 784–91 (1941); Harrow, *Helvering v. Horst: Some Notes on Recent Applications of the Doctrine*, 6 N.Y.U. TAX INST. 1127 (1948); Miller, *Gifts of Income and of Property: What the Horst Case Decides*, 5 TAX L. REV. 1 (1949).

17. *Id.* at 115.

18. *Ibid.*

19. 348 U.S. 426 (1955). See p. 15 *supra*.

on "administrative convenience." The definition of income used in *Eisner* v. *Macomber*—"the gain derived from capital, from labor or from both combined"—was put aside as not intended "to provide a touchstone to all future gross income questions." [20] However, the requirement of realization, in its post–*Bruun* and *Horst* form, was acknowledged when the Court, in holding punitive damages to be income, observed: "Here we have instances of undeniable accessions to wealth, *clearly realized,* and over which the taxpayers have complete dominion." [21] (Italics added.)

Finally, in *United States* v. *Davis*,[22] a decision which was discussed in Chapter III, the Court approached the problem (whether the transfer of appreciated property by a husband to his wife by reason of their divorce in satisfaction of her marital property rights resulted in gain to the husband) from the standpoint of ascertaining the existence of a "taxable event." While *Davis* arguably would not pose a close constitutional issue even under the *Eisner* v. *Macomber* view of realization, it is instructive because of the manner in which the "taxable event" issue was approached. This issue was viewed as involving simply the determination of *when* an economic gain *should* be taxed. Arguments based on analogous transactions, the nature of the wife's property interest and previous administrative and judicial practice, were marshaled.[23] No constitutional rigidities appeared to constrain analysis. Thus, although

20. 348 U.S. 426, 431 (1955).

21. *Ibid.* See Wright, *The Effect of the Source of Realized Benefits upon the Supreme Court's Concept of Taxable Receipts,* 8 STAN. L. REV. 164 (1956).

22. 370 U.S. 65 (1962).

23. See pp. 39–62 *supra* for the discussion of the manner in which the *amount* of gain was determined.

realization remains a requirement, the bonds of *Eisner* v. *Macomber* have been exchanged for those of fairness and convenience.

The foregoing, however, is little more than a tranquil tableau set in a much larger tapestry. When this tapestry is viewed as a whole, it is clear that gain can be more easily deferred than the Court's interpretation of realization might suggest. Although *Marr* v. *United States*[24] and the subsequent decisions of the Court make clear that a change in the form or extent of the taxpayer's investment[25] is an appropriate occasion for the realization of gain, the Code, and to some extent administrative practice, are far less demanding. Thus, despite the fact that under the Court's view an exchange of property for property of a like kind,[26] property for all the stock of a newly organized corporation,[27] stock for stock in another corporation,[28] and stock for property in a corporate liquidation even when a continuation of the business[29] results in gain or loss, the Code presently contains provisions which under certain circumstances[30] treat these and similar transactions as instances where gain or loss is not *recognized* although technically *realized*. Some of these provisions trace their ancestry back to the Revenue Act of 1921[31] and the regula-

24. 268 U.S. 536 (1925).

25. MAGILL, TAXABLE INCOME 65–80 (rev. ed. 1945).

26. California Delta Farms, Inc., 6 B.T.A. 1301 (1927) (land for land); Cooper-Brannan Naval Stores Co., 9 B.T.A. 105 (1927).

27. Jefferson Livingston, 18 B.T.A. 1184 (1930); C. A. O'Meara, 11 B.T.A. 101 (1928).

28. Ralph Andrew Applegate, 10 B.T.A. 705 (1928).

29. Langstaff v. Lucas, 9 F.2d 691 (W.D.Ky. 1925), *aff'd* 13 F.2d 1022 (6th Cir. 1926), *cert. denied* 273 U.S. 721 (1926).

30. Liquidation followed by reincorporation may be considered a reorganization in which gain or loss is not recognized.

31. Revenue Act of 1921, § 202 (c)(1) permitted exchanges of property of a like kind, stock and securities for stock and securities in a corporate

tions of an even earlier date.[32] Exchanges of property for property of a like kind,[33] formation of corporations or partnerships,[34] reorganizations of corporations (involving either stock for stock or assets for stock exchanges under circumstances carefully detailed in the Code),[35] liquidation of partnerships and, to a limited extent, corporations [36] may result in no recognition of gain or loss.

Even the virtual equivalent of the receipt of compensation income is not recognized when contributed by the employer to qualified option, profit-sharing, stock bonus, and annuity plans.[37] The recent enactment of somewhat similar provisions designed for the self-employed and partners,[38] as well as the existence of several do-it-yourself techniques,[39] further underscore the breadth and scope of

---

reorganization, and property for stock of a controlled corporation without recognition of gain or loss. Their sophisticated descendants may be found in Int. Rev. Code of 1954, §§ 351, 354, 355, 361, 368, 1031.

32. See the discussion in Helvering v. Walbridge, 70 F.2d 683 (2d Cir. 1934), *cert. denied* 293 U.S. 594 (1934) of the Treasury's position in respect of realization on formation and liquidation of partnerships as reflected in Regulations dating back to 1919. Magill examines this area very fully. TAXABLE INCOME 134–38 (rev. ed. 1945).

33. Int. Rev. Code of 1954, § 1031.

34. Int. Rev. Code of 1954, §§ 351, 721.

35. Int. Rev. Code of 1954, §§ 354, 355, 361, 368.

36. Int. Rev. Code of 1954, §§ 333, 731.

37. Int. Rev. Code of 1954, §§ 402, 403.

38. Int. Rev. Code of 1954, § 483 (added by the Revenue Act of 1964, Pub. L. 88–272, tit. II, § 224).

39. The principles of accounting applicable to tax cash-basis taxpayers may be used to fashion a deferred compensation plan outside the framework of qualified plans. Rev. Rul. 60–31, 1960–1 C.B. 174. Also, professional corporations or associations organized under state law may provide accountants, doctors, lawyers, and other professional groups access to the qualified plan structure. See United States v. Kintner, 216 F.2d 418 (9th Cir. 1954). The present regulations, however, leave little scope for the effective operation of this technique. Treas. Reg. § 301.7701–2 (1960), as amended by T.D. 6797, 1965–1 C.B. 553. This position of the regulations has been criticized severely. See Scallen, *Federal Income Taxation of Professional Associations and Corporations*, 49 MINN. L. REV. 603 (1965).

techniques which function to defer recognition of gain which has been realized.

The principles of realization, when joined with these and other non-recognition techniques,[40] result in significant amounts of gain being deferred and in some instances escaping tax altogether. Thus, a taxpayer whose property has appreciated in value may choose to defer the tax on the gain by not selling, and this gain can escape tax where no taxable disposition occurs before death. Where the property is stock or securities, the non-recognition provisions relating to corporate organizations and reorganizations make possible substantial alterations in the nature of the investment without constituting a taxable disposition.[41] Earnings of closely held corporations to a certain extent can be held in the business [42] and not realized at the shareholder level until those in control deem it expedient to do so. Employees may tuck away a portion of their earnings until retirement, and gifts of appreciated property either shift to others the burden of the tax imposed on the gain or, when given to charity, permit both a deduction equal to the fair market value of the property and the non-realization of the gain.[43]

To understand the contrast between the Court's erosion of the constitutional requirement of realization and the

40. *E.g.*, Int. Rev. Code of 1954, § 1033 (involuntary conversions), § 1034 (sale of residence).

41. For a lively analysis of this general problem and some particular suggestions for improvement, see Hellerstein, *Mergers, Taxes, and Realism,* 71 HARV. L. REV. 254 (1957).

42. Improper accumulations of surplus and personal holding company status will lead to severe tax penalties. Int. Rev. Code of 1954 §§ 531–37, 541–47.

43. The statement relating to charitable gifts assumes no problem with percentage limitations on charitable gifts. For a recent and unusual illustration of this technique, see Sheppard v. United States, 66–1 USTC 9461 (Ct. Cl. 1966). Income is realized, however, when the gift constitutes an assignment of income. *E.g.*, Friedman v. Comm'r, 346 F.2d 506 (6th Cir. 1965).

openhanded manner of Congress in the area of non-recognition, it is first necessary to recall that the Court was seeking to establish that Congress had broad constitutional power to tax income while Congress was concerned with how that power was to be used. However, the contrast cannot be explained entirely on this basis. Fundamentally, it rests on the differences with which the macrocriteria have been ordered by the Court and Congress. These differences will now be examined.

It should be clear that Equity requires that taxpayers be put on an inventory basis with respect to all their assets.[44] While the Court has not said so explicitly, it is very probable that there is no present constitutional bar to prevent Congress from adopting such a procedure.[45] However, realization, as presently enunciated by the Court, does not require such a procedure. Many difficulties would exist were it to do so. Adequate market information frequently is not available, and the necessity of annual estimates based on conjecture has little appeal to Government or taxpayers.[46] It seems fair to say that the Court, in working out its notions of realization, has been guided by what it considered to be the proper balance between Equity and Practicality.

44. Under such a system appreciation and depreciation are reflected by, as Simons put it, ascertaining " 'wealth' at the end of the period and then subtracting 'wealth' at the beginning." PERSONAL INCOME TAXATION 50 (1938). In the same work Simons states at p. 100, "Strictly speaking, the calculation of income demands complete revaluation of all assets and obligations at the end of every period. Practically, the question is: How shall the requisite value estimates be obtained? This is where the realization criterion may properly be introduced as a practical expedient. But the problem here is one of administration, not of definition."

45. Bittker has put it this way. "Despite *Eisner* v. *Macomber*, I think all taxpayers could be put on an annual inventory basis with appreciation and depreciation being tallied up and taken into the tax return at year's end." *Charitable Gifts of Income and the Internal Revenue Code*, 65 HARV. L. REV. 1375, 1380 (1952).

46. SIMONS, PERSONAL INCOME TAXATION 56 (1938).

Reduced Economic Inequality and Political Order probably also have played a part in shaping the Court's view. The dissenters in *Marr* v. *United States,* by insisting that realization depended upon a material change in the business and assets [47] of the corporation being reorganized, were concerned both with limiting the power of Congress to tax income and protecting wealth from too frequent depletion by taxation. The majority then was, and in subsequent realization cases have been, less committed to these objectives.

Congress, lacking authority to determine the scope of its own power, has been able to shape non-recognition rules without regard to questions relating to its taxing power. Also, the attachment of Congress to Reduced Economic Inequality has varied in intensity as the political winds changed and, on balance, usually has been less intense than that of the Court. It was, to illustrate, during a Republican era that the first steps were taken to put in statutory form many of the non-recognition rules applicable to exchanges of property of a like kind and corporate organizations and reorganizations.[48] It was during a New Deal Democratic era that these provisions were significantly restricted in scope.[49]

47. In the dissent by Justices Van Devanter, McReynolds, Sutherland, and Butter, it was said: "The practical result of the things done was but the reorganization of a going concern. The business and assets were not materially changed, and the stockholder received nothing actually severed from his original capital interest—nothing differing in substance from what he already had." 268 U.S. 536, 542 (1925).

48. Revenue Act of 1921, § 202 (C), 42 Stat. 227. Revenue Act of 1924, § 204 (a)(8), 43 Stat. 253.

49. Revenue Act of 1934, §§ 112 (b), (d), (g), 48 Stat. 683. The form of corporate division known as a "spin-off" was banished from the circle of tax-free reorganizations. See BITTKER, FEDERAL INCOME TAXATION OF CORPORATIONS AND SHAREHOLDERS 322–28 (1959). Magill has an authoritative discussion of these statutory changes. TAXABLE INCOME 145–74 (rev. ed. 1945).

Practicality, however, also has been a dominant force in Congressional thinking. In the reorganization area, for example, the effort has been to impose the tax only when money or property other than certain stock and securities changes hands.[50] A similar thought has played a part in the framing of provisions relating to exchanges of property of a like kind [51] and qualified pension plans.[52] Difficult valuation problems were reduced, if not eliminated, in this manner.

Congress also has been concerned with a criterion which probably played little part in the thinking of the Court— Free Market Compatibility. To grasp this point it must be understood that to the extent that realization does not require taxpayers to inventory their assets, the functioning of a free market is impaired. Inasmuch as realization, as worked out by the Court, imposes no such requirement, it would, if not altered, encourage shareholders to resist those corporate organizations and reorganizations which from the standpoint of the market would be desirable. Not being willing to embrace the taxation of unrealized gains on an annual basis, Congress could eliminate this resistance only by enactment of fairly comprehensive non-recognition provisions. This it did in the first decade of the life of the present tax.

50. MAGILL, TAXABLE INCOME 144 (rev. ed. 1945).

51. *Cf.* MERTENS, LAW OF FEDERAL INCOME TAXATION § 20.22 (1957); HOLMES, FEDERAL TAXES 528 (1923 ed.); BLAKEY, THE FEDERAL INCOME TAX 220 (1940).

52. The proper treatment by an employee of a distribution of stock having unrealized appreciation in value by a stock-bonus, profit-sharing, or pension plan has posed a problem since the beginning of the income tax. The Revenue Act of 1928, § 165, first provided for a deferral of tax on such appreciation. S. REP. No. 960, 70th Cong., 1st Sess., 21 (1928). This was removed in 1932. The Revenue Act of 1932, § 165, 47 Stat. 169. At the present time it is excluded. Int. Rev. Code of 1954, § 402 (a)(1). For a discussion of present rules which date from 1951, see 4 MERTENS, LAW OF FEDERAL INCOME TAXATION, § 25 B. 50–51 (1957).

It is tempting to speculate on another aspect of Free Market Compatibility which is suggested by the breadth of non-recognition and deferral techniques in the present law. It will be recalled that John Stuart Mill observed that "no income tax is really just from which savings are not exempted. . . ."[53] Among economists, arguments generated by this viewpoint persist to this day. It is generally agreed, however, that a general income tax which includes interest and similar income from investment within its definition of gross income differentiates against saving and in favor of consumption. Pigou put it as follows:

An income tax, on the other hand, differentiates against saving, by striking savings both when they are made and also when they yield their fruits. Thus a general permanent income tax at the rate of X percent strikes the part of income that is spent at this rate. But if $100 of income is put away for saving, this tax removes $X at the moment and, thereafter, removes also some parts of the fruits yielded to it.[54]

This "announcement effect," to use Pigou's term, may be eliminated by either the adoption of a general expenditure tax[55] or the exemption of investment income from income taxation.[56]

53. Principles of Political Economy, Book V, ch. 11, § 4 (1848).

54. Pigou, Public Finance 118–19 (3d rev. ed. 1962). Musgrave makes the same point. See his discussion of a model where it is assumed there is pure competition and only one product. The choice is between consuming now or later. The Theory of Public Finance 152–53 (1959). He then concludes that an income tax on all income regardless of source "reduces the rate of substitution of future for present consumption." *Id.* at 159. For a spirited development of the point, see Kaldor, An Expenditure Tax 79–101 (1955).

55. The possible structure of an expenditure tax can be grasped by examining the following extract from Kaldor, An Expenditure Tax 191–93 (1955). "It was left to Irving Fisher to show that comprehensive records of personal expenditure are in fact unnecessary for the administration of the tax since expenditure could in principle be computed as the difference between certain money incomings and outgoings. Fisher's idea was that since what a man spends is nothing else but the difference between what he had available for spending and what he is left with,

personal expenditure can be computed for tax purposes by taking his income (as at present) *adding* monies received from the sale of capital assets, depletion of bank balances, etc., and *deducting* sums spent on the purchase of capital assets and on 'non-personal' or 'non-chargeable' expenditure.

"This method of assessment can perhaps best be understood by seeing what a tax return would look like. The return would be drawn up on the following broad lines:

(1) Bank balances and cash at beginning of year

(2) Receipts (in money or money's worth) such as wages and salaries, business drawings, interest and dividends, and all other kinds of income to which the present Income Tax applies; in addition, bequests, gifts, winnings, etc.

(3) Money borrowed, or money received in repayment of loans

(4) Proceeds of sales of investments (including houses)

            Total receipts   _____

Less:

(5) Money lent or money paid in repayment of previous borrowing

(6) Purchase of investments (including houses)

(7) Bank balance and cash at end of year

           Gross expenditure   _____

Less:

(8) Exempted expenditure

(9) Allowance for spreading of expenditure on durable goods

Add:

(10) Proportion of expenditure on durable goods incurred in previous years and chargeable in the current year

         Chargeable expenditure   _____

"Items (1) – (4) represent the total amount of money at the taxpayer's disposal from all possible sources; items (5) – (7) represent the total amount of money which is applied in ways other than personal spending. The difference between the two represents the 'gross personal expenditure' from which, after a number of deductions and adjustments, net chargeable expenditure is arrived at.

"Looking at the matter in another way a man obtains spending cash (a) from regular income sources—such as a wage or salary,

Is it not reasonable to suggest that the extensive departures from Equity, with its emphasis on accretion, reflected by the provisions here discussed have been semiconsciously inspired by a desire to reduce the extent of differentiation against saving theoretically possible in an income tax? [57] In fact, is it far-fetched to say that we do not have an income tax; that it is rather a hybrid resulting from the joinder of an income and an expenditure tax? Moreover, it is by no means certain that the expenditure tax characteristics are diminishing in importance. Perhaps some day our attachment to the Simons-type income tax will appear quite primitive.

---

interest and dividends, etc.; (b) from gifts and bequests or winnings; (c) by depleting his cash balances or bank accounts; (d) by selling capital assets (stocks and shares, real property, etc.) *in excess* of his purchases; (e) by borrowing. Some of these items can be negative or positive. At present only (a) figures on the income tax return. Under an expenditure tax on the lines suggested by Fisher the liability would still be assessed in a similar manner—starting from 'income' so to speak—but there would be a series of additions and deductions the net result of which should make spendings, and not earnings, the basis of the charge."

Also see Expenditure Tax Act, Act Number 29, 1957 (India); chap. v, pp. 79–81 *infra*.

56. Pigou rejected the first as impractical and the second on the basis of the excess of investment income over savings in England in 1938 and the distributional effects which would favor the rich. PUBLIC FINANCE 122–33 (3d rev. ed. 1962). Kaldor did not find these objections nearly as persuasive. AN EXPENDITURE TAX, chs. ii, vii (1955). These two techniques, of course, yield different results where savings and investment income are not equal. PIGOU, *op. cit. supra*, at 130. In the models employed by Musgrave, a general consumption tax and an income tax excluding interest are treated as equivalents. Musgrave, *op. cit.* n. 54 *supra*.

57. The exchange of stock for stock in a corporate reorganization, for example, would not constitute under Kaldor's structure, n. 55 *supra,* either receipts or the proceeds of the sales of investments. Similarly, compensation for personal services invested in retirement plans would disappear from Kaldor's taxable base because the receipt would be balanced by the purchase of an investment. See items (2) and (6), n. 55 *supra*.

B. Consumption, Status, and the
Sixteenth Amendment

V. Gain in the Form of Consumption

THE OBJECT of this chapter is to focus on Gain in the Form of Consumption, the second of the two main headings under which the analysis of gross income offered here is organized. At the risk of tedium, you will recall that the Simons definition goes as follows:

Personal income may be defined as the algebraic sum of (1) the market value of rights exercised in consumption and (2) the change in the value of the store of property rights between the beginning and end of the period in question.[1]

Present concern is with that portion of the definition which reads "the market value of rights exercised in consumption."

At the threshold it must be pointed out that the consumption of capital, or dis-saving, is not income even though rights are being exercised in consumption. When this occurs, the positive figure representing "the market value of rights exercised in consumption" is precisely offset by a decrease "in the value of the store of property rights" at the end of the taxable period. Thus, the elderly person who uses savings of yesterday to purchase a meal today has no income as a result of this transaction. However, when the existing store of property rights is not being depleted, after all proper adjustments, the exercise of

1. SIMONS, PERSONAL INCOME TAXATION 50.

79

property rights in consumption does result in gross income.

In this respect the present income tax differs from an expenditure tax under which this form of consumption would be taxable.[2] This follows because under an expenditure tax the task is to fix the amount of aggregate consumption (as opposed to investment) from whatever source and apportion this amount to the appropriate period.

The difference between an income and expenditure tax can be further illustrated by reference to the purchase and enjoyment of a work of art which appreciates rapidly in value subsequent to its purchase. Under an income tax the problem is to devise, if possible, a means whereby the value of the owner's enjoyment, determined by reference to values prevailing at the time of such enjoyment, can be measured.[3] Even though, in view of the appreciation in value, no part of the enjoyment constitutes a return of

2. KALDOR, AN EXPENDITURE TAX 221–22 (1955) recognizes that the taxation of consumption from savings by retired persons would present a particularly difficult problem during a period of transition from an income tax to an expenditure tax. He was concerned about the taxation under an income tax of the sums which went into savings and their taxation under an expenditure tax when consumed. To meet this problem, he proposed a special exemption for persons in retirement at the time of the transition from an income tax to an expenditure tax. To the extent savings were not subject to the income tax when put by, to that extent taxation as consumed under an expenditure tax involves no hardship. Indeed, there is little difference in that case between an income tax incurred when savings are drawn down and an expenditure tax. Thus, because of the extensive use of qualified pension, profit-sharing, and stock bonus plans in this country, the transition to an expenditure tax would be easier than it otherwise would be. Thus, the hybrid features of the present system are highlighted again. See chap. iv, nn. 55 and 57.

3. SIMONS, PERSONAL INCOME TAXATION 119 (1938). "Consumption, presumably, should be measured in terms of values at the time of consumption; but to ignore changes in value between time of purchase and time of use will ordinarily make very little difference. The difference might be large, of course, where a man purchased choice beverages and allowed them to acquire the quality and distinction of ripe age—especially if prohibition came in the interim."

capital, it remains true that the measurement of the value of enjoyment poses difficult problems.

The issues faced by an expenditure tax are different. They are: first, did the acquisition of the work constitute consumption or investment; and second, if consumption, to what taxable period, or periods, should it be attributed, or, if investment, to what extent should the value of enjoyment be treated as consumption in each taxable period.[4] Only the latter issue involves a task similar to that faced by an income tax; that is, the determination of the value of enjoyment once the purchase is found to have been an investment.

As will be pointed out, practical income tax law by and large has avoided tasks such as evaluating the enjoyment derived from an object of art. Nonetheless, the burden of dealing with the "market value of rights exercised in consumption" cannot be escaped because, even if theory could be ignored, the frequency with which compensation is in a form that immediately satisfies consumer needs makes such avoidance impossible.

1. Compensation in Kind Which Satisfies Consumer Needs

Instances of this form of compensation are numerous. Payment by employer of living and other personal expenses of employees,[5] use of tangible property owned by

4. KALDOR, AN EXPENDITURE TAX 195–201 (1955) discusses these issues under the heading of "Consumers' 'Capital' Expenditures."

5. Rudolph v. United States, 370 U.S. 269 (1962) (pleasure trip provided by insurance company for agents and their wives) ; Silverman v. Comm'r, 253 F.2d 849 (8th Cir. 1958) (reimbursement of travel expenses of wife of employee) ; Campbell Sash Works, Inc. v. United States, 217 F. Supp. 74 (N.D. Ohio 1963) (vacation trip furnished by employer) ; Harris W. Bradley, 39 T.C. 652 (1963) (reimbursement of loss by employee on sale of his residence) . Meals and lodging, when not excluded by the provisions of Int. Rev. Code, § 119, fall within this category.

employer,[6] and contributions to protection of families of employees by payment of life insurance costs [7] are three which readily come to mind.

6. Dean v. Comm'r, 187 F.2d 1019 (3d Cir. 1951) (occupancy by president of residence owned by corporation income to extent of "fair value of occupying") ; Chandler v. Comm'r, 119 F.2d 623 (3d Cir. 1941) (lodge owned by corporation used by employee and family) ; R. A. Heintz Construction Co. v. United States, 65-2 U.S.T.C. ¶ 9455 (D. Ore. 1965) (rental by controlling shareholder of residence owned by corporation compensation to extent fair rental value exceeded rental paid) ; O'Neill v. Patterson, 65-1 U.S.T.C. ¶ 9436 (N.D. Ala. 1964) (personal use of employer-owned auto). *But cf.* Richards v. Comm'r, 111 F.2d 376 (5th Cir. 1940) (rented value of property treated as gift). These cases raise additional interesting questions. Where the employee is also a shareholder of the corporate employer, it must be determined for some purposes (e.g., whether the employer is entitled to a deduction) whether the payment is compensation or a dividend. See Greenspon v. Comm'r, 229 F.2d 947 (8th Cir. 1956) , where expenses incurred by corporation in enhancing value of home of employee and major shareholder treated as corporate dividend rather than compensation. The problem has been significantly reduced in importance by Int. Rev. Code of 1954, § 274 (a)(1)(B) , enacted in 1962, which prevents deduction of expenses incurred in connection with a "facility" used with an "activity" constituting "entertainment, amusement, or recreation" except where (1) "used primarily for the furtherance of taxpayer's trade or business" and "is directly related to the active conduct of such trade or business" or (2) used primarily for the benefit of employees other than substantial shareholders and highly compensated employees. However, where use of tangible property owned by a corporation constitutes a corporate distribution in the nature of a dividend, the effect of the transaction on corporate income and earnings and profits remains troublesome.

7. This result is quite clear where the policy is ordinary life and is owned by the employee. Treas. Reg. § 1.61–2 (d)(2) . *Cf.* Yuengling v. Comm'r, 69 F.2d 971 (1934) (premiums paid by employer on ordinary life insurance policies where insured employee had power to designate beneficiary) . The right to designate the beneficiary, however, does not always make premium payments either compensation or dividend income. In Rev. Rul. 59–184, 1959–1 C.B. 65, the Service held "that whenever a corporation purchases life insurance on the lives of its shareholders, the proceeds of which are to be used in payment for the stock of any shareholder, the premiums on such insurance do not constitute income to any stockholder even though the stockholder has the right to designate a beneficiary, if such right of the beneficiary to receive proceeds is conditioned upon the transfer of the corporate stock to the corporation." This constitutes Service acceptance of the holdings of Sanders v. Fox, 253 F.2d 855 (10th Cir. 1958) ; Premier v. Comm'r, 248 F.2d 818 (1st Cir. 1957) ; Casale v. Comm'r, 247 F.2d 440 (2d Cir. 1957) . For a different view, see Sneed, *A Defense of the Tax Court's Result in Premier and Casale*, 43 CORNELL L.Q. 339 (1958) .

Premiums are compensation income where members of employee's family are designated as beneficiaries by corporation which obtained policies and reserved no power to change such designations. Comm'r v. Bonivet, 87 F.2d 764 (2d Cir. 1937). The premiums are generally not taxable to the employees or shareholders where the beneficiary is the corporation and all incidents of ownership, including the power to change the beneficiary, are held by the corporation. An earlier ruling, however, held that premiums paid on insurance whose proceeds "inure directly to the benefit of the employee's wife or other dependents or his estate, notwithstanding the insured employee may not be permitted to designate the beneficiary," were taxable to the insured employee. G.C.M. 16069, XV-1 C.B. 84 (1936). See George M. Adams, 18 B.T.A. 381 (1929) (premiums taxable to employee where corporation not beneficiary of policy and no discussion of whether corporation could change beneficiary); N. L. Danforth, 18 B.T.A. 1221 (1930) (premiums taxable to employee where wife beneficiary and no discussion of whether corporation could change beneficiary). *But see* Lewis v. O'Malley, 140 F.2d 735 (8th Cir. 1944) (premiums on single premium policy not taxable to insured where insured's son and later a charity were designated beneficiary even though insured had power to designate beneficiary).

So-called split-dollar arrangements between employers and employees also result in taxable income to the employee to the extent the value of the insurance protection afforded him exceeds the amount of premiums he provides. Rev. Rul. 64–328, 1964–2 C.B. 11. Dividends under these arrangements also may result in gain to the employee. Rev. Rul. 66–110, 1966, Int. Rev. Bull. No. 20, at 6.

Where the corporation obtains the policy and retains all the incidents of ownership, the tax treatment of the payment of the proceeds to a designated beneficiary other than the corporation is somewhat uncertain. Ducros v. Comm'r, 272 F.2d 49 (6th Cir. 1959) (proceeds not a dividend distribution). The Service refuses to follow *Ducros.* Rev. Rul. 61–134, 1961–2 C.B. 250.

See Lawthers, *Sixth Cir. in Durcos Departs from Basic Corp. Insur. Cases,* 12 J. Tax. 92 (1960); Steinberg, *Funding Stock Redemption Agreements With Life Insurance,* 35 Taxes 669 (1957); Swados, *Death and Nonsense: The Decline and Fall of the Buy-Sell Agreement,* 26 Fordham L. Rev. (1957); Strecker, *Corporate Buy-Sell Agreements: Tax Problems in Drafting,* 15 Wash. & Lee L. Rev. 18 (1958); Note, 71 Harv. L. Rev. 687 (1958); Note, 1958 U. Ill. L. F. 135.

Where insurance protection involves a buildup of cash-surrender values, the gain to the employee is not exclusively in the form of current consumption. Until recently, however, premiums paid on group term insurance by employers were not taxable to employees. A series of rulings established this position. Rev. Rul. 54–165, 1954–1 C.B. 17; Mim. 6477, 1950–1 C.B. 16; G.C.M. 16069, XV-1 C.B. 84 (1936); L.O. 1014, 2 C.B. 88 (1920). The justification for this exclusion appeared to have rested primarily on practicality. See L.O. 1014, 2 C.B. 88, 89 (1920). It is difficult with group term insurance to ascertain the precise gain of any individual employee. Because abuses in the area developed, the 1964 Revenue Act provided for inclusion in the employee's income of the cost of such insurance to the extent it exceeds a reasonably generous exclusion. The limit was the cost of $50,000 of such insurance and the amount (if any) paid by the employee toward the purchase of such insurance. In addition, there are several exceptions to the inclusion. Int. Rev. Code of 1954, § 79. *(Continued on next page.)*

It is by no means true, however, that all employer-furnished consumption rights are included in gross income. The exclusion of meals and lodging furnished for the convenience of the employer [8] and the deductibility of certain transportation costs, meals, and lodging while away from home in pursuit of a trade or business [9] allow an indefinite amount of income in the form of rights exercised in consumption to escape tax. That is, in most instances in which the exclusion or deduction is available there is some amount, although frequently difficult to measure, which represents consumption gain unaccompanied by any diminution in value of the store of property rights. The interminable litigation in these areas primarily reflects a continuing conflict over the scope of this omission from the base of the tax. The Government, seeking to narrow this scope, is ascendant in one decade; the taxpayer, having the opposite purpose, in another.

A less well-known area in which perhaps consumption gain escapes tax is where an interest-free loan is made by an employer to an employee.[10] Initially, the failure to include in the income of the employee-borrower a sum equal to a reasonable interest rate appears inexcusable. The use of the employer's money seems no different from the use of his tangible property. However, the issue is made complex by the presence of a deduction for "all interest paid or accrued within the taxable year on in-

---

Fairly arbitrary provisions for fixing the amount of cost attributable to each employee are provided. Int. Rev. Code of 1954, § 79 (c) .

8. Int. Rev. Code of 1954, § 119.

9. Int. Rev. Code of 1954, § 162 (a)(2) .

10. The position of the text is supported by J. Simpson Dean, 35 T.C. 1083 (1961) , which involved an interest-free loan by a corporation to a shareholder. Presumably, the same result (i.e., no income to the borrower) is reached where the employer lends and the employee borrows.

debtedness." [11] This becomes clear when a simple case of an interest-free loan by an employer to an employee intended as part of the latter's compensation is considered. If it be assumed that the loan is for one year and in the amount of $1,000 and that a reasonable rate of interest is 5 per cent per annum, the employee's economic benefit from the loan is $50. At first, it would appear sensible to increase the employee's taxable compensation by $50. Hesitancy is suggested, however, when two things are realized. The first is that the economic equivalent of the interest-free loan just described (for convenience, here designated as transaction A) is a loan by the employer to the employee of $1,000 for one year, bearing interest at 5 per cent per annum accompanied by an increase in compensation of $50 per annum (for convenience, here designated as transaction B). The second is that *where the interest paid by the employee in transaction B is deductible,* the tax consequences of transaction A can be made equivalent to those of transaction B only by either (1) excluding from the employee's income in transaction A taxable compensation of $50 per annum or (2) including such compensation in transaction A and also permitting a deduction for interest which is, in fact, neither owed nor paid.

This may be put graphically with simple figures. An employee, X, with compensation income of $5,000 suffers neither an increase nor decrease of this sum by reason of a loan of $1,000 for one year at interest of 5 per cent per annum where (1) the interest is deductible and (2) his compensation is increased in an amount precisely equal to the interest paid. The $50 in increased compensation is wiped out by a deduction in the same amount. Employee Y, also receiving $5,000 in compensation income, who

11. Int. Rev. Code of 1954, § 163 (a).

obtains an interest-free loan of $1,000 for one year will suffer an increase in compensation income if (1) he is required to include in his income $50 and (2) is not afforded a deduction in the same amount. Under such circumstances Y's compensation income is $5,050, while X's remains $5,000. Because it is difficult, to say the least, to obtain an interest deduction for interest neither paid nor owed,[12] the best way to make these two economically equivalent transactions yield similar tax results is to exclude from the gross income of employee Y the economic benefits of an interest-free loan.[13] Although the Tax Court's opinion in *J. Simpson Dean* is somewhat cryptic, its analysis, in holding an interest-free loan by a corporation to its shareholder did not result in gain to the borrower, is consistent with that just set forth.[14]

12. Interest can be deducted only when paid when the taxpayer is on the cash basis. Mere accrual is not enough. Lewis C. Cristensen, 40 T.C. 563 (1963); Oscar G. Joseph, 32 B.T.A. 1192 (1935). An accrual-basis taxpayer is not entitled to deduct interest until his liability therefor becomes fixed. Security Flour Mills Co. v. Comm'r, 321 U.S. 281 (1943); Central Cuba Sugar Co. v. Comm'r, 198 F.2d 214, 217 (2d Cir. 1952).

13. While the same result could be reached by including in the employee's income a reasonable rate of interest and permitting a deduction in the same amount, § 163 of the Code presents an obstacle. It speaks of a deduction for "all interest paid or accrued within the taxable year on indebtedness." To argue that an interest-free loan generates a deduction for interest "paid" requires an affection for paradoxes, which many do not possess.

14. The relevant portion of Judge Raum's opinion in J. Simpson Dean, 35 T.C. 1083 (1961), is as follows: "These cases bear a superficial resemblance to the present case, but reflection convinces us that they are not in point. In each of them a benefit was conferred upon the stockholder or officer in circumstances such that had the stockholder or officer undertaken to procure the same benefit by an expenditure of money such expenditure would not have been deductible by him. Here, on the other hand, had petitioners borrowed the funds in question on interest-bearing notes, their payment of interest would have been fully deductible by them under section 163, I.R.C. 1954. Not only would they not be charged with the additional income in controversy herein, but they would have a deduction equal to that very amount. We think this circumstance differentiates the various cases relied upon by the Commissioner, and perhaps explains why he has apparently never taken this position in any prior case.
"We have heretofore given full force to interest-free loans for tax purposes, holding that they result in no interest deduction for the

It is obvious, therefore, that it is the deduction for interest paid or accrued which justifies exclusion of gain to the borrower where the loan is interest-free. From this it follows that where the deduction is *not* available, an exclusion of gain must be legitimated on other grounds.

This can be illustrated in the following manner. An exclusion of gain from the compensation income of employee Y, the recipient of an interest-free loan, would place him in a better position than employee X, who received a similar loan at interest with compensation increased to cover the interest charge, where both loans were incurred to purchase obligations yielding tax-exempt interests. Not being able to deduct the interest paid, X's compensation income would be $5,050. Y, on the other hand, would have only $5,000 of such income provided the exclusion is permitted. Aside from the practical difficulties attending any effort to include gain in Y's income, there is no good reason why Y's compensation income should be less than X's. To permit it to be so is to give Y the equivalent of an interest deduction which is not permitted under section 265 of the Code.

---

borrower, *A. Backus, Jr. & Sons*, 6 B.T.A. 590; *Rainbow Gasoline Corporation*, 31 B.T.A. 1050; *Howell Turpentine Co.*, 6 T.C. 364, reversed on another issue 162 F.2d 316 (C.A. 5); *D. Loveman & Son Export Corporation*, 34 T.C. 776, nor interest income to the lender, *Combs Lumber Co.*, 41 B.T.A. 339; *Society Brand Clothes, Inc.*, 18 T.C. 304; *Brandtjen & Kluge, Inc.*, 34 T.C. 416. We think it to be equally true that an interest-free loan results in no taxable gain to the borrower,[3] and we hold that the Commissioner is not entitled to any increased deficiency based upon this issue."

Footnote 3 of the opinion reads as follows: "3. As recently as 1955, this was also the view of the Commissioner. In Rev. Rul. 55–713, 1955–2 C.B. 23, in sanctioning the so-called split-dollar insurance scheme, it is said at page 24: 'In the instant case, the substance of the insurance arrangement between the parties is in all essential respects the same as if Y corporation makes annual loans without interest, of a sum of money equal to the annual increases in the cash surrender value of the policies of insurance taken out on the life of B. The mere making available of money does not result in realized income to the payee or a deduction to the payor.' "

The entire matter comes to this. Where the loan proceeds of an interest-free loan are used in a manner which would not preclude a deduction for any interest that might have been paid had the loan been at interest, an exclusion is justified. On the other hand, where the loan proceeds of an interest-free loan are used in a manner which would preclude a deduction for any interest that might have been paid had the loan been at interest, an exclusion is *not* justified. Thus, the test should be this. *Is the interest-free loan such that had it been at interest a deduction for such interest would have been available?* If the answer is affirmative, an exclusion is justified; otherwise, it is not. While some may regard use of this test as the equivalent of inclusion accompanied by an offsetting deduction, it avoids direct confrontation with the problem of justifying a deduction for interest neither paid nor owed in fact.

2. *Use of Owned Property*

Taxpayer use of property he owns, to the extent the value of such use exceeds the capital being consumed, would seem to constitute another form of gain based on "the market value of rights exercised in consumption." This form of gain, often described as imputed income,[15] generally is not taxed, however. It is distinguishable from income derived in the use of an employer's property, for example, because the latter, as well as most transactions generating taxable income, arises in an ordinary market transaction.[16]

15. Imputed income has been defined "as a flow of satisfactions from durable goods owned and used by the taxpayer, or from goods and services arising out of the personal exertions of the taxpayer on his own behalf." Marsh, *The Taxation of Imputed Income,* 58 POL. SCI. Q. 514 (1943).

16. Marsh employed this distinction. *Ibid.*

The volume of imputed income is difficult to calculate. Although the use of consumer durables, such as automobiles, furniture, art works, and houses, generates some amount of imputed income, it is clear that the greatest single source of such income is homeownership.[17] The exclusion of gain from this source discriminates against those who rent.[18] Tersely put, and without refinements, the latter satisfy their shelter wants from income subject to tax while the former accomplish the same end with tax-free income. Although correction of this discrimination by subjecting to tax this imputed income would create rather complex practical problems,[19] it is clear that the desire to

17. Marsh estimated the net imputed rent in 1940 at $1,898,900,000. *Id.* at 522. See Pechman, *Erosion of the Individual Income Tax,* 10 NAT'L TAX J. 1, 14 (1957).

18. *E.g.,* SIMONS, PERSONAL INCOME TAXATION 112 (1938); VICKREY, AGENDA FOR PROGRESSIVE TAXATION 18–19 (1947).

19. The tasks are to isolate the amount of net gain from use of home and to make certain that the treatment of the homeowner and the tenant is equal. Isolation of net gain requires (1) an approximation of the gross return from the investment in the home, (2) a determination of the extent to which this return constitutes a return of capital in the form of depreciation, and (3) an accounting for those current expenses, such as repairs and taxes, which were ordinary and necessary to the production of that return.

The gross return could be derived from the fair rental value of the premises, *i.e.,* what the owner would have to pay to obtain occupancy of similar premises in the market. Perhaps some reduction of this sum is justified in view of the responsibilities of, and lack of mobility caused by, home ownership. These three steps can almost be reduced to one by merely adopting a fixed percentage of either (a) the value of the taxpayer's equity in the home, or (b) the fair market value of the unencumbered premises as an approximation of the *net* gain. In using a percentage against full value, a deduction for interest paid on the mortgage debt is necessary. Only the excess over the interest charge represents net gain. Such a deduction is not necessary where the percentage is applied against the equity of the taxpayer. Obviously, the use of arbitrary percentages gives Practicality ascendancy over Equity.

In any event, the second task must be faced. Is imposition of a tax on the net gain from home ownership sufficient to eliminate discrimination between tenants and homeowners? Or does discrimination still exist? It has been suggested that to eliminate all discrimination against the tenant it is necessary to provide him with deductions for "vicarious" expenses incurred by the landlord identical in character to those which the home-

encourage homeownership presently prevents the elimination of this discrimination. Equity, Free Market Compatibility, and, perhaps to some degree, Reduced Economic Inequality [20] all suggest a change.

These same considerations are applicable in determining the extent to which benefits from other consumer durables should be included in income. However, the practical difficulties of inclusion are even greater here than in the case of homeownership.[21]

---

owner is permitted to deduct (or which are accounted for in fixing the percentage to be used by the homeowner) in determining net gain. Marsh, *The Taxation of Imputed Income,* 58 POL. SCI. Q. 514, 531, n. 42. The logic of this suggestion can be illustrated in the following manner. If it is assumed an investment of X sum in a home yields Y *net* gain, then only Y is subject to tax. The investment of X sum in securities yields, it can be assumed, $Y + Z$ sum. This amount is taxable. Its use to pay rent would reduce the amount subject to tax to Y only if a deduction in the amount of Z were available. The amount Z should equal the deductions for depreciation, taxes, insurance, repairs, etc., available to the homeowner who invested X and derives a net gain of Y. Can this discrimination be overcome by taxing the homeowner on more than his *net* gain?

Are there other ways to approach the problem of putting the homeowner and the tenant on equal footing? To what extent is this achieved by eliminating the deductions available to the homeowner for interest and taxes? See VICKREY, AGENDA FOR PROGRESSIVE TAXATION 22–24 (1947), where it is said this elimination will greatly reduce present inequities. *But see* White, *Proper Income Tax Treatment of Deductions for Personal Expense, Tax Revision Compendium, House Committee on Ways and Means,* 86th Cong., 1st Sess. part 1, 365–6 (1959), where presence of interest deduction in respect to home mortgage debts is defended. To what extent, if any, would the discrimination be reduced by the proposal in the President's 1963 Tax Message to limit itemized deductions to those in excess of 5 per cent of adjusted gross income? President's 1963 Tax Message, 88th Cong., 1st Sess., 15 (Comm. Print 1963). Would discrimination be eliminated, or its cutting edge merely reversed, if tenants were permitted to deduct their rent? Should such a deduction include the entire rent where the landlord assumed the obligation to pay the telephone bill?

20. Omission of this form of gain diminishes the effectiveness of progression. While the distribution of tenancy by income classes is not available, it is probable that a large proportion of tenants are in the lower-income groups.

21. See Marsh, *Taxation of Imputed Income,* 58 POL. SCI. Q. 514 (1943). The practical difficulties can be reduced through the use of fixed rates of return applied to estimated capital values. Nonetheless, it is doubtful that even this rough technique will work evenly under a self-assessment system; and the idea of revenue agents subjecting house-

Another form of income in kind derived from the ownership of property which, at least to a degree, presently escapes tax is that derived by the lender who makes an interest-free loan. Thus, the employer who compensates his employee by providing interest-free loans not only may generate, in theory at any rate, interest income for the employee but also for himself as well. Generally, this would not be prejudicial to the employer because the imputation of income would be offset by a business expense deduction.[22] Interest-free loans to shareholders of the lender not for the purpose of compensation or other deduction-generating purposes, however, stand on a different footing. Failure to include interest in corporate income effectively reduces the taxable income of the corporation while affording shareholders benefits measurable in money terms.[23] Nonetheless, most authority which exists holds that the lender has no income as a result of an interest-free loan.[24]

---

hold effects, including jewelry, books, and works of art, to close scrutiny in a routine audit remains unappealing. Despite this, it probably is true that the failure to impute income in this area leads to greater investment in jewelry and art by the wealthy than otherwise would be the case. To a degree this may reflect another microcriterion—encouragement of the arts; but this is extremely speculative. Kaldor, for example, vigorously objects to this method of advancing the arts. AN EXPENDITURE TAX 199 (1955).

22. Disallowance of the deduction because total compensation was unreasonable, however, would make imputation harmful to the employer.

23. Earnings and profits, although increased by the imputation of interest income, would be reduced by a like amount when the imputed interest income is, in effect, distributed to the shareholders as a dividend.

24. J. Simpson Dean, 35 T.C. 1083 (1961) (dictum); Brandtjen & Kluge, Inc., 34 T.C. 416 (1960) (loans to officers and employees); Wilbur Security Co., 31 T.C. 938 (1958) (withdrawal by shareholder); Society Brand Clothes, 18 T.C. 304 (1952) (loan to subsidiary corporation); Combs Lumber Co., 41 B.T.A. 339 (1940) (loans to shareholders for their personal use). *But see* Rev. Rul. 65-199, 1965-2 C.B. 20 (advance premium payments on life insurance which generate increments in value applied to payment of premiums result in taxable income). At least a partial explanation of the result in these cases is that the issue was approached frequently as a matter of tax accounting for accrual-basis

Finally, neither (1) the holding of checking accounts sufficiently large to eliminate bank service charges nor (2) advance payments for goods or services to be made available in the distant future generate interest income.[25] The

taxpayers. *E.g.*, Society Brand Clothes, *supra*. Since the right to interest under an interest-free loan never becomes "fixed," no interest is includable. The issue, however, is not whether the right to receive has become fixed but rather whether the lender should be treated as having received a benefit which, in turn, is made available to the borrower.

The rule that a lender has no income as a result of an interest-free loan contrasts rather sharply with § 483 of the Code, enacted in the 1964 Revenue Act. This section in respect of "any payment on account of the sale or exchange of property which constitutes part or all of the sales price," requires that a part thereof be treated as interest when under the complex provisions of that section there exists what is described as "total unstated interest." According to Treas. Reg. § 1.483–1 (d)(2) (1966), § 483 does not apply "if the interest payments specified in a contract are at a rate of at least 4 per cent per annum, whether simple or compounded." After determining that § 483 does apply, it is then necessary to fix the "total unstated interest." This is done by discounting payments due in the future at a rate of interest to be fixed by the secretary or his delegate. In any event, the section applies only to payments due more than six months after the date of the sale or exchange under a contract which provides for some or all of the payments to be made more than one year thereafter.

It is clear that § 483, because of its restriction to payments "on account of a sale or exchange of property," does not constitute general statutory recognition of interest or income derived from the ownership of property. Nonetheless, the similarity of its techniques to those which would be used to calculate interest income to the maker of an interest-free loan, for example, and its almost certain application to efforts to avoid its reach by selling property for cash followed by an interest-free loan by the seller to the buyer, suggest that the era when lenders were taken at their word may be nearing an end. However, stipulation of the minimum rate of interest necessary to preclude the operation of § 483 followed at an appropriate interval by an interest-free loan, designed to compensate the buyer for the loss of an interest deduction of a greater amount, may not invoke Governmental wrath since the same adjustment can be made through the purchase price.

25. The rendition of services by the bank in which the deposit exists constitutes a gain in the form of consumption. The exclusion of the value of these services from the income of the depositor discriminates against the depositor who pays service charges from the interest income earned by sums invested rather than held in a non-interest-bearing checking account. The manner in which assets are held is also influenced. Thus, the existing exclusion violates the criteria of Equity and Free Market Compatibility. Advance payments, such as subscriptions, prepaid insurance, and club memberships, involve a discounting of the value of the service back to the time of payment. This discount is, in effect, the interest income earned the sum paid over. It also represents the cost to the payee of obtaining the use

work of the Treasury is done with screens which catch little imputed income arising from use of owned property.

3. Service to Self and Family

Gain in the form of rights exercised in consumption also results from service to self and family. The carpenter who repairs his roof, the housewife who serves the family, the farmer who grows vegetables for family consumption, the lawyer who maintains his lawn and garden, and even the rebel who eschews employment and devotes his leisure to the study of Zen experiences gain in the form of consumption. Generally speaking, despite unanimous recognition of the existence of this type of gain, it is seldom brought within the tax base. The reasons for this are not difficult to understand. The restraint imposed by the economic pressure to specialize,[26] the difficulties of valuation and enforcement, the proportionately large amount of this kind of income in the lower income groups,[27] and the

---

of the funds prior to his performance of the service. See VICKREY, AGENDA FOR PROGRESSIVE TAXATION 32–35 (1947). Advance premium payments which result in an increment in value applied to premiums or made available for withdrawal result in taxable income to the policyholder. Rev. Rul. 65–199, n. 24 *supra.* This position is developed through guidelines in Rev. Rul. 66–120, 1966 Int. Rev. Bull. No. 20 at 8.

26. "In a modern industrial economy with division of labor carried to considerable lengths, such cases [as where the accountant does his own plumbing repairs instead of working more hours in his profession] are not likely to be frequent enough to constitute a serious problem." VICKREY, AGENDA FOR PROGRESSIVE TAXATION 44 (1947). Again, it is made clear that an income tax is highly compatible with an industrialized economy. See pp. 41–45 *supra.*

27. Simons points out that what he calls "earned income in kind," "bulks large only in the cases of classes exempt from tax or subject to only the lowest rates." SIMONS, PERSONAL INCOME TAXATION, 113 (1937). This may be an overstatement, but probably it remains essentially valid today. He concludes that the exclusion increases exemptions and to a somewhat steeper rate of progression than is reflected by the rates.

unavoidability of fairly arbitrary distinctions,[28] all support this exclusion.

There exists in the tax law, nonetheless, a number of cases and rulings involving situations lying along the border between this type of gain and gain conventionally taxed, such as compensation income paid in kind. One of the most recent of these held that an insurance agent or broker who procured or kept in force policies of insurance upon his life had income as a result of receiving commissions in respect of such policies. No distinction was drawn between an agent who is an employee and one who is an independent contractor.[29] Several similar cases [30] exist although the Tax Court once held otherwise.[31]

Such results, while theoretically sound, do require a determination of the point at which the exclusion of gain from self-service commences. If such commissions to an insurance broker are income, what of the reduction in cost made possible when a stock broker who is a member of an exchange purchases stock on his own account? [32] Or the

28. Some wives are better homemakers than others. Must all such services be valued at the same rate? What is the minimum leisure to which one should be entitled before being charged with income from the use of leisure? What acts of self-service should be excluded on the ground that they maintain a level of personal hygiene necessary to physical and mental health?

29. Comm'r v. Minzer, 279 F.2d 338 (5th Cir. 1960).

30. Comm'r v. Daehler, 281 F.2d 823 (5th Cir. 1960) (real estate commission received by employee real estate agent from his employer on sale of property to himself held taxable income); Ostheimer v. United States, 264 F.2d 789 (3d Cir. 1959) (commission received in respect of policies agent placed on lives of his partner, key employees, and children taxable income to agent).

31. Both *Daehler,* n. 30 *supra,* and *Minzer,* n. 29 *supra,* were decided differently by the Tax Court. Kenneth W. Daehler, 21 T.C. 722 (1959); Sol Minzer, 31 T.C. 1130 (1959). The Tax Court now follows Comm'r v. Minzer, 279 F.2d 338 (5th Cir. 1960). See George E. Bailey, 41 T.C. 663 (1964).

32. The illustration is taken from the Tax Court opinion in Sol Minzer, 31 T.C. 1130 (1959).

lawyer who prepares his own will? Essentially, the task of drawing lines here is arbitrary.

This is nicely illustrated by two intriguing examples of cases touching upon the problems relating to this type of gain, *Joy Manufacturing Co.* v. *Commissioner* [33] and *Commissioner* v. *Fender Sales Inc.*[34] Somewhat simplified, the issue in *Joy Manufacturing* was whether stock issued by a wholly-owned subsidiary corporation to its parent in exchange for beneficial services rendered by the parent to the subsidiary, pursuant to an agreement not describing the debt in terms of a liquidated sum, constitutes income. In holding that it did not, the court observed that, although the parent obtained an "economic advantage" attributable to its services, such "advantage" did not constitute realized gain.[35] On the other hand, in *Fender Sales Inc.* the issuance of equal amounts of stock to two individual shareholders, each of whom owned one-half the outstanding stock, in discharge of equal salary claims, not previously reported in gross income, constituted gross income in the same amount to each shareholder. In both cases, however, the efforts of the taxpayer shareholders resulted in an increase in their wealth; but only in *Fender Sales Inc.*, the case in which a liquidated sum was discharged, was the tax imposed. Seldom does one encounter a situation better designed to illustrate that when drawing arbitrary lines, form must prevail over substance.

Problems arising down on the farm and in the mom-and-pop business also reveal an unwillingness to tax gain from self-service. The consumption of home-grown produce by the farm family and canned peaches from the

33. 230 F.2d 740 (3d Cir. 1956).

34. 338 F.2d 924 (9th Cir. 1964).

35. 230 F.2d at 742.

stock of the mom-and-pop grocery by Mom and Pop raise the issues. Is the value (and, if so, what value?) of the farm produce income to the farmer? Is the retail price of the peaches income to Mom and Pop? If no income results in either case, what of the out-of-pocket costs incurred in growing the home produce or purchasing the canned peaches? The answers are fairly simple. If the peaches and produce are taken into income, the costs should be deductible; but where there is no inclusion in income, then clearly no deduction should be available.[36] The case law and rulings accept the latter alternative; that is, the deduction is denied [37] and there is no inclusion in income.[38] The result is a denial of a deduction for personal expenditures and an exclusion from gross income of any gain attributable to self-service.[39]

36. The validity of these conclusions can be demonstrated in the following manner. Consider taxpayer *A* who incurs expenses of $5X earning compensation income of $25X. He spends $25X on farm produce which he consumes. His taxable income is $20X. It is unaffected by the fact that he spends $25X on farm produce. Taxpayer *B,* a farmer, spends $5X and considerable personal effort growing farm produce worth $25X which the family consumes. If the farm produce is considered taxable, *B's* taxable income is $20X. Both *A* and *B* consume the same amount of produce and pay the same tax. Also, both have consumed capital in the amount of $5X. If, however, *B* has no income as a result of raising and consuming the produce, the tax burden of *A* is greater than that of *B* even though their "standard of living" is the same. This disparity is further enhanced if *B* is given a deduction for the cost of raising the produce.

37. **P. P. Sweten,** 2 B.T.A. 37 (1925) (cost of goods withdrawn from grocery store inventory added to taxpayer's income) ; J. Calamaras, 19 T.C.M. 1045 (cost of meals consumed by family of restaurant operator not deductible) . Cf. Rev. Rul. 28, 1953–1 C.B. 20.

38. T.D. 2665, 20 Treas. Dec. Int. Rev. 45, 47 (1918) .

39. Another example is the disallowance of a deduction of the costs of owner-consumed meals and lodging even though the taxpayer's business, conducted as a sole proprietorship or partnership, requires him to take his meals and maintain his lodging on the business premises. Comm'r v. Doak, 234 F.2d 704 (4th Cir. 1956) (board and lodging furnished partners for convenience of partnership business not deductible) ; Comm'r v. Moran, 236 F.2d 595 (8th Cir. 1956) . The view that any gain from self-service is excluded from income was made explicit recently when the Tax Court observed that, in disallowing partnership expenses attributable to the

personal consumption of the partners, the issue was amount of such expenses and not the money value of the benefits received by the taxpayers. Richard E. Moran, 17 T.C.M. 18 (1958). Only by inclusion of the value of such benefits would the gain from self-service be brought within the base. See n. 36 *supra*.

The non-conformity with Equity which exclusion of this type of gain induces may be reduced by extension of certain compensating advantages to others. Thus, allowances of one type or another may be given to families who are deprived of the imputed income of the housewife. VICKREY, AGENDA FOR PROGRESSIVE TAXATION 45–48 (1947) sets forth some of the alternatives available. An earned income credit measured as a certain percentage of income of a fixed amount earned by a working wife, an exclusion of income earned by the wife up to a modest amount, and a deduction for certain additional expenses made necessary by outside employment of the wife are some possibilities discussed by Vickrey. Other suggestions include an additional exemption, a special deduction proportional to wife's income but diminishing as income increases, or the use of special rate tables for two-job families which diminish the magnitude of the concession as income increases. See GROVES, FEDERAL TAX TREATMENT OF THE FAMILY 80–81 (Brookings Inst. 1963). Int. Rev. Code of 1954, § 214, as amended by the 1964 Revenue Act, permits a deduction for expenses for the care of dependents, subject to certain dollar-amount limitations, incurred to permit a wife, widower, or husband whose wife is incapacitated or is institutionalized to be employed gainfully.

Also, a limited earned income credit may be used to offset the imputed income of leisure. Vickrey puts it this way. "A treatment which not only produces results in accord with this theory, but has the practical advantage of being symmetrical with the treatment of working wives, is to reduce the personal exemption for persons not gainfully occupied, and provide an earned income credit based on earnings which will bring the total exemption up to the former value by the time the earnings reach a sum which can be presumed to indicate full-time employment." AGENDA FOR PROGRESSIVE TAXATION, 50 (1947). At best these adjustments amount only to rough approximations, but this provides little comfort to those who defend the existing situation.

VI. Gains from Status

ALTHOUGH the discussion to this point has assumed that a clear line exists between gain in the form of an increase in the value of property rights and that represented by consumption, in fact the line is often faint and difficult to trace. Certainly *Joy Manufacturing Co.* and *Fender Sales Inc.* make clear that the expenditure of effort and skill may enhance the taxpayer's property values. Also, it is shortsighted to insist that all services of the housewife must be regarded as a form of current consumption. The truth is that the division of gain between accumulation and consumption is often arbitrary to a significant degree.[1]

This is particularly apparent when the increments derived from status are considered. Does a life of rectitude which makes possible esteem, affection, and, generally, a better life (sometimes, even, in material ways) involve a series of acts which must be viewed as either consumption or accumulation? Do efforts which result in a marriage above one's previous station in life represent accumulation, consumption, or both? Moreover, does it make any difference which it represents? Perhaps many would conclude that issues of this sort are too nebulous to warrant concern by a tax system which must be guided by Practicality. There is much truth in this, but in fact no income

1. Simons recognized this. PERSONAL INCOME TAXATION 54 (1938).

tax can wholly ignore the existence of gain from status. This is true because drawing the line between taxable and non-taxable receipts related to status cannot be avoided. Before turning to an examination of the manner in which tax law has dealt with status, a few words about its meaning are necessary. A taxpayer always stands in a particular relationship to other individuals—his employer and fellow employees, his spouse and family, the religious organization of which he is a member, the state and nation, and so on. These relationships may, for example, entitle the taxpayer to demand that John pay him $100, or that all other individuals refrain from doing certain things in respect of Blackacre, or that protection from thieves be provided. In the aggregate they constitute much of what is called identity. Status is a part of this aggregate.

In general, *status refers to those relationships which infrequently become subject to a market place exchange.* For example, although the individual may negotiate for positions which carry with them a vast array of peripheral relations, this array, in whole or in part, is seldom severable and capable of transfer in the market place. It is a part of the taxpayer's status. The fact that a wife may have, in effect, negotiated diligently in obtaining a favorable marriage does not entitle her to enter the market place and sell her right to support to the highest bidder. This right is a part of her status. Similarly, a husband, despite the care with which an antenuptial agreement may have been negotiated, is not entitled to put his relationship with his wife up for sale. It is, thus, a part of his status.

What follows is an examination of certain benefits derived from status to observe how tax law has fixed the line between such gains and receipts conventionally taxed.

The Configurations of Gross Income

1. Gains from Status Distinguished from Gains Ordinarily Taxed

The factory roof over the industrial worker's head contributes to his well-being while at work; but, of course, it is not considered as income to him, nor is it usually thought of as an aspect of status. However, the somewhat leisurely paced assembly line, the rights, privileges, and immunities of seniority, the spotless and affluently appointed lounge, accessibility to a convenient parking place, and the employee's golf course maintained at the expense of the employer depict a series which moves perceptibly from obvious "working conditions" to a perquisite which might reasonably be considered as compensation paid in kind. The point at which the Government assumes the burden of charging employees with taxable gain is both a practical and sociological problem. The will to undertake the tasks of valuation, withholding, etc., depends to a substantial degree upon whether the community classifies a particular item as compensation rather than "working conditions." These classifications, however, change over time. As a consequence, it is not possible to mark out a theoretically precise line which can long endure. It can only be observed that as the community grows richer and the employer, rather than the market place, increasingly comes to be regarded as the source of consumption items in kind, the scope of "working conditions" increases while that of compensation decreases. Over the years the tax law has been forced to classify such fringe benefits as meals and lodging,[2] recreational facilities,[3] va-

2. The story is a long one and need not be related here. Int. Rev. Code of 1954, § 119 now deals specifically with these items. The magnitude of meals furnished employees is difficult to estimate. MACAULAY, FRINGE

cation trips,[4] courtesy discounts,[5] Christmas hams and turkeys,[6] insurance coverage,[7] and so on.[8]

From the standpoint of the macrocriteria, these decisions
have involved a balancing of Practicality, Equity, Free

BENEFITS AND THEIR FEDERAL TAX TREATMENT 161 (1959). This source
cites figures of the Chamber of Commerce of the United States as of 1953
which estimate the cost of meals at 1 per cent of the total cost of fringe
benefits. However, according to the Wall Street Journal, May 14, 1963, p.
1, col. 8, the cost of fringe benefits has more than doubled since then. This
source quotes a "Government expert" as believing that the practice of
"free lunches" has reached "Gargantuan proportions." See chap. xvii *infra*.

3. These consist of a wide range of facilities. Macaulay, *id*. at 174–75,
puts it this way. "Planned recreation for employees financed by employers
is another type of expenditure which is growing and which is considered
by some as a fringe benefit. The expenditures may take many forms,
ranging from the mere provision of grounds where athletic contests may
be held to the provision of directors of recreation, expensive recreation
facilities and equipment, and even to allowing employees to engage in
these activities on company time. In this field, as in medical care, unions
are also taking steps to provide services financed primarily by payments
direct from the employer to the union and by tax-exempt union dues." In
1962 there was some effort to control this area by enacting a provision to
curb deductions by employers. Int. Rev. Code of 1954, § 274.

4. Rudolph v. United States, 291 F.2d 841 (5th Cir. 1961), *petition for
cert. dismissed* 370 U.S. 269 (1962). See also Bell Electric Co., 45 T.C. 158
(1965).

5. VICKREY, AGENDA FOR PROGRESSIVE TAXATION 41–43 (1947); Landman,
The Taxability of Fringe Benefits, 33 TAXES 173, 183 (1955). It is
frequently asserted that "courtesy discounts" do not constitute taxable
income. *But see* Treas. Reg. § 1.61–1 (d) (1957). These discounts are
not considered as wages subject to withholding. Treas. Reg.
§ 31.3401 (a) –1 (b) 10 (1957). Also observe that Treas. Reg., § 1.421–6 (a)
(1959) applies to options granted by employers to employees "to purchase
stock of the employer or other property."

6. Rev. Rul. 59–58, 1959–1 C.B. 17 treats such items as gifts. This ruling
was relied upon in Hallmark Cards, Inc. v. United States, 200 F. Supp. 847
(W.D. Mo. 1961), a case which refused to read Comm'r v. Duberstein, 363
U.S. 278 (1960) as being entirely inconsistent with Rev. Rul. 59–58.

7. See p. 82 *supra*.

8. See generally Guttentag, Leonard, and Rodewald, *Federal Income
Taxation of Fringe Benefits: A Specific Proposal*, 6 NAT'L TAX J. 250
(1953); Bittker, *The Individual as Wage Earner*, 11 N.Y.U. TAX INST. 1147
(1953); Comment, *Tax Treatment of Compensation in Kind*, 37 CALIF. L.
REV. 628 (1949); Murphy, Jr., *Introduction to Management Compensation*, 1958 U. ILL. L.F. 1.

Market Compatibility,[9] Adequacy, and, perhaps in some attenuated way, Political Order.[10] In any event, a status-oriented society obviously clashes with any political theory built on assumptions derived from an individualistic, market-oriented society. Although the criterion of Stability might suggest a very flexible policy with regard to employer-furnished consumption items, which would encourage their substantial increase in slack times, little attention has been given to this possibility.[11]

On the whole, the Government might have done worse in holding the line against pressures to expand the scope of "working conditions."[12] But, like many parents, the

9. For an excellent discussion of the allocation effects of tax-free fringe benefits, see MACAULAY, FRINGE BENEFITS AND THEIR FEDERAL TAX TREATMENT, chap. iii (1959). The author's approach may be reflected somewhat by the following extracts. "It has been pointed out that the presence of tax-free fringe benefits is likely to lead to a changed pattern of production and consumption from that which would exist if workers were paid only in taxable cash. This alteration stems from two causes: (1) some workers will probably be given more of the fringe benefit than they would voluntarily have purchased, and (2) a net tax saving may accrue to employer, employee, or certain consumers. . . .

"If there is this change in the allocation of resources, is there any criterion of resource allocation which may be used for comparison? If competitive conditions are assumed, the price of a good will equal its marginal cost of production or the sum of marginal returns to factors of production just sufficient to overcome their marginal disutilities or opportunity costs in producing this unit of output. At the same time this price will represent the marginal worth of the good to the purchaser, or its ability to create additional utility when used by the purchaser. In money terms, then, the disutility due to production and the utility stemming from consumption of the marginal unit are equal. Any time, then, that the recipient of a good values the good at less than its market price, the equality between marginal utility and disutility in money terms is violated." *Id.* at 61–62.

10. *Cf.* Ratchford, *Practical Limitations to the Net Income Tax— General*, VII J. FINANCE 211 (1952).

11. However, because most "fringe benefits" are in a form which increase savings more than present consumption, the use of such benefits as compensation probably results in a level of consumption below what it would be if the compensation were paid in cash. MACAULAY, FRINGE BENEFITS AND THEIR FEDERAL TAX TREATMENT 78–85 (1959). For stabilization purposes, all fringe benefits need not be treated alike.

12. Mr. Justice Goldberg, when general counsel of the CIO, urged that

rigor of its preachments to outsiders is softened when applied to its own. Thus, military personnel, particularly, have an impressive array of benefits which escape tax.[13] More modest exclusions are enjoyed by other Government employees.[14]

These allowances, however, become insignificant when contrasted with the vast magnitude of benefits which are provided through Government to those under its rule. The status of citizenship, and to a lesser extent that of residency, does provide a source of gains (such as immunity from enemy attack, a relatively stable currency, freedom of movement within the limits of the nation, educational and recreational opportunities, etc.) which in most instances defy valuation and are certainly beyond the limits of gross income.

Yet, it must be acknowledged that the ambit of non-marketable citizenship benefits, like that of "working conditions," can be expanded almost infinitely. From free, or under cost, access to a state or national park to free, or under cost, medical services and housing is not a leap which is beyond comprehension. The community, through

---

non-taxable conditions of employment be expanded. See SURREY & WARREN, FEDERAL INCOME TAXATION 120–21 (1960 ed.) .

13. The following allowances, among others, escape tax. Allowances for subsistence or in lieu of subsistence, Mim. 3413, V–1 C.B. 29 (1926) ; R.O.T.C. subsistence allowances, Rev. Rul. 66–3, 1966 Int. Rev. Bull. No. 1, at 12. Communication and rental value of quarters, Jones v. United States, 60 Ct. Cl. 552 (1925) ; uniform allowances, I.T. 3455, 1941–1 C.B. 193; I.T. 3603, 1943 C.B. 69; I.T. 3597, 1943 C.B. 69; transportation allowances, Rev. Rul. 54–429, 1954–2 C.B. 53; combat pay for service in combat zones, Int. Rev. Code of 1954, § 112; mustering-out payments, Int. Rev. Code of 1954, § 113; cost-of-living allowance to member of uniformed services while doing foreign service, Rev. Rul. 61–5, 1961–1 C.B. 8; gratuity pay, Rev. Rul. 55–330, 1955–1 C.B. 236.

14. Certain "foreign areas allowances," cost-of-living allowances paid under the Overseas Differentials and Allowances Act, and certain Peace Corps Allowances are excluded under Int. Rev. Code of 1954, § 912.

Government, can establish the level of benefits it wishes. Seldom is our attention drawn to the fact that these benefits are a source of wealth generally excluded from gross income. This is not the case, however, when a receipt includes an item which either is transferable, or is substantially identical to items (such as money or property) which are freely traded. Social Security payments are this type of receipt. Tax law must determine whether this gain is to enjoy the immunity from tax accorded most status benefits. As is well known, a ruling provides that such payments do enjoy such immunity.[15]

In addition to attributes of employment, citizenship, and domicile, a number of familial relationships are likewise exempt from tax. The "good name," the "connections" nurtured over several generations and, in some few

15. Monthly payments from the Federal Old Age and Survivors Insurance Trust Fund, I.T. 3447, 1941–1 C.B. 191; certain "lump sum payments under Social Security, I.T. 3194, 1938–1 C.B. 114; I.T. 3229, 1938–2 C.B. 136; unemployment compensation by state agencies from Federal Unemployment Trust Fund established by the Social Security Act, I.T. 3230, 1938–2 C.B. 136; similar unemployment compensation paid to federal employees, Rev. Rul. 54–190, 1954–1 C.B. 46.
United States v. Kaiser, 363 U.S. 299 (1959) does not entirely support the view that status benefits receive tax immunity. There the taxpayer argued that "subsistence relief," whether in cash or property, was excludable from gross income. This view was not accepted, and Mr. Justice Frankfurter's concurring opinion was devoted to demonstrating that no such broad principle had been established beyond question by the Commissioner's rulings. Moreover, Mr. Justice Frankfurter refused to permit the exclusion of social security payments to justify an exclusion of other welfare receipts. He put it this way in his concurring opinion in 363 U.S. at 313–14: "To say that the Social Security rulings control private welfare schemes is to say that the Commissioner has not been entitled to find in the policy of the Social Security legislation, in relation to the tax statutes, a reason for excluding its benefits from taxation, while this policy does not apply to other payments." Nonetheless, two rulings exist which suggest that disaster relief based on need is not income although it may reduce the amount of the casualty loss deduction. Special Ruling, May 11, 1952, 1952–5 CCH Fed. Tax Rep. ¶ 6196; Rev. Rul. 131, 1953–2 C.B. 112. Perhaps it can be said that such receipts are the performance by the social group of its guarantee of minimal protection against disaster to each member of the group and that such protection is merely another aspect of the individual's status within the group.

cases, the family charisma make up a source of personal satisfactions no less real than, and by no means unrelated to, economic gain. More susceptible to measurement in the market place, but still not taxable gain, is the right each spouse has in the presence and comfort of the other [16] and the right to support which a child, wife, or certain incompetents may have.[17] This very incomplete catalogue of attributes of status [18] can be closed by pointing out that there are certain attributes relating to the physical and mental well-being of the individual which not only are protected from destruction by others but also contribute immensely to happiness and economic productivity. Good health, a worthy reputation, the right of privacy, and the security of all from unlawful attack are values widely recognized although not a part of the income tax base.

2. *The Voluntary and Involuntary Conversion of Status*

Sometimes the wealth represented by status is converted into cash or property having an ascertainable fair market value. When this happens, it is necessary to determine

16. Sol. Op. 132, I–1 C.B. 92 (1922).

17. United States v. Davis, 370 U.S. 65 (1962).

18. Among the many other examples that might be cited are the status benefits derived from co-operative endeavors. No income results in car pools even though instead of sharing the responsibility for furnishing transportation one person uses his own automobile and is reimbursed by other members of the pool to the extent of their agreed-upon share of the costs. Rev. Rul. 55–555, 1955–2 C.B. 20. Similarly, patronage dividends attributable to the purchase of personal, living, or family items are excluded from gross income. Int. Rev. Code of 1954, § 1385 (b)(2). Under this view, if it be assumed that the taxpayer's income is $100 and his consumption expenditures $60, before being aided by co-operative endeavor, a reduction in out-of-pocket consumption costs by $5 made possible by such endeavor results in increasing savings of the taxpayer from $40 to $45. Treatment of the $5 as income would be based on the theory that the taxpayer's level of consumption remained at $60, of which $55 was paid by the taxpayer and $5 by others. Thus, the total income of the taxpayer would be $105 and his savings, as before, $45.

whether the previous immunity attaches to the proceeds of the conversion. This determination is difficult in several respects.

In the first place, it is generally impossible to establish a basis in the interest which has been converted inasmuch as no investment can be traced thereto. As a result, the assertion that the proceeds of conversion constitute a return of capital rings false.[19] Second, as long as it was thought necessary that income be derived from capital, labor, both combined, or from the conversion of a capital asset,[20] it was difficult to attribute the proceeds of an involuntary conversion of status benefits to such a source. Finally, it is obvious to all that these conversions, looked at simply as an economic matter, often did not make the taxpayer richer than before.[21] The result is that over the years there

19. *Cf.* pp. 17–23 *supra.* Nonetheless, the return-of-capital idea was used to exclude from gross income damages, including proceeds of accident policies, received for personal injuries prior to enactment of what is now Int. Rev. Code of 1954, § 104. S.M. 1384, 2 C.B. 71 (1920). This ruling refused to apply the return-of-capital idea to damages for alienation of the wife's affections not causing physical sickness. This ruling was revoked by Sol. Op. 132, I–1 C.B. 92 (1922), which excluded damages for alienation of affections. In O.D. 501, 2 C.B. 70 (1920) damages for breach of promise to marry were treated as income on the ground that such did not constitute a return of capital. The Commissioner later took a contrary position based upon the definition of income in Eisner v. Macomber, 252 U.S. 189 (1920). I.T. 1804, II–2 C.B. 61–62 (1923). I.T. 1804, however, was revoked by I.T. 2170, IV–1 C.B. 28 (1955), which relied upon S.M. 2042, IV–1 C.B. 26. The Board of Tax Appeals excluded such damages from income, Mrs. Lyde McDonald, 9 B.T.A. 1340 (1928). Thereafter, S.M. 2042 was revoked by G.C.M. 4363, VII–2 C.B. 185 (1928), and O.D. 501 and I.T. 2170 were revoked by I.T. 2422, VII–2 C.B. 186 (1928).

20. Eisner v. Macomber, 252 U.S. 189 (1920) was thought to have established this source requirement. It was relied on in Sol. Op. 132, I–1 C.B., 92 (1922), n. 19 *supra.* The demise-of-the-source requirement is traced in Wright, *The Effect of the Source of Realized Receipts upon the Supreme Court's Concept of Taxable Receipts,* 8 STAN. L. REV. 164 (1956).

21. Sol. Op. 132, I–1 C.B. 92 (1922) relied on this in holding that damages for alienation of affections or defamation of personal character or surrender of the custody of a minor child do not amount to income. It was put this way: "If an individual is possessed of a personal right that is not assignable and not susceptible of any appraisal in relation to market

have been many rulings and cases dealing with the problem and, as yet, no plainly stated and accepted general principles have emerged. What follows in this chapter is an attempt to state such principles and to illustrate their application by reference to the authorities.

The first of these principles is that, in the case of an *involuntary* conversion of status benefits, a "payment which compensates for a loss of something which would not itself have been an item of gross income is not a taxable payment." These words, taken from Mr. Justice Frankfurter's concurring opinion in *United States* v. *Kaiser,* express a view which is consistent with the manner in which other damage recoveries are treated.[22] The second is that the *voluntary* conversion of status benefits does constitute gain to the full extent of the amount realized.[23]

This distinction between the *voluntary* and *involuntary* may be justified, although perhaps not satisfactorily explained, by recognizing that the taxpayer who enters the market to sell an interest not usually traded thereon ought to accept all the burdens, including taxation, of a trader as the price of obtaining the benefits of the market place. Under these two principles the critical issues become, first, was the disposition *voluntary,* and, second, if not, was the interest disposed of something which would not have been an item of income. The results reached by the authorities are not entirely consistent with these principles, but the degree of inconsistency is not great.

---

values, and thereafter receives either damages or payment in compromise for an invasion of that right, it cannot be held that he thereby derives any gain or profit."

22. 363 U.S. 299, 311 (1959).

23. This assumes, as is almost always the case, that the interest sold has no basis.

For example, it has held that compensatory damages for injuries caused by libel and slander,[24] alienation of affections of the taxpayer's spouse,[25] breach of promise to marry,[26] entering a marriage procured by fraud and deceit sought in connection with an annulment of the marriage,[27] loss of the taxpayer's husband by reason of the sinking of the "Lusitania," [28] and wrongful death [29] are not income. In addition, there is an exclusion of the mortality gain present in life insurance proceeds when paid by reason of death to a member of the insured's family. In each the conversion was involuntary, and the sole doubt pertains to whether the receipt in each case was for an interest which would not have been an item of income had it not been converted. While one cannot be dogmatic on this issue, it is reasonable to assert that the interests were of that nature. If so, these results support the first principle stated above.

Certain other rulings also appear to offer corrobora-

24. C.A. Hawkins, 6 B.T.A. 1023 (1927); Sol. Op. 132, I–1 C.B. 92 (1922); Rev. Rul. 58–418, 1958–2 C.B. 18. The latter ruling makes clear that punitive damages awarded in connection with an action of slander or libel is taxable gain. See p. 15 *supra*. Exemplary damages are not regarded as the amount realized upon the involuntary conversion of status. The taxpayer is not being compensated for an interest of which he has been deprived; rather, he is the instrument through which the purposes of such damages are being accomplished.

25. Sol. Op. 132, I–1 C.B. 92 (1922).

26. S.M. 2042, IV–1 C.B. 26 (1925) distinguished a payment of an annuity by reason of a breach of promise to marry from damages for alienations on the ground that the former represented gain through the exercise of one's physical or mental faculties whereas the latter does not.

27. I.T. 1852, II–2 C.B. 66 (1923).

28. I.T. 2420, VII–2 C.B. 123 (1928). This ruling states: "In the instant case, the award is, in fact, the undertaking on the part of the Government of Germany, by the substitution of a sum of money for the life that was lost, is [*sic*] to restore *A* to substantially the same financial and economic status as she possessed prior to the death of her husband."

29. Rev. Rul. 54–88, 1954–1 C.B. 177 (1954). This ruling relied on the "Lusitania" ruling, n. 28 *supra*.

tion.[30] Two of these deserve special mention. One holds that relocation payments to taxpayers for moving expenses and actual direct losses of property resulting from displacement by an urban renewal project are not income.[31] The other holds similarly as to payments by a school board to parents for transporting children to school where no bus service is available.[32] The rulings may be viewed as either, first, examples demonstrating that the scope of the status of citizenship can be expanded to include certain cash payments [33] or, second, as instances of payments being made as the result of an involuntary conversion of interests which otherwise would have been enjoyed tax-free. If the latter is an appropriate characterization, the involuntary conversion principle receives additional support.

When one turns to voluntary conversions of tax-free aspects of status, the Faustian legend comes to mind. The tax law, generally conforming to the legend, exacts its price. The embezzler realizes taxable gain as does the

30. For example, compensation for wartime maltreatment which deprives the taxpayer of the minimum rights attaching to his status represents the involuntary conversion of interests the enjoyment of which would not have been income. See Rev. Rul. 56–518, 1956–2 C.B. 25; Rev. Rul. 55–132, 1955–1 C.B. 213.

31. Rev. Rul. 60–279, 1960–2 C.B. 11. The ruling also holds that expenses incurred by individuals in excess of the tax-free allowances are personal expenses and not deductible. Since the gains from status are not income, the losses suffered by reason of an impairment of status should not be deductible.

32. Rev. Rul. 60–280, 1960–2 C.B. 12.

33. Both rulings were based upon the notion that the payments involved constituted the discharge of a governmental obligation assumed in connection with the performance of a governmental function. This alone is hardly sufficient to justify an exclusion. The relationship between the government and the payee must be considered. If the payee has rendered personal service, the payment is income to him even though it also represents the discharge of a governmental obligation assumed in connection with performance of a governmental function. Only when the government performance is regarded as providing a feature of status which the individual is entitled to enjoy tax-free is an exclusion justified.

extortioner, the bribe recipient, the vote seller, the procurer, the prostitute, and probably all others who live in that subculture of the lawless.[34] Even when the conversion is lawful, the result is generally gain. Thus, the relinquishment of seniority rights and termination of employment in a particular position for a lump-sum payment constitutes gain.[35] Similarly, taxable gain results when certain somewhat imprecisely defined interests pertaining to the story of the life of a family member are sold for dramatic or literary uses.[36] Furthermore, the Tax Court in dictum has stated that "one may receive compensation for allowing medical experiments upon his body in circumstances

34. The list of illegal activities which yield taxable gain is much too long to be set forth. It includes, however, in addition to those items mentioned in the text, income from influence peddling, M. L. Reichert, 19 T.C. 1027 (1953); "kickbacks," United States v. Wyss, 239 F.2d 658 (7th Cir. 1957); M. S. Somers, 14 T.C.M. 793 (1955); proceeds from narcotic sales, A. Farina, 58–2 U.S.T.C. ¶ 9938. Also see Rev. Rul. 62–194, 1962–2 C.B. 57 announcing Service's intention not to follow M. E. Pew, 20 T.C.M. 1377 (1961), which held certain kickbacks excludable from income.

35. Rev. Rul. 59–227, 1959–2 C.B. 13. Furthermore, the gain is ordinary income and not capital gain according to this ruling.

36. Runyon v. United States, 281 F.2d 590 (5th Cir. 1960) (proceeds treated as ordinary income and court expressed doubt taxpayer had a property right in father's name and life story); Miller v. Comm'r, 299 F.2d 706 (2d Cir. 1962) (proceeds ordinary income because taxpayer, in permitting the production of a movie on the life of Glenn Miller, sold "the chance that a new theory of 'property' might be advanced and that a lawsuit predicated on it might be successful"); Starrels v. Comm'r, 304 F.2d 574 (9th Cir. 1962) (payments for taxpayer's consent to permit production of a movie based on life of taxpayer's father not excluded as damages received on account of personal injuries); Ehrlich v. Higgins, 52 F. Supp. 805 (S.D.N.Y. 1943) (sum paid for use of certain material relating to Ehrlich family taxable income); Franklin D. Roosevelt, Jr. 43 T.C. 77 (1964) (payments for taxpayer's consent to production of play based on the life of taxpayer's father not excludable as damages for invasion of privacy). Cf. Meyer v. United States, 173 F. Supp. 920 (E.D. Tenn. 1959) (sum received for possible future injuries to reputation of taxpayer by reason of making motion picture taxable income). In *Starrels, Ehrlich, Roosevelt,* and *Meyer* each court pointed out that no injury to taxpayer was shown by the facts and that it was doubtful that the exclusion for damages for personal injuries was applicable to payments made for release of claims arising from possible future injuries.

that would constitute a tort if his prior consent had not been given." [37]

However, voluntary conversion does not always result in taxable gain. The voluntary surrender of custody of a child in exchange for cash or property, for example, may not result in taxable income.[38] In addition, the voluntary surrender of marital rights or right of support results in no gain.[39] These exceptions to the second principle stated here may be justified by observing that in each the distinction between voluntary and involuntary conversion lacks the force it usually has. There is no open market for such rights, and often the exchange has its coercive aspects. In

37. Maurie Starrels, 35 T.C. 646 (1961), *aff'd*, 304 F.2d 574 (9th Cir. 1962). Presumably, the taxpayer who sells a small quantity of his blood for cash has income.

38. Sol. Op. 132, I–1 C.B. 92 (1922). The ruling does not address itself to the voluntary-involuntary issue. Taken in context, the ruling may refer to involuntary surrenders; but it is not expressly so limited. Ehrlich v. Higgins, 52 F. Supp. 805 (S.D.N.Y. 1943) in dictum treated the ruling as applying to voluntary transfers.

39. In Davis v. United States, 370 U.S. 65 (1962), Mr. Justice Clark writing for the majority stated in footnote 3 of the opinion: "Under the present administrative practice, the release of marital rights in exchange for property or other consideration is not considered a taxable event as to the wife." See 8 U.C.L.A. L. REV. 593, 601 (1961). The taxpayer whose right to support is voluntarily liquidated by a lump-sum cash payment clearly realizes no income. Gould v. Gould, 245 U.S. 151 (1917); Rev. Rul. 55–457, 1955–2 C.B. 527; 8 U.C.L.A. L. REV. 593, 601 (1961). Int. Rev. Code of 1954, § 71 makes the wife taxable on "periodic payments" which discharge certain obligations imposed because of the marital or family relationship. It is doubtful that an absolute discharge of an obligation to support a minor child by means of a lump-sum payment is possible. See Note, *Federal Tax Aspects of the Obligation to Support* 74 HARV. L. REV. 1191, 1192, 1219 (1961).

See generally, Holland, Piper, Bailey & Sander, *Matrimony, Divorce, and Separation,* 18 N.Y.U. TAX INST. 901 (1960); McDonald, 17 U. PITT. L. REV. 1 (1955); Note, *Tax Aspects of Alimony Trusts,* 66 YALE L. J. 881 (1959); Kragen, Oliver, Stoke & Buchley, *The Marriage Undone Taxwise,* 42 CALIF. L. REV. 408 (1954); Logamarcino, *Federal Tax Consequences of Alimony and Separate Maintenance Payments,* 3 BUFFALO L. REV. 179 (1954); Jackson, *Divorce and Federal Income Taxes,* 37 MINN. L. REV. 413 (1953).

any event, the case for the existence of the two principles previously stated is quite strong.

It should now be abundantly clear that the reach of gross income is very flexible. This fact is of utmost importance to an understanding of the constitutional problems pertaining to the income tax to which the next chapter is devoted.

VII. The Constitutional Problems

THE MAJOR PURPOSE of this chapter is to demonstrate that no substantial constitutional barrier exists that is inconsistent with the malleable quality of gross income which the preceding chapters have revealed. Superficially, such an undertaking appears to be an exercise in absurdity. How, it might be asked, can it be thought that such an inconsistency exists in the face of decades of judicial and administrative flexibility in the interpretation of the meaning of gross income? The answer to this question is not as simple as might be supposed.

To commence with fundamentals, the taxing power of Congress is based on article I, section 8, clause 1 of the Constitution, which provides:

The Congress shall have Power to Lay and Collect Taxes, Duties, Imposts, and Exercises, to pay the Debts and provide for the common Defense and general Welfare of the United States; but all Duties, Imposts, and Exercises shall be uniform throughout the United States.

Article I, section 2, clause 3 provides that "direct taxes shall be apportioned among the several states" and article I, section 9, clause 4, that "no capitation, or other direct tax shall be laid, unless in proportion to the census or enumeration hereinbefore directed to be taken." As stated in *Pollock* v. *Farmers' Loan & Trust Co.*,[1] these provisions

1. 157 U.S. 429, 557 (1895).

recognize two great classes of taxes, *direct* and *indirect.* Their imposition must be governed by two rules: "The rule of apportionment as to direct taxes, and the rule of uniformity as to duties, imposts and excises." [2]

The distinction between direct and indirect taxes looms large in the constitutional history of the income tax. Prior to *Pollock,* indirect taxes had been held to include a tax "levied, collected, and paid upon all carriages for the conveyance of persons, which shall be kept by or for any person for his or her own use, or to be let out to hire or for the conveyance of passengers," [3] taxes on the insurance business,[4] on the issue of notes by a bank,[5] on being prepared to distil spirits,[6] and on income, gains, and profits.[7] It was commonly thought that the only direct taxes were capitation taxes and taxes on real estate.[8]

However, in *Pollock* it was held that "an annual tax upon the annual value or annual user of real estate appears . . . the same in substance as an annual tax on the real estate, which would be paid out of the rent or income." [9] The theory was simple. A tax on the value of the land is a direct tax. The value of land is fixed by the income therefrom. Therefore, a tax on income from land is equivalent to a direct tax on the value of the land. In

2. *Ibid.*

3. Hylton v. United States, 3 U.S. 171 (1796).

4. Pacific Insurance Co. v. Soule, 74 U.S. 433 (1869).

5. Veazie Bank v. Fenno, 75 U.S. 533 (1869).

6. United States v. Singer, 82 U.S. 111 (1872).

7. Springer v. United States, 102 U.S. 586 (1880). See POWELL, CONSTITUTIONAL ASPECTS OF FEDERAL INCOME TAXATION: THE FEDERAL INCOME TAX (Haig, ed. 1921) for an immensely readable and still pertinent discussion of this early period. Also see Powell, *Stock Dividends, Direct Taxes and the Sixteenth Amendment,* 20 COLUM. L. REV. 536 (1920).

8. Springer v. United States, 102 U.S. 586, 602 (1880).

9. Pollock v. Farmers' Loan and Trust Co., 157 U.S. 429, 581 (1894).

addition, a tax on the income from municipal bonds was held to be invalid because it amounted to a "tax on the power of the States and their instrumentalities to borrow money, and consequently repugnant to the Constitution."

On rehearing, the holding as to a tax on income from realty was reaffirmed by a divided Court and extended to bring within the direct tax category a tax on the income of personal property.[10] Finally, because of these invalid provisions, which the Court considered as part of "one entire scheme of taxation," [11] the entire income tax was declared invalid. Thereafter, a number of different taxes came before the Court and were declared to be indirect,[12] including one on carrying on business as a corporation, the base of which was the net income of the corporation.[13]

On February 25, 1913, the sixteenth amendment became a part of the Constitution.[14] Its language is spare and direct:

The Congress shall have power to lay and collect taxes on incomes, from whatever source derived, without apportionment among the several States, and without regard to any census or enumeration.

Notwithstanding this simplicity, there has not always been complete unanimity about the precise consequences of this amendment. Mr. Chief Justice White, a dissenter in *Pol-*

10. Pollock v. Farmers' Loan and Trust Co., 158 U.S. 601, 635, 637 (1895).

11. *Id.* at 637.

12. See Powell, *op. cit.,* n. 7 *supra.*

13. Flint v. Stone Tracy Co., 220 U.S. 107 (1911).

14. An extremely readable account of the *Pollock* decision and the history of the sixteenth amendment may be found in Chapters II and III of PAUL, TAXATION IN THE UNITED STATES (1954). For additional historical insights, see RATNER, AMERICAN TAXATION (1942); SELIGMAN, THE INCOME TAX (1911).

lock, explained its consequences on behalf of the Court in *Brushaber* v. *Union Pacific Railroad Co.*[15] in the following manner:

It is clear on the face of this text that it does not purport to confer power to levy income taxes in a generic sense—an authority already possessed and never questioned—or to limit and distinguish between one kind of income taxes and another, but that the whole purpose of the Amendment was to relieve all income taxes when imposed from apportionment from a consideration of the source whence the income was derived. . . . The purpose [of the amendment] was not to change the existing interpretation except to the extent necessary to accomplish the result intended, that is, the prevention of the resort to the sources from which a taxed income was derived in order to cause a direct tax on the income to be a direct tax on the sources itself and thereby take an income tax out of the class of excises, duties and imposts and place it in the class of direct taxes.[16]

Similar views, stated again by Mr. Chief Justice White, are present in *Stanton* v. *Baltic Mining Co.*[17] The sum of these expressions is that the imposition of an income tax has always been within the power of Congress; that an income tax "inherently belonged" to the indirect class of taxation; that *Pollock* required that the classification of an income tax as direct or indirect turn on the source of the income; that the sixteenth amendment prevents this resort to sources and returns the income tax to the indirect tax fold; and that the power to impose an income tax is but part of the very broad powers of Congress to levy excises, duties, and imposts.

15. 240 U.S. 1 (1916).
16. *Id.* at 17, 19.
17. 240 U.S. 103 (1916).

The Configurations of Gross Income

A very different tack was taken in *Eisner* v. *Macomber*,[18] however, where the issue was whether Congress had the power to tax as income to the shareholder a stock dividend of common stock on common stock. In holding that Congress did not have such power, the Court approached its task from the standpoint of determining the extent to which the limitation of apportionment of direct taxes was reduced in scope by the sixteenth amendment. Its view was that the limitation of apportionment was inapplicable if the tax was imposed upon "income." If, however, the tax in question was not imposed upon "income," the limitation of apportionment remained in effect. That is, the tax being examined was a direct tax.

Thus, a definition of "income" within the meaning of the sixteenth amendment became necessary. The Court proceeded to define income in terms of sources as " 'gain derived from capital, from labor, or from both combined,' provided it be understood to include profit gained through a sale or conversion of capital assets. . . ." As previously pointed out, it also interpreted "derived" as something "proceeding from," "severed from," or "received or drawn by the recipient for his separate use, benefit and disposal." [19] Thus, income must arise from specified sources, and the realization requirement became

18. 252 U.S. 189 (1920). One of the surprising aspects of this case is that, although it adopts an approach different from that of *Brushaber* and *Baltic Mining Co.*, Mr. Chief Justice White voted with the majority. Did this represent a recantation of his former position? Does his death the following year suggest that fatigue dulled his sensitivity to the structure of the argument in the majority opinion? If the latter is the case, the history of constitutional litigation might well have been different had *Eisner* v. *Macomber* arisen a few years earlier. It is a fact that Mr. Chief Justice White's physical powers declined during the last year of his life and that he suffered from cataracts and increasing deafness in this period. KLINKHAMER, EDWARD DOUGLAS WHITE: CHIEF JUSTICE OF THE UNITED STATES, 60, 240 (1943).

19. *Id.* at 207.

a part of the constitutional definition of income. And, of much greater importance, this entire definitional apparatus was fastened to the income tax statute enacted by Congress through the assertion that Congress in enacting such a statute intended to exercise the full constitutional power which it possessed to tax income.[20]

It has already been pointed out how the realization requirement was converted to a test which merely insisted that there be some recognizable change in the interest of the taxpayer prior to assessment of the tax on any appreciation in value of the taxpayer's property.[21] The necessity that constitutionally taxable income be derived from particular sources likewise has been worn away in a process which has been traced by others.[22] Commencing with the expression of doubts by lower courts concerning the finality of the sources enumerated by *Eisner* v. *Macomber*,[23] the process, among other things, included a lack of concern with source in cases involving illegal gains such as *Rutkin*

20. *Id.* at 203. The following extract from MAGILL, TAXABLE INCOME, 5 (rev. ed. 1945) is interesting and reveals the extent to which it was thought the constitutional definition of income limited Congressional power. "So far as the federal government is concerned, each income tax statute since 1913 purports to be an exercise of the power conferred upon Congress by the Sixteenth Amendment 'to lay and collect taxes on incomes, from whatever source derived.' The power to define income, to prescribe the time of realization, and to designate the person who shall be taxable in particular transactions thus rests with Congress in the first instance. An aggrieved taxpayer may, however, present to the federal courts the question whether Congress has exceeded the bounds of the power conferred by the Amendment; e.g., has defined as income something which is not income in the eye of the court. Thus it may be said that, in the last analysis, Congress cannot enlarge the scope of the term 'income' as defined by the courts, but Congress can narrow it."

21. See pp. 63–68 *supra.*

22. See Wright, *The Effect of the Source of Realized Benefits upon the Supreme Court's Concept of Taxable Receipts,* 8 STAN. L. REV. 164, 193–201 (1956).

23. C. A. Hawkins, 6 B.T.A. 1023, 1024 (1927); Park & Tilford Distillers Corp. v. United States, 123 Ct. Cl. 509, 107 F. Supp. 941 (1952), *cert. denied,* 345 U.S. 917 (1953).

v. *United States*,[24] careful scrutiny to determine the "source" of governmental subsidies granted to taxpayers,[25] and finally *Commissioner* v. *Glenshaw Glass Co.*[26] There the Court seized upon an apparent concession by the taxpayer (to the effect that it was within the power of Congress to tax punitive damages without regard to the sixteenth amendment since to do so would not constitute a direct tax within the meaning of *Pollock*) as the means by which its focus was shifted from the Constitution to the Code. Scrutiny of the Code then revealed that "Congress applied no limitations as to the source of taxable receipts, nor restrictive labels as to their nature." [27] Furthermore, the *Eisner* v. *Macomber* definition of income was put aside with the observation that "it was not meant to provide a touchstone to all future gross income questions." [28]

A brief description of where this history places us at the present time is now in order. It appears that it is proper to believe that there has been a return to a position resembling the views Mr. Chief Justice White expressed in *Brushaber* and *Baltic Mining Co.* concerning the function of the sixteenth amendment in respect of the taxing power of Congress.[29] Thus, in examining a provision of the Code

24. 343 U.S. 130 (1952).

25. *Cf.* Edwards v. Cuba R.R., 268 U.S. 628 (1925) (subsidy paid to railroad not income under the 16th amendment) ; Texas & Pacific Ry. v. United States, 286 U.S. 285 (1932) (payments by Government to defray deficiencies in operating revenue taxable income).

26. 348 U.S. 426 (1955).

27. *Id.* at 429–30.

28. *Id.* at 431.

29. Observe how the Tax Court in Penn. Mutual Indemnity Co., 32 T.C. 653 (1959) used both decisions as supporting pillars in its holding that a special tax "on the gross amount received from interest, dividends, rents, and net premiums," imposed as part of a comprehensive scheme of taxation of mutual insurance companies, was an indirect tax and thus constitutional even though not apportioned.

which *specifically* imposes a tax on a *particular* item which does not constitute gain "clearly realized," the *first* inquiry must be whether the tax is an indirect or direct tax, *not whether the item taxed is "income."* If indirect, the tax is constitutional even if not on "income" and not apportioned. Only where the tax is direct, taking into account the teaching of *Pollock,* is it necessary to consider the scope of the sixteenth amendment. If the tax is not saved by that amendment, interpreted as in *Brushaber,* then it is unconstitutional unless apportioned. It is obvious that under this approach a tax will be seldom classified as direct. Presumably, the same approach should be used in determining the *constitutionality* of inclusion of a particular item under section 61.[30]

This approach, although sound from the standpoint of the constitutional power of Congress to tax, does not unmistakably chart the *statutory* limits of section 61. It does, however, suggest that caution be exercised in the interpretation of the language in *Glenshaw Glass Co.,* which sweepingly asserts that Congress intended in what is now section 61 "to bring the taxing power to bear on all *receipts* constitutionally taxable." [31] (Italics added.) The broad power of Congress to tax "receipts" includes, among other things, the power to tax the gross receipts of various

30. This scheme of analysis was employed in Penn. Mutual Indemnity Co., *ibid.* Thus, after concluding that the tax there involved was an indirect tax, it was stated in dictum that even if it were direct, it was saved from apportionment by the sixteenth amendment.

31. 348 U.S. 426, 429 (1955). The Court pointed out that § 61 of the 1954 Code simplified the language of § 22 (a) of the 1939 Code but that "the all-inclusive nature of statutory gross income has not been affected thereby." See, footnote 3 of the Court's opinion. The Court's language in the body of the opinion quoted in the text is broader than the assertions which appear in the references cited in the footnote. The latter consist of the House Report accompanying the 1954 Code. As quoted in the footnote, this Report merely states that the word "income," appearing in § 61 (a), is used in its constitutional sense.

forms of business, the gross receipts from sales, and gross premiums from insurance.[32] Obviously, such a power is not limited to items which, reasonably considered, constitute gain.[33] This means that the *entire* scope of Congressional power to tax "receipts" was *not* exercised to the full extent by section 61—*one* section, albeit a fundamental one, of *one* (and only *one*) scheme of taxation. Furthermore, the absence of a constitutional objection to inclusion in an income tax of an indirect tax in the form of an excise on an item other than one representing gain [34] suggests that even section 61 may be less tightly tied to *economic* gain than might be supposed.[35]

If these views are sound, the proper approach to the statutory limits of section 61, in contrast to that applicable to the constitutional power to tax, may be stated in the form of three propositions. First, the section should be regarded as presumptively embracing all items which reasonably may be described as "clearly realized" gain. Second, it should be recognized that some such items may be excluded because of the forceful operation of one or more of the macrocriteria set forth in Chapter I.

32. Pacific Insurance Co. v. Soule, 74 U.S. 433 (1868) ; Spreckels Sugar Rfg. Co. v. McClain, 192 U.S. 397 (1904).

33. In the companion case to *Glenshaw Glass Co.*, General American Investors Co. v. Comm'r, 348 U.S. 434 (1955), the Court, in holding "insider profits" taxable income to the corporation which received them pursuant to the Securities Exchange Act of 1934 and the Investment Company Act of 1940, stated that § 61 was designed "to reach all gain constitutionally taxable." This substitution of "gain" for "receipts" which was used in *Glenshaw Glass Co.* contributes nothing to the clarity of the Court's meaning.

34. This is precisely what occurred in Penn. Mutual Indemnity Co., 32 T.C. 653 (1959).

35. See POWELL, CONSTITUTIONAL ASPECTS OF FEDERAL INCOME TAXATION: THE FEDERAL INCOME TAX 51, 64–69 (Haig ed. 1921) where the taxation of distribution of corporate accumulations prior to 1913 as dividends, which was permitted in Lynch v. Hornby, 247 U.S. 339 (1918), was regarded as an example of taxing *legal* gain rather than *economic* gain.

Finally, inclusion of an item arguably not "clearly realized" gain should encounter constitutional objections only when a tax thereon would be direct under the scope of that class of tax and the function of the sixteenth amendment adopted by *Brushaber* and *Baltic Mining Co.*

There should be little doubt in the light of the preceding discussion of the structure of gross income that this approach is in fact the one which has been used throughout the history of the income tax. The only obstacle to a forthright expression of this approach is the oft-repeated assertion that section 61 and the constitutional power to tax *income* under the sixteenth amendment are coterminous.[36] This should be taken to mean, as Mr. Chief Justice White long ago suggested, that in the interpretation of section 61 no restrictions based upon the meaning of a direct tax developed by *Pollock* exist. It should not mean that each refusal to include an item under section 61 must rest on congressional impotence.

It must be acknowledged that this approach sacrifices two purposes which have been served by the assertion that section 61 exhausted congressional power to tax income. The assertion reduced to an indeterminate extent the *exclusionary* flexibility available to the courts and Government in administering the section; [37] and, second, it probably enlarged, also to an indeterminate extent, the scope of direct taxation by preserving the shadow of *Pollock* as

36. This was asserted in Eisner v. Macomber, 252 U.S. 189, 203 (1920); Helvering v. Stockholms Enskilda Bank, 293 U.S. 84, 89 (1934); Helvering v. Clifford, 309 U.S. 331 (1940). This was undoubtedly the meaning of the loose language in *Glenshaw Glass Co.* See nn. 31, 33, *supra.*

37. Although reduced, it has not precluded the Government from overlooking the imputed income derived from ownership of residential realty which is clearly taxable under the Constitution as amended by the sixteenth amendment. The assertion, of course, has enabled the courts and Government to *expand* the scope of § 61 in the face of supposed constitutional or policy objections.

interpreted in *Eisner* v. *Macomber*.[38] It is believed the first, although perhaps valued highly by some liberals, is both unnecessary and undesirable and that the second, for which some conservatives have affection, is unjustified in view of the decrepitude of *Eisner* v. *Macomber* and the reduction of the role of the sixteenth amendment to that described by *Brushaber* and *Baltic Mining Co.*

Recently, in the separate opinion of Mr. Justice Harlan in *Rudolph* v. *United States*,[39] where a previously granted petition for certiorari was dismissed as improvidently granted, there appeared recognition of the possibility that the statutory exclusions from gross income may not be "exhaustive." [40] Since such exceptions do exist, it is hoped that this view gains acceptance. Only a rusty remnant of *Eisner* v. *Macomber* prevents it. This remnant should be consigned to the junk yard of judicial history, and, if it is important to do so, the narrow holding of the case to the effect that taxation as income of a common stock dividend on common stock is a direct tax can be preserved. There

38. An exclusion, even if justified on the grounds of one or more of the macrocriteria, will, if the assertion is not properly understood, be considered as a likely candidate for the direct tax category. It is possible, of course, for there to be an exclusion from the reach of § 61 which, even if included, would amount to an indirect tax. However, the failure of the taxpayer in *Glenshaw Glass Co.* in an effort of this kind does not provide much reason for supposing that this class will be very large as long as the statutory reach of § 61 must match the constitutional power of Congress to grasp.

39. 370 U.S. 269 (1962).

40. *Id.* at 274. This was based upon a position taken by the Government in its brief. It was there asserted that following *Glenshaw Glass Co.* the approach to gross income issues should shift from "excluded unless specifically included" to "included unless specifically excluded." Brief for Government, p. 44. It was thought that this shift would require the emphasis to be placed "on questions whether there are sufficiently strong reasons of tax policy for excluding any particular kind of receipt." *Ibid.* Thus, non-statutory exceptions to gross income could exist which are plainly within the constitutional power of Congress to tax.

are other ways to skin the stock-dividend cat.[41] The result will be freedom to interpret section 61 in a rational manner unimpaired by inhibitions derived from *Pollock* and *Eisner* v. *Macomber*. Tax lawyers and students should welcome the opportunity to argue section 61 questions as issues of *statutory* rather than *constitutional* interpretation.

41. *Cf.* Int. Rev. Code of 1964, §§ 305, 306, 307.

PART TWO

SOME STATUTORY MODIFICATIONS AND REFINEMENTS OF THE STRUCTURE OF GROSS INCOME

A. Gifts, Inheritances, and
Related Receipts

VIII. The Exclusion of Gifts, Bequests, Devises, and Inheritances in General

1. Possible Approaches to Gratuitous Transfers

THE CODE PRESENTLY EXCLUDES from gross income "the value of property acquired by gift, bequests, devise or inheritance." [1] A substantially similar exclusion [2] has been in existence since the adoption of the present income tax in 1913; however, the income tax declared unconstitutional by *Pollock* v. *Farmers' Loan & Trust Co.* did include within the scope of income all personal property acquired by gift or inheritance.[3] Although doubts existed for many years concerning the constitutional power of Congress to tax such receipts,[4] the analysis of Chapter VII indicates that presently there is no foundation for this uncertainty. Gains without regard to their source can be taxed as income.

1. Int. Rev. Code of 1954, § 102 (a) .

2. Income under the Revenue Act of 1913 did not include "the value of property acquired by gift, bequest, devise or descent." Revenue Act of 1913, ch. 16, § II (B) , 38 Stat. 167.

3. Tariff Act of 1894, ch. 349, § 28, 28 Stat. 553. Presumably, the exclusion of gifts of real property was on constitutional grounds. See 26 CONG. REC. 1736 (1894) . In 1926 Congress rejected an amendment which would have made subject to the income tax all gifts in excess of $5,000. 67 CONG. REC. 3831–36, 3843–51 (1926) .

4. Hess and Guterman, *Annuity Trusts and the Federal Income Tax,* 55 HARV. L. REV. 329, 330 (1942) , suggest that in excluding gifts, Congress was "mindful of the limits of the powers granted it by the Sixteenth Amendment. . . ." Magill suggested that there is a "slight inference" that gifts would constitute gross income in the absence of a special exclusion. TAXABLE INCOME 407 (rev. ed. 1945) . *Cf.* Rice v. Eisner, 16 F.2d 358, 360 (2d Cir. 1926) , *cert. denied,* 273 U.S. 764 (1927) .

This, however, contributes little to the issue of whether the present exclusion is justified. This is not a simple question. Generally speaking, there are at least four approaches to the gift transaction which can be adopted by an income tax. The first, and the one which the federal income tax has followed since its inception, is to exclude the gift from the income of the recipient and to treat it as not a taxable event in respect to the donor. Thus, a gift of appreciated, or depreciated, property results in neither gain nor loss to donor and donee. The second provides an opposite result. It regards the gift as a taxable event to the donor and treats the donee as being in receipt of taxable gain. Simons, guided by his definition of income, advocated this approach.[5] No deduction is allowable to the donor under this approach.[6] A third way, one somewhat in keeping with the philosophy of an expenditure tax,[7] is to provide the donor with a deduction [8] in respect to the gift

5. PERSONAL INCOME TAXATION 125–147 (1938). The argument, somewhat unfairly condensed, is that the donee experiences an accretion to wealth and the donor has "consumed" the gift property. Since any "disposition" of property was, in his view, an appropriate occasion for determining gain, "consumption" would constitute a taxable event. *Id.* at 212.

6. *Id.* at 138–42. Moreover, Simons would disallow "estimated losses on property transferred by gift." *Id.* at 212.

7. The resemblance exists because the donee is considered as the ultimate consumer of the property. A gift is, thus, a form of saving by the donor. *Cf.* VICKREY, AGENDA FOR PROGRESSIVE TAXATION 201 (1947). Kaldor observes, "The basic conception of the spendings tax as a tax on per caput consumption would justify the exemption of all genuinely one-sided transfers whether in the form of casual gifts, bequests or regular allowances to other persons, and treat these as taxable (or rather accountable for tax purposes) in the hands of the beneficiaries." AN EXPENDITURE TAX 201 (1955). He recognizes, however, that some limit on the exemption is necessary when "capital" gifts are involved in the absence of a "rational" system of taxing the transmission of family wealth. *Id.* at 203, 204.

8. The deduction could be limited to the donor's adjusted basis in the property or its fair market value, whichever is lower, where the disposition by gift is not treated as a taxable event to the donor. Where it is so treated, the deduction should correspond to the fair market value of the property and the donor's gain or loss should be measured by the difference

and tax the donee on its full value at the time of receipt. Finally, it is possible to exclude the gift from the income of the donee but regard the donor as making a taxable disposition, at least with respect to appreciated property, at the time of the gift.

The problems under the second or third approach are both theoretical and practical. In the realm of theory, inclusion of gifts and inheritances in the income of the recipient immediately raises the issue whether taxation of gratuitous receipts in this manner is preferable to other forms of taxation, such as an estate and gift tax or inheritance tax. To this, Simons gave an unequivocal affirmative response.[9] Vickrey took a different position and suggested that the essentials of a rational successions tax required a

---

between this value and the donor's adjusted basis. Absent some capital gain–ordinary income differentiation, the effect would be a net deduction to the donor equal to the adjusted basis. Where there has been depreciation, consistency would require that the deduction and the loss equal the adjusted basis at the time of the gift.

9. He regarded a separate tax on gifts and inheritances as possessing the "shortcomings of the 'analytic' income tax." In expressing his preference for absorbing the function of these separate taxes in the income tax, he painted the following picture. "Thus, to make a somewhat sensible system out of existing death duties would require elaborate and extensive reconstruction; and the possible results, at best, fail to warrant much enthusiasm about the undertaking. Reconstruction along the lines of our proposal for broadening the income-tax base seems hardly more difficult to carry out and far more satisfying in terms of its probable effects. The income tax would become more equitable among persons; the tax base would become conceptually simpler and more objective; errors and uncertainties of assessment would, because of prospective counteraction later on, become less serious; the diseconomies involved in the elaborate and devious business of tax avoidance would be diminished; and the treasury would be placed in a position to require full accounting by taxpayers for every acquisition and disposition of property. With complementary arrangements to be noted later on, we should have a system full of internal checks, with provision for wholesale cancellation of errors automatically, and with a minimum of opportunities for successful falsifying of returns. These special virtues and potentialities of the income-tax device are of immense practical importance and deserve to be carefully exploited." PERSONAL INCOME TAXATION 133–34 (1938).

structure quite different from the one which would result were gifts and inheritances brought within the income tax.[10] Both recognized, however, that the present estate and gift tax structure do not conform to the ideal of such taxes and that a major purpose in the taxation of such receipts is the reduction of economic inequality in a manner most compatible with the free market. The truth is that this purpose can be served reasonably well under either approach, providing the structure in both cases is sound.

Indeed, to a substantial extent the structural problems under both approaches are the same. The treatment of gifts between spouses and members of the same generation, for example, poses a stubborn issue of theory without regard to whether the setting is that of an income tax or a transfer tax. A highly individualistic application of Equity under the income tax suggests disregarding the relationship between the donor and donee; but, as a matter of fact, Equity contributes little to determining the proper tax-paying entity. Whether an exclusion of interspousal transfers from income of the donee spouse conforms with Equity depends upon whether spouses are treated as one or two taxpayers. Equity, however, does not supply a ready answer. In the setting of a transfer tax, the issue of freedom from tax of interspousal transfers is posed in slightly different terms. It is whether transfers within the same generation justify imposition of a tax which, in broad outline, is designed to reach gifts and bequests from an older to a younger generation. However, in both settings the exclusion issue must be faced.

10. AGENDA FOR PROGRESSIVE TAXATION 202–23 (1947).

A related structural problem common to both settings is the treatment of expenditures incurred in rearing and educating children. An income tax which includes gifts within its base, as well as a transfer tax, must confront the issue whether such receipts are taxable. Again the reasoning required to resolve the issue is slightly different in each setting, but the problem is similar.

Inclusion of gratuitous transfers in the income tax base also generates practical problems which are exceedingly numerous and complex. The valuation difficulty is particularly acute where gifts in trust are made which provide for contingent future interests and discretionary distributions to classes of beneficiaries.[11] It is true, of course, that the annual character of the income tax makes possible either adjustments for faulty valuation in subsequent taxable periods [12] or the postponement of taxation until values become fixed, made necessary by faulty valuation at the time of the gift. Nonetheless, it is also true that maintenance of a tolerable margin of error and the prevention of undue deferrals poses a difficult administrative task.

In addition, it would be necessary to develop some form of annual exclusion which would eliminate from the tax base the nuisance of reporting small and insignificant tokens of esteem and affection that commonly pass between taxpayers. Finally, there is the problem of fragmentation of gifts which inclusion of gifts in income would enhance. Apportioning larger gifts over numerous tax periods and by-passing generations would become imperative. In turn,

11. This is also the type of problem which an accessions tax must face. See Rudick, *A Proposal for an Accessions Tax,* 1 TAX. L. REV. 25 (1945).

12. See excerpts from SIMONS, n. 9 *supra.*

special levies to counteract these practices would be called for.[13]

The upshot is that taxation of gratuitous receipts as income is not manifestly superior to other means of reaching these receipts. The contribution income taxation of these receipts would make to Reduced Economic Inequality can be made as well by other modes of taxation. Inclusion in income, moreover, raises serious practical problems which are probably best handled under a structure independent of the income tax. And, although Equity strongly suggests income tax treatment, any revenue deficiencies and misallocation of human talent to wasteful leisure and resources to voluptuous pursuits can be reasonably well checked by a suitably designed transfer tax system. Thus, the exclusion of gifts, bequests, devises, and inheritances from income is not a loophole which demands immediate attention. Other matters are far more pressing.

One of these is the proper treatment of the donor. Present law, as has been pointed out, affords the donor the choice of shifting gain on appreciated property to the donee by making an *inter vivos* gift or securing forgiveness of the tax on the gain by means of a transfer at death.[14] Losses, however, may not be shifted by means of lifetime

13. *Cf.* the cumulative supplementary levy designed to remove the profit from gradual giving proposed by Simons. PERSONAL INCOME TAXATION 144–45 (1938). Bypassing could be handled through a penalty tax structure. An accessions tax, see n. 11 *supra,* also would be faced with these problems.

14. See p. 70 *supra.* Int. Rev. Code of 1954, § 1015 (a), provides that the basis of gift property "shall be the same as it would be in the hands of the donor or the last preceding owner by whom it was not acquired by gift. . . ." Section 1014 (a) provides that the basis of property acquired from a decedent shall "be the fair market value of the property at the date of the decedent's death. . . ." As pointed out previously, this provision provides the taxpayer who acquires appreciated property from a decedent a "constructive investment" in the property.

gifts and are expunged from the tax records entirely when transferred at death.[15] Hence, depreciated property frequently is sold by the donor and the loss taken, while appreciated property is transferred by *inter vivos* or testamentary transfer. A more favorable arrangement from the standpoint of the taxpayer is difficult to imagine.

There has long been agreement in public finance circles that a final disposition of property, whether by gift or otherwise, constitutes an appropriate time for taking into account gains and losses experienced during the donor's holding period.[16] Former President Kennedy recommended in 1963 that Congress adopt the principle of "constructive realization." [17] His proposals provided for a number of exceptions which, taken together, illustrate some of the difficulties in charging a gratuitous transferor with gain or loss. For example, exceptions were provided for transfers of personal and household effects, residences, the first $15,000 of gain, transfers to the surviving spouse, and charitable gifts. In addition to the practical difficulties of administration which these exceptions create, they also reflect the fact that "constructive realization" imposes sub-

15. Int. Rev. Code of 1954. § 1015 (a), imposes a prohibition on losses by making an exception to its general rule which reads as follows: ". . . Except that if such basis (adjusted for the period before the date of the gift as provided in section 1016) is greater than the fair market value of the property at the time of the gift, then for the purpose of determining loss the basis shall be such fair market value." The "fair market value at date of death" basis provided for property acquired from a decedent effectively removes the loss from the tax records.

16. Simons certainly advocated this. PERSONAL INCOME TAXATION 167 (1938). *Cf.* MUSGRAVE, THE THEORY OF PUBLIC FINANCE 165–68 (1959); DUE, GOVERNMENT FINANCE 191 (3d ed. 1963); Groves, *Taxation of Capital Gains* in *Tax Revision Compendium, House Committee on Ways and Means*, 86th Cong., 1st Sess., pt. 2, 1193, 1199 (1959).

17. *President's 1963 Tax Message, Hearings Before the House Committee on Ways and Means*, 88th Cong., 1st Sess., pt. 1, at 20, 122–40 (1963).

stantial additional tax burdens on small- and medium-size estates.[18] It appears, therefore, that such realization may require a substantial reduction of income and/or estate tax rates.

Nonetheless, Equity strongly supports "constructive" realization. Assuming rate structure adjustments and some reasonable means to solve any "liquidity" problem which might arise from the necessity of meeting large income and estate tax obligations caused by unforeseen death, there is little doubt but that Free Market Compatibility and Reduced Economic Inequality point in the same direction. To the extent that realization at death or gift increases the tax burden of the upper-middle class to a greater extent than that of other groups, an observer who values the political and social contribution of that class is encouraged to resist "constructive" realization. Practicality, moreover, can also be marshaled for support of the existing structure because *simple* generosity to the taxpayer is its hallmark.

2. *What Is a Gift and Who Determines What?*

The point of simplicity, however, can be overstated because the vexing problem of what constitutes a gift

18. See Steger, *Economic Consequences of Substantial Changes in the Method of Taxing Capital Gains and Losses* in *Tax Revision Compendium, House Committee on Ways and Means*, 86th Cong., 1st Sess., pt. 2, p. 1261 (1959). In summary Steger observes: "Were unrealized gains included at death, the total taxes to be paid at death would increase by 40 per cent over the old estate tax. The percentage increase would be greatest for smaller estates and would decrease rapidly as estates increase in size. The effective tax rates would increase more for smaller estates also. However, liquidity difficulties would appear primarily in estates greater than $300,000. Most of these estates would be forced to liquidate assets of less than the highest liquidity. This would severely increase the problems of small- and medium-sized businesses on the death of one of the owners. All this is true if capital gains are taxed at 25 per cent; the problem would be severely intensified were they included in income in full with averaging."

transaction thus far has defied solution in a simple, straightforward, and consistent manner. Furthermore, such a solution does not appear imminent. One aspect of the confusion is the tendency, reflected in the decisions and legislation, to fragment the problem. That is, intra-family lifetime transfers constitute one area; death benefits paid to beneficiaries (usually widows) of deceased employees by employers another; payments upon retirement of ministers and employees of churches another; prizes, scholarships, and fellowships another; bounties or subsidies by government another; and testamentary transfers yet another. Other similarly specialized areas also exist. The discussion which follows is organized along the lines of this fragmentation even though this scheme contributes little to advance discovery of an all-embracing synthesis for which many have searched.

Despite this fissioning, there are some things that can be stated which have general application. The term "gift" for income tax purposes, for example, does not have the meaning it has at common law. Thus, a transfer without consideration, although a gift for common-law purposes, may not constitute an excludable gift. While a transfer primarily induced by the constraining "force of any moral or legal duty" does not constitute a gift for income tax purposes,[19] the absence of any such obligation does not make this classification imperative.[20] A transfer primarily induced by anticipated benefits of an economic nature is outside the gift classification,[21] but the fact the transferor

19. Comm'r v. Duberstein, 363 U.S. 278 (1960); Bogardus v. Comm'r, 302 U.S. 34 (1937).

20. Old Colony Trust Co. v. Comm'r, 279 U.S. 716, 730 (1929); Tomlinson v. Hine, 329 F.2d 462 (5th Cir. 1964).

21. Comm'r v. Duberstein, 363 U.S. 278 (1960).

derives no economic benefit does not provide tax immunity to the transferee where the payment was in exchange for services by the latter.[22] Although enduring formulations of an affirmative test are unlikely, the present posture is that gifts must emanate from "detached and disinterested generosity"[23] and be given "out of affection, respect, admiration, charity or like impulses."[24] The proper object of judicial search is "the dominant reason that explains his [the transferor's] action in making the transfer."[25] This is a fact issue to be determined on a case-by-case basis with appellate review quite restricted.[26] Where the factual determination is by a judge without a jury, his findings prevail unless "clearly erroneous." A jury's finding where proper instructions were given can be set aside only where it is one which reasonable men could not reach.

These generalizations were made the guiding principles of the gift area by the Supreme Court in *Commissioner* v. *Duberstein*.[27] There a Tax Court finding, which treated the receipt of a Cadillac automobile as income where it was given to recompense the taxpayer for making known to the transferor potential customers for his products, was not considered "clearly erroneous." In doing this, the Court rejected a test proposed by the Government which would have treated as gifts "transfers of property for personal as distinguished from business reasons." The proposed test was considered based on "maxims of experi-

22. Robertson v. United States, 343 U.S. 711 (1952).

23. Comm'r v. Lo Bue, 351 U.S. 243 (1956).

24. Robertson v. United States, 343 U.S. 711 (1952).

25. Comm'r v. Duberstein, 363 U.S. 278 (1960).

26. *Ibid.*

27. *Ibid.*

ence" rather than "principles of law," and to have imposed a standard which improperly narrowed the scope of relevant factors. While it is true that the Government's test rested on questionable premises,[28] it is also true that the Court's reliance upon the "fact-finding tribunal's experience with the mainsprings of human conduct" countenances the strong probability of unequal administration of the gift exclusion.[29] Although the determinations of the fact-finders will be more or less uniform within certain courts,[30] it is likely that greater national uniformity will not be achieved in the absence of further action by the Supreme Court or Congress.

28. See Note, *Gift v. Income: A More Definite Test?*, 29 GEO. WASH. L. REV. 555, 573 (1961).

29. Dean Griswold regarded *Duberstein* as overrating the function of the fact-finder and shirking the function of a court. The result, he asserted, was "to fail to administer justice rationally, consistently, and soundly." What he regarded as a better approach is set forth in the following sentence: "Where the transaction clearly has commercial or economic elements, where there is a *quid pro quo*, and no aspect of family love and affection, it would be more satisfactory, it seems to me, to rule as a matter of law that property transferred is not a 'gift,' rather than to leave each such case to the apparently unguided surmise of the trier of facts." *The Supreme Court, 1959 Term, Foreword: of Time and Attitudes—Professor Hart and Judge Arnold,* 74 HARV. L. REV. 81, 89 (1960). This approximates the test proposed by the Government and would narrow somewhat the gift exclusion.

30. The Court in *Duberstein* observed: "Doubtless diversity of result will tend to be lessened somewhat since federal income tax decisions, even those in tribunals of first instance turning on issues of fact, tend to be reported, and since there may be a natural tendency of professional triers of fact to follow one another's determinations, even as to factual matter." 363 U.S. at 290. The issue is whether diversity will be lessened sufficiently by this process.

IX. Application of Gift Exclusion to Certain Troublesome Areas

1. Employee Death Benefits

NOWHERE is this mixture of uniformity within courts, districts, or circuits and diversity within the nation more pronounced than in the employee death benefit area. The factual pattern of this area, although different in detail, involves a number of constants. In almost all instances the employer has made a substantial payment in cash to a beneficiary, usually a widow, of an important deceased executive. No contractual obligation impels payment, and the sum involved usually bears some significant relationship to the compensation being received by the employee prior to his death. Finally, rarely has the beneficiary rendered any personal service to the employer of the deceased.

At this point variations in detail commence. The payment may bear such a close resemblance to payments on previous occasions to similarly situated beneficiaries as to suggest that a "plan" to make such payments exists.[1] It may or may not have been adjusted to the "needs" of the beneficiary.[2] A deduction as an ordinary and necessary

1. *Cf.* Gaugler v. United States, 312 F.2d 681, 684 (2d Cir. 1963); Bounds v. United States, 262 F.2d 876, 881 (4th Cir. 1958) (absence of "plan" indicated gift); Simpson v. United States, 261 F.2d 497 (7th Cir. 1958) (presence of "plan" indicated not a gift).

2. *Cf.* Froehlenger v. United States, 63–1 U.S.T.C. ¶ 9492 (D. Md. 1963).

business expense in the amount of the payment may have been claimed by the employer.[3] The beneficiary receiving payment may be a major shareholder of the corporate employer.[4] The corporate resolution authorizing the payment may speak in terms of compensation,[5] "disinterested generosity," or both. Other minor factual variations exist of course, but these, together with the constants, are the primary data of the employee death benefit area.

Prior to *Duberstein*, the Tax Court adopted a fairly generous attitude toward these benefits. The presence of five factors tended to insure gift classification. These were: (1) the payments had been made to the wife of the deceased employee and not to his estate; (2) there was no obligation on the part of the corporation to pay any additional compensation to the deceased employee; (3) the corporation derived no benefit from the payment; (4) the wife of the deceased employee performed no services for the corporation; and (5) the services of her husband had been fully compensated."[6] Since *Duberstein*, however, the Tax Court is prepared to put all of these aside when other circumstances (such as the existence of a "plan" to provide such benefits, the irrelevance of "need" of the recipient to the amount of the payment, and the commanding shareholder position occupied by the widow and family),

3. *Cf.* Simpson v. United States, 261 F.2d 497, 501 (7th Cir. 1958) (existence of deduction indicates not a gift).

4. *Cf.* Estate of Pierpont, 35 T.C. 65 (1960), *rev'd sub nom.* Poyner v. Comm'r, 301 F.2d 287 (4th Cir. 1962), where deceased employee was a major shareholder of corporation. See Estate of Doumakes, 22 T.C.M. 1247 (1963).

5. *Cf.* Estate of Olsen v. Comm'r, 302 F.2d 671 (8th Cir. 1962) (resolution recognized employee's previous services); Estate of Kuntz v. Comm'r, 300 F.2d 849 (6th Cir. 1962) (resolution speaks of "additional compensation"). Despite the wording of the resolutions in these cases, the receipts were characterized as gifts.

6. Florence Luntz, 29 T.C. 647 (1958).

indicate that the dominant motive of the employer was not "detached and disinterested generosity." [7] This shift of focus has narrowed substantially the scope of the gift exclusion in this court.

It is not so narrow in some of the circuits. In some there is a willingness to be influenced by factors such as the five which formerly guided the Tax Court.[8] In others there exists tolerance of fact-finders who give significant weight to these five; [9] while in yet others there exists tolerance of fact-finders who give little weight to these five.[10] Finally, the second circuit has designated as "clearly relevant" the following six factors: "(1) the inconsistent accounting and tax treatment by the Company; (2) the existence of a previous practice of making similar payments to widows of high officials of the Company; (3) the computation of the payments in terms of the salary which would have been paid had decedent survived and continued his employment; (4) the fact that the payments were made by a business corporatoin and sound business reasons were considered in making them; (5) the 'moral duty' implicit in the special circumstances of the widow's need to readjust to a lower standard of living; (6) the Company's failure

7. See Estate of Pierpont, 35 T.C. 65 (1960), *rev'd sub nom.* Poyner v. Comm'r, 301 F.2d 287 (4th Cir. 1962); Mary C. Westphal, 37 T.C. 340 (1961); Estate of Rosen, 21 T.C.M. 317 (1963); Estate of Doumakes, 22 T.C.M. 1247 (1963). Nonetheless, even the Tax Court is willing to find a gift under some circumstances. Estate of Enyart, 24 T.C.M. 1447 (1965).

8. *Cf.* United States v. Frankel, 302 F.2d 666 (8th Cir. 1962); Estate of Olsen v. Comm'r, 302 F.2d 671 (8th Cir. 1962); Estate of Kuntz v. Comm'r, 300 F.2d 849 (6th Cir. 1962); United States v. Kasynski, 284 F.2d 143 (10th Cir. 1960).

9. United States v. Pixton, 326 F.2d 626 (5th Cir. 1964) (also there was no past history of death benefit payments); Poyner v. Comm'r, 301 F.2d 287 (4th Cir. 1962). The fifth circuit does not speak with one voice. See Tomlinson v. Hine, 329 F.2d 462 (5th Cir. 1964).

10. Smith v. Comm'r, 305 F.2d 778 (3d Cir. 1962); Martin v. Comm'r, 305 F.2d 290 (3d Cir. 1962).

to investigate the actual financial circumstances and needs of the widow." [11]

Out of this emerges one useful generalization. Since *Duberstein*, the scope of relevant factors in the employee death benefit area has expanded, and those less favorable to the taxpayer have assumed a greater importance than previously was the case. The evolution is, however, clearly not finished. In due course the gift exclusion may be effectively withdrawn from the employee death benefits area, and their only shelter then will be that provided by section 101 (b) of the 1954 Code.[12] This can be accomplished in large measure by making the second, third, and sixth factors designated by the second circuit the legally controlling factors. At present, however, this is not the position of current case law; [13] moreover, such a result would not be consistent, strictly speaking, with the teaching of *Duberstein*. In the meantime the present situation fails to measure up to the criteria of Practicality, Equity, and Reduced Economic Inequality.

2. *Tips and Other Commercial Gratuities*

The regulations have long provided that tips, which have been described judicially as "token[s] of better serv-

11. Gaugler v. United States, 312 F.2d 681, 684 (2d Cir. 1963).

12. The provision excludes amounts received by the beneficiaries which are paid by an employer and "by reason of the death of an employee." The exclusion is limited to $5000 and does not apply where "the employee possessed, immediately before his death, a non-forfeitable right to receive the amounts while living." At one time the Government argued that this provision overrode § 102 so that employee death benefits which qualified as gifts were limited to an exclusion of $5000. Rev. Rul. 60–326, 1960–2 C.B. 32. This position, after several judicial defeats, was later abandoned. Rev. Rul. 62–102, 1962–2 C.B. 37. It continues to argue that the extension in 1954 of § 101 (b) to payments not pursuant to contractual obligations indicates that Congress assumed that such payments did not qualify as gifts. There is little in the Committee reports to indicate this intent.

13. The Second Circuit, for example, has shown no tendency to read

ice received," [14] are included in gross income.[15] The case law uniformly has supported this view.[16] At present the litigation pertaining to tips involves the issue of whether the Commissioner's determination of the amount of tips received by the taxpayer is proper.[17]

The proper treatment of other commercial gratuities is not as clear. While it is generally true that Christmas bonuses and other payments which are in some fashion correlated with the recipient's service to the payor are income,[18] it is also true that Christmas hams and turkeys given to employees are presently treated as gifts.[19] Presumably, the annual office Christmas party also falls within this "Bob Cratchit" exclusion. Also excluded as gifts are

---

Gaugler v. United States, 312 F.2d 681 (2d Cir. 1963), in a manner which would make the second, third, and sixth factors mentioned in the text controlling. At present, it appears to follow faithfully the *ad hoc* approach of *Duberstein*. Fanning v. Couley, 66–1 USTC ¶ 9240 (2d Cir. 1966).

14. Judge Yankwich in Roberts v. Comm'r, 176 F.2d 221, 226 (9th Cir. 1949), used these words: "It may be more in keeping with the attitudes prevailing in some areas to suggest that tips are to insure even minimum service should the payor and payee ever chance to meet again."

15. Treas. Reg. § 1.61–2 (a) (1959). All regulations since 1918 have provided that tips are includable in gross income. See T.D. 2831, art. 32, 21 Treas. Dec. 170, 180 (1919).

16. Roberts v. Comm'r, 176 F.2d 221 (9th Cir. 1949); Andrews v. United States, 295 F.2d 819 (Ct. Cl. 1961). *Duberstein* cited the *Roberts* case with approval.

17. *E.g.*, Carroll F. Schroeder, 40 T.C. 30 (1963); Dorothy L. Sutherland, 32 T.C. 862 (1959); Quintillian C. Borden, 22 T.C.M. 1214 (1963); Elmer Hornburg, 22 T.C.M. 459 (1963). The Commissioner appears to be successful when his estimates run from 10 per cent to 15 per cent of the cost of the service rendered. *Cf.* Pedro E. Martinez, 23 T.C.M. 1263 (1964). An estimate of 20 per cent is probably too high. *Cf.* Herbert Payne, 23 T.C.M. 170 (1964). Obviously, these cases constitute one of the best guides for tipping in existence. On withholding with respect to tips, see T.I.R. No. 823 (1966).

18. Miller v. Comm'r, 327 F.2d 846 (2d Cir. 1964); Tietelbaum v. Comm'r, 294 F.2d 541 (7th Cir. 1961); Painter v. Campbell, 110 F. Supp. 503 (N.D. Tex. 1953); I.T. 1600, II–1 C.B. 184 (1923). *But see* I.T. 3726, 1945 C.B. 63, distinguished in T.I.R. No. 527.

19. Rev. Rul. 59–58, 1959–1 C.B. 17.

147

passes issued by railroads to their employees,[20] and it is possible for contributions made for presentation at a testimonial dinner to be considered gifts.[21]

The gift exclusion, however, is not large in the area of commercial gratuities. A useful generalization is that receipts by taxpayers engaged in rendering services, contributed by those with whom the taxpayers have some personal or functional contact in the course of the performance of their services, are taxable income when in conformity with the commercial custom of the particular area and capable of reasonably accurate valuation. In reaching this point, tax law is only reflecting accurately the impersonal relationship which now characterizes the rendition of service. It is difficult for the briskly efficient (or, for that matter, the dully inefficient) waitress, employee, garage attendant, doorman, milkman, paper boy, etc. to appear before the Government in tax matters in the functional garments of a beloved family retainer. To repeat an old theme of this book, tax law takes society as it finds it.

3. Payments "In Appreciation" Made upon Termination of Services

This skepticism regarding claims of "disinterested generosity" in a highly specialized, market-oriented society is also present when gift classification is sought for payments "in appreciation" made upon termination of services. Where the payment is by the former employer, the intention to reward the employee more generously than is re-

20. O.D. 946, 4 C.B. 110 (1921).

21. Max Kralstein, 38 T.C. 810 (1962) (union official received at a testimonial dinner a large sum made up from contributions from many sources which was part gift and part income.) *Cf.* J. Marion Wright, 30 T.C. 392 (1958).

quired by existing legal obligations does not suffice to make the payment a gift.[22] Indeed, the fact that the payor is the former employer creates a presumption that the payment is not a gift.[23] Designation of the payment as bonus, honorarium, or gift, of course, does not guarantee exclusion as a gift.[24] The classification of the payment is not significantly influenced by the reason for the termination of employment. Thus, not ill health,[25] liquidation of employer,[26] dismissal with or without cause,[27] or loss of benefits under a pension plan [28] provides a reason sufficient to merit exclusion. Finally, classification as a gift is not achieved by the payor's failure to treat the payment as compensation.[29]

Occasionally, however, a former employee is successful.[30] Not a little surprising is that the most recent taxpayer victory occurred in *Stanton* v. *United States*,[31] a companion case to *Duberstein*. The taxpayer, an employee of the Trinity Church in New York City, received a

22. Willkie v. Comm'r, 127 F.2d 953 (6th Cir. 1942) ; Fisher v. Comm'r, 59 F.2d 192 (2d Cir. 1932) ; L. Gordon Walker, 25 T.C. 832 (1956).

23. Poorman v. Comm'r, 131 F.2d 946 (9th Cir. 1942) ; Bass v. Hawley, 62 F.2d 721 (5th Cir. 1933).

24. L. Gordon Walker, 25 T.C. 832 (1956).

25. *Ibid.*

26. Carragan v. Comm'r, 197 F.2d 246 (2d Cir. 1952).

27. Harris W. Watkins, 6 T.C.M. 652 (1947).

28. Poorman v. Comm'r, 131 F.2d 946 (9th Cir. 1942).

29. Nickelsburg v. Comm'r, 154 F.2d 70 (2d Cir. 1946).

30. For an early case which reflects a judicial tolerance to gift classification not present today, see Cunningham v. Comm'r, 67 F.2d 205 (3d Cir. 1933).

31. 363 U.S. 278 (1960). Almost equally surprising is that the same chain of circumstances involved in *Stanton* also were involved in Harris W. Watkins, 6 T.C.M. 652 (1947). The payments to Watkins were treated as income while those to Stanton ultimately received the gift immunity. The payment to Watkins, however, was not designated as a "gratuity" by the employer.

sum of money upon his resignation almost equal to his annual salary as comptroller of the Church corporation and president of the Trinity Operating Company, a subsidiary corporation formed to manage the extensive real estate holdings of the Church. Although there was some indication that Stanton's resignation was not viewed with unqualified regret by the directors of the Operating Company,[32] the corporate resolution designated the payment a "gratuity." In the initial proceedings the District Court held the payment was a gift. This finding was considered improper by the Circuit Court,[33] but the Supreme Court reversed and remanded "for further proceedings not inconsistent with this opinion." [34] Upon remand the District Court adhered to its previous position [35] and, in so doing, emphasized that Trinity Operating Company was a unique corporation and that the relationship between Stanton and the directors was less commercial and more personal than is usually the case because he had "enabled them the more adequately to perform" the duties of their stewardship made exacting by "a sensitive conscience that each is assumed to have possessed." [36] This finding was then affirmed by the Circuit Court on the ground that it was not "clearly erroneous." [37]

To a much greater extent is the relationship between minister and congregation removed from that which normally prevails in the market place. It is not surprising,

32. The dismissal of Watkins, see n. 31 *supra,* was resisted by Stanton. To avoid embarrassment, Stanton then resigned.

33. Stanton v. United States, 268 F.2d 727 (2d Cir. 1959).

34. 363 U.S. at 293.

35. Stanton v. United States, 186 F. Supp. 393 (E.D.N.Y. 1960).

36. *Id.* at 395–96.

37. United States v. Stanton, 287 F.2d 876 (2d Cir. 1961).

therefore, to find that certain payments by congregations "in gratitude and appreciation" to ministers upon termination of their ministry enjoy immunity from tax.[38] These payments, sometimes in addition to regular pensions,[39] spring from a desire to provide the minister with additional financial security within the limits of the congregation's means. Whether these circumstances make the dominant motive of the payor one of "detached and disinterested generosity" no doubt does present an issue whose solution requires "experience with the mainsprings of human [and perhaps spiritual?] conduct to the totality of the facts of each case." It can only be said for certain that a congregation's feeling for its minister is quite likely to be different from that between a commercial corporation and its retiring president.[40]

Somewhere between these two types of sentiment may lie that which prevails when an "in appreciation" payment is made by one other than the former employer. In *Bogardus* v. *Commissioner*[41] the Supreme Court concluded that such a payment was a gift. Prior to the sale of

38. Abernethy v. Comm'r, 211 F.2d 651 (D.C. Cir. 1954); Mutch v. Comm'r, 209 F.2d 390 (3d Cir. 1954); Schale v. Comm'r, 174 F.2d 893 (5th Cir. 1949).

39. Pension payments under an established plan to which contributions by a number of congregations were made and where no personal relationship between the recipient and many of the contributing congregations existed are taxable income. Alvin T. Perkins, 34 T.C. 117 (1960). It is interesting to note that in Mutch v. Comm'r, 209 F.2d 390 (3d Cir. 1954), the court observed that a continuation of the taxpayer's salary was clearly taxable even though the "honorarium" was not.

40. The Service has indicated that it will no longer litigate cases involving facts similar to those in the cases cited in n. 39 *supra*. Rev. Rul. 55-422, 1955-1 C.B. 14. The feeling between the donor and his mistress is also unlike that which prevails in most market places. Perhaps this is a reason which can be asserted in defense of a Tax Court decision which found certain payments to the taxpayer mistress to be gifts. See Greta Starks, 25 T.C.M. 676 (1966).

41. 302 U.S. 34 (1937).

the stock of the highly successful employer corporation, a new corporation was "spun off" from the employer. The new corporation was owned by the same shareholders, and in the same proportion, as was the employer corporation. Thereafter, all the stock of the employer was sold to a third corporation. The new corporation then made payments, described as a "gift or honorarium," to certain present and former employees [42] of the employer corporation. Despite the fact that the transactions somewhat resembled the actions of joint-venturers "splitting a melon," the Supreme Court found "spontaneous generosity" as the moving cause of the payment. And perhaps it was. Certainly shareholders and directors in the early thirties did not view corporate gains as impressed with any moral or economic claim held by its employees. Nonetheless, the sophisticated, realizing the probability of a different result had the payments been made as a lump sum prior to the sale of the stock of the employer, will always have difficulty accepting the *Bogardus* result.

This has not prevented *Bogardus* from having substantial influence. It has been followed in a number of instances where the facts are substantially similar.[43] Furthermore, its emphasis upon the "intention" with which the payment was made [44] influenced the Court in *Duberstein* in formulating its "proper criterion," viz., "what the basic reason for his conduct was in fact." Its influence, however,

42. One recipient was the sister of a deceased employee.

43. Hall v. Comm'r, 93 F.2d 1005 (4th Cir. 1938); Simpkinson v. Comm'r, 93 F.2d 1015 (5th Cir. 1937); Bert P. Newton, 11 T.C. 512 (1948).

44. The majority opinion emphasized "intention," but the point was put more succinctly by the dissenters: "What controls is the intention with which payment, however voluntary, has been made." 302 U.S. at 45. It was this statement which the Court in *Duberstein* used as the "*Bogardus* criterion."

is waning. *Duberstein,* itself, more reflects the views of the dissenters in *Bogardus* than those of the majority.[45] Another straw in the wind is that a Tax Court finding of taxable income, where payments were made by the acquiring corporation to former employees of an acquired corporation, was sustained under the authority of *Duberstein* by a Circuit Court which plainly felt that a contrary finding was more reasonable.[46]

4. Strike Benefits

Consideration of payments made to those who are employees of others leads to strike benefits. In both there are elements of self-interest on the part of the payor. For many years the Government adhered to the policy that payments made by labor unions to individual members while on strike were taxable income.[47] This position was extended in 1957 to payments on the basis of need without regard to union membership.[48] However, in *United States* v. *Kaiser*[49] the Supreme Court affirmed a reversal by the

45. This is based on the fact that in *Duberstein* the role of the fact-finder was elevated to that which was advocated by the dissenting opinion in *Bogardus*. There it was said: "We think there was a question of fact whether payment to this petitioner was made with one intention or the other. A finding either in his favor or against him would have had a fair basis in the evidence. It was for the triers of the facts to seek among competing aims or motives the ones that dominated conduct. Perhaps, if such a function had been ours, we would have drawn the inference favoring a gift. That is not enough. If there was opportunity for opposing inferences, the judgment of the Board controls . . . ." 302 U.S. at 45.

46. Joshel v. Comm'r, 296 F.2d 645 (10th Cir. 1961). Some of the recipients, although not all, became employees of the acquiring corporation. The acquisition grew out of efforts by Shell Chemical Corporation, the acquiring corporation, to protect its interests in certain insecticides. The retention of the loyalty of the recipients was thought to be helpful in these efforts.

47. O.D. 552, 2 C.B. 73 (1920); I.T. 1293, I-1 C.B. 63 (1922).

48. Rev. Rul. 57-1, 1957-1 C.B. 15.

49. 363 U.S. 299 (1960).

Circuit Court of a judgment entered n.o.v. by the trial court after a jury finding that strike benefits paid on the basis of need to one not a member of the striking union were gifts. This decision by the Supreme Court was rendered on the same day as *Duberstein* and was based upon the primacy of the role of the fact-finder established therein.[50] No doubt the factual and procedural setting of *Kaiser* influenced the establishment of this primacy. Following this decision, the Revenue Service stated "that in cases presenting facts substantially like those in the *Kaiser* case, strike benefit payments will be regarded as gifts and, therefore, exempt from Federal income tax." [51] In addition, a troublesome point concerning the scope of *Kaiser* was put aside by observing that "the fact that benefits are paid only to union members will not, in and of itself, be considered determinative of whether such benefits will be regarded as gifts or as gross income." Thus, despite the fact that *Duberstein* appreciably narrowed the gift exclusion in many cases, it and *Kaiser* appear to have expanded it somewhat in the area of strike benefits.

Perhaps because the words "out of affection, respect, admiration, charity, or like impulses," the hallmark of excludable gifts, stick in the throat when the effort is made to apply them to certain strike benefits, an exclusion of all strike benefits from gross income has not been given judicial approval. Instead, the courts have commenced the difficult task of separating those which are "income" from

50. Justices Frankfurter and Clark concurred in the result on the ground that there was "sufficient evidence . . . to support the theory that in making these payments the union was exercising a wholly charitable function." *Id*. at 305, 316. Justice Douglas concurred and stated that the case was sufficiently clear to have entitled the taxpayer to a directed verdict had he requested it. He admitted that his view of the gift exclusion was broader than that of other members of the Court. *Id*. at 325–27.

51. Rev. Rul. 61–136, 1961–2 C.B. 20.

those which are "gifts." The indicia of "income" strike benefits include (1) restriction of benefits to union membership, (2) existence of a legal or moral obligation on the part of the union to make payments and the striker to perform duties incident to the strike, (3) irrelevance of the financial condition or need of the striker, (4) presence of a clear relationship between the amount of benefits and the normal salary of the striker, (5) payments in money rather than in "chits" redeemable only for food or rent, and (6) any other evidence which tends to show that both the union and striker are advancing their economic interests and that the benefits are merely incident thereto.[52] It remains to be seen whether *Kaiser* will beget numerous progeny or remain a sterile precedent regularly distinguished by "fact finders."

In any event, it is probable that *Kaiser* cannot be explained completely without resort to the criterion of Political Order. Obviously, the position of the strikers in *Kaiser* elicited a response which was not divorced from the Court's attitude toward the position of labor in the political and economic structure. Moreover, the Kohler strike, the one in which the benefits dealt with in *Kaiser* were paid, was an extremely bitter labor dispute. The "pull" of sympathy with the goals of labor undoubtedly will lead some to approach the gift exclusion, as applied in this area, with "generosity" other than "detached," while others, having different sympathies, will adopt the mien of the most severe publican and seriously doubt that a single drop of kindness and mercy can be wrung from the hard union heart. This being true, perhaps something can be

52. Halsor v. Lethert, 240 F. Supp. 738 (D. Minn. 1965); Godwin v. United States, 65-1 U.S.T.C. ¶ 9121 (W.D. Tenn. 1964); John H. Hagar, 43 T.C. 468 (1965).

said for turning the problem over to the fact-finders after all. Even Equity and Practicality must step aside at times.

5. *Governmental Grants*

The difficulty encountered in searching for the warm heart of a corporation or union is multiplied when a similar search is made for that of Government. Fortunately, the presence of *Edwards* v. *Cuba Railroad Co.* [53] has greatly reduced the necessity for this endeavor. Subsidies, when not capital contributions, are considered income. In one instance, however, a governmental grant has been classified as a gift. Fittingly enough, that instance is the homestead acquired from the Government by public grant.[54] A more appropriate coincidence of American mythology and sentiment in taxation is difficult to imagine.

53. 268 U.S. 628 (1925). For a discussion of the contribution of capital area see Sneed, *The Criteria of Federal Income Tax Policy*, 17 STAN. L. REV. 567, 604–13 (1965).

54. O.D. 601, 3 C.B. 50 (1920).

X. Statutory Descendants of the Gift Exclusion: Prizes, Awards, Scholarships, and Fellowships

1. Prizes and Awards

UNDER the 1939 Code the gift exclusion afforded some modest immunity from taxation of prizes and awards. Its scope was uncertain, however. In addition, in drawing the limits of this immunity, attention was focused not on the state of mind of the payor but rather on the actions of the recipient, both before and after receiving the boon, and the legal relationship between the payor and payee. Thus, in *Robertson* v. *United States* [1] the Supreme Court, speaking through Justice Douglas, who presently appears willing to find gift-generating generosity when his brethren behold only self-interest,[2] rather summarily held that a prize won by a composer in a contest to select the "three best symphonic works written by native-born composers of this hemisphere" constituted taxable income. In doing so, the Court tersely observed that the relationship between a contestant and the sponsor of the contest is contractual and that performance by the latter of its duty to pay the prize was "in no sense a gift." [3] It was acknowledged, however, that the gift exclusion would extend to awards "in recognition of past achievements or present abilities." [4]

1. 343 U.S. 711 (1952).

2. See n. 50, chap. ix, *supra*.

3. 343 U.S. at 713.

4. *Ibid.* Thus, the Pulitzer Prize did not constitute income. Rev. Rul. 54–110, 1954–1 C.B. 28. Similar awards in other fields were excluded. Rev.

The lower courts did not extend the contractual analysis to situations resembling what the economists designate as "money rain." That is, where the prize winner did nothing to enter a contest, submitted to no rules, gave up no rights, produced nothing, performed no services, granted no permission for the use of his name, but merely received a prize awarded on the basis of chance, the amount was excluded as a gift.[5] On the other hand, where the prize winner, or his donor, purchased a "chance" or "ticket" entitling him to a prize awarded substantially on the basis of chance, his winnings constituted income.[6]

In the 1954 Code the somewhat unique character of this area was recognized by enactment of a special section.[7] Its general rule is that all prizes and awards are income. An exception is made for those "primarily in recognition of religious, charitable, scientific, educational, artistic, liter-

---

Rul. 55–314, 1955–1 C.B. 235 (chemistry). After initial resistance, it was conceded in 1959 that the Stalin Peace Prize was excludable under the 1939 Code. I.R.-277 (Feb. 4, 1959).

5. Ray W. Campeau, 24 T.C. 370 (1955) (prize awarded by radio show "Hollywood Calling—Film of Fortune" to one who answers telephone number picked at random and who answered correctly two questions); Pauline C. Washburn, 5 T.C. 1333 (1945) (prize awarded by radio show "Pot O'Gold" to one who answers telephone number picked at random). In Glenn v. Bates, 217 F.2d 535 (6th Cir. 1954), the same result was reached even though the prize winner in response to an advertisement went to an automobile dealer's showroom and registered for the purpose of a drawing for a new automobile to be awarded as the prize. Prizes won by participating in quiz shows were considered income. I.T. 3987, 1950–1 C.B. 9.

6. Riebe v. Comm'r, 124 F.2d 399 (6th Cir. 1941), *affirming* 41 B.T.A. 935 (1940) (sweepstakes or lottery winnings are income); Reynolds v. United States, 118 F. Supp. 911 (N.D. Cal. 1954) ("Lucky 49er Sweepstakes" conducted by San Francisco's *Call-Bulletin* taxable income); Diane M. Solomon, 25 T.C. 936 (1956) (winning ticket at church bazaar taxable income); Clewell Sykes, 24 T.C. 1156 (1955) (winning ticket at a drawing at the annual club function taxable income); Max Silver, 42 B.T.A. 461 (1940) (Irish Sweepstakes winnings taxable income).

7. Int. Rev. Code of 1954, § 74.

ary or civic achievement." However, this exception does not apply unless (1) "the recipient was selected without any action on his part to enter the contest" and (2) he "is not required to render substantial future services as a condition to receiving the prize or award." Thus, gross income has been expanded to include the receipts considered in the "money rain" type case, but it still does not embrace prizes such as the Nobel and Pulitzer.[8]

The focus of attention now becomes whether the circumstances surrounding a particular receipt bring it within the exception for religious, charitable, or other similar achievement. Thus, it has been argued on behalf of a taxpayer that the cash prize for winning a fishing derby sponsored by a brewery constituted an amount received primarily in recognition of a "civic achievement." [9] This bit of tax-inspired nonsense proved unconvincing. Also unconvincing, but involving a much closer issue, was the argument that an award under the Government Employee's Incentive Awards Act, given to the taxpayer for his work in developing a rate formula for use in fixing proper railroad freight charges for transporting rockets and projectiles, was in recognition of "scientific achievement." [10] The court felt the taxpayer's achievement rose only to the level of the "technical," at least one rung below the "scientific." The two qualifying conditions nec-

---

8. Treas. Reg. § 1.74–1 (1955).

9. Simmons v. United States, 308 F.2d 160 (4th Cir. 1962).

10. Griggs v. United States, 314 F.2d 515 (Ct. Cl. 1963). Discretionary awards by government department leads to "employees who 'contribute to the efficiency, economy, or other improvement of Government operations or who perform special acts or services in the public interest in connection with or related to their official employment'" are not excludable from income of the recipients. Denniston v. Commr., 343 F.2d 312, 312–13 (D.C. Cir. 1965).

essary for the exception to be operative also can be expected to become a productive source of disputes.[11]

Without doubt, the 1954 Code solved some problems in this area, but it is equally clear that others were created. In fact, confidence in the ability of tax legislation to reduce the scope of problems may be shaken when it is observed that notwithstanding the 1954 changes it remains difficult to be certain about the tax treatment of a sum paid by an uncle to his nephew as a reward for having abstained, pursuant to the uncle's request, from smoking and drinking until reaching the age of twenty-one.[12] Is it a gift in view of *Robertson?* An excluded prize or award? Or simply compensation income?

2. *Scholarships and Fellowships*

Another instance of 1954 legislation producing a nest of problems different from those which existed when the transactions involved were dealt with under the gift exclusion occurs in the scholarship and fellowship area.[13] Under the 1939 Code the issue in the scholarship and fellowship area was to separate the "gift" sheep from the "compensation" goats. As might be expected, there were more goats than sheep. While Guggenheim grants received gift immunity,[14] fellowships which required participation in super-

11. As to what constitutes action "to enter a contest or proceedings," see Rev. Rul. 57–67, 1957–1 C.B. 33, holding filing a written form and the appearance for a personal interview does not constitute such action. *But see* Max Isenbergh, 31 T.C. 1046, 1052 (1959). Submission of an entry and obtaining endorsement of employer does constitute entering the contest. Rev. Rul. 65–161, 1965–1 C.B. 38. The uncertain scope of "substantial future service as a condition to receiving the prize or award" is obvious. See Mueller, 41 T.C. 639, *aff'd,* 338 F.2d 215 (1st Cir. 1964).

12. See Hamer v. Sidway, 124 N.Y. 538 (1891).

13. Int. Rev. Code of 1954, § 117.

14. George W. Stone, 23 T.C. 254 (1954) (A); Rev. Rul. 57–286, 1957–1 C.B. 497.

vised research on a particular project were treated as compensation even though such work enabled the recipient to prepare papers which were accepted in full, or partial, satisfaction of certain degree requirements.[15] Postdoctoral fellowships involving supervised research fared as badly,[16] although grants solely for the training and education of recipients were tax free.[17] The lines obviously were shadowy. Guggenheim grants were distinguished on the grounds that (1) the research was done in a field selected by the recipient, (2) the foundation did not direct or control the manner in which the research was done, (3) no rights to the research were bargained for or obtained by the foundation, and (4) there was no commitment of a contractual nature on the part of the foundation.

The 1954 Code fashioned a new and somewhat elaborate structure to deal with this area. Realizing that the then existing law did not provide "a clear cut method of determining whether a grant is taxable," [18] Congress enacted section 117. It commences with the general rule that gross income does not include scholarships received "at an educational institution (as defined in section 151 (e)(4)) " and fellowship grants.[19] Also excluded are amounts received to cover expenses for travel, research, clerical help, or equipment which are incident to the grant and are so expended.[20] The balance of the section

15. Ephraim Banks, 17 T.C. 1386 (1952) ; Robert F. Doerge, 11 T.C.M. 475 (1952).

16. Ti Li Loo, 22 T.C. 220 (1954) ; I.T. 4056, 1951–2 C.B. 8.

17. *Cf.* I.T. 4056, 1951–2 C.B. 8; I.T. 3756, 1945 C.B. 64.

18. S. REP. No. 1622, 83d Cong., 2d Sess., 189–90.

19. Int. Rev. Code of 1954, § 117 (a)(1).

20. Int. Rev. Code of 1954, § 117 (a)(2). This additional exclusion is available in the case of grants after July 28, 1956, only if "the amount received by the individual is specifically designated to cover expenses for

deals with limitations through which runs a common theme. That is, all can be said to constitute an effort to eliminate, or at least significantly reduce, the possibility of amounts received as compensation for services escaping tax as a scholarship or fellowship.

The consequence is that the old problem of distinguishing between gifts and compensation for services has been transmuted to those of (1) distinguishing between such compensation and scholarships and fellowships and (2) interpretation of the statutory limitations designed to facilitate this task. The solutions of the latter are no more simple than was the former. The improvements, if such they be, are that the issues are more sharply delineated, although greater in number than previously was the case, and that some previously troublesome situations have been eliminated.

The limitations are divided into two sets—one set applicable to degree candidates and the other to non-degree candidates. The first set makes the exclusion inapplicable to "any amount received which represents payment for teaching, research, or other services in the nature of part-time employment required as a condition to receiving the scholarship or fellowship grant." [21] This limitation is, however, made inapplicable where such services are required of all degree candidates without regard to whether they are receiving grants. Therefore, the "part-time employ-

---

travel, research, clerical help, or equipment." Treas. Reg. § 1.117–1 (b)(2) , as amended by T.D. 6456, 1960–1 C.B. 43. The cut-off date reflects the fact that Max Isenbergh, 31 T.C. 1046, 1055 (1959) , held that such a provision could not be made applicable to grants made before the regulations applicable to § 117 were adopted. These became final, although subsequently amended, on June 29, 1956.

21. Int. Rev. Code of 1954, § 117 (b)(1) .

ment" limitation is not applicable where a learning-through-working program is a required part of a college's scholastic program leading to a degree.[22] Furthermore, it is inapplicable where a fellowship is received which facilitates research necessary to obtaining a degree and which is similar to that required of all degree candidates.[23]

Nonetheless, the Tax Court has expressed the view that requiring services of all degree candidates will not insulate all sums paid in respect thereto from tax.[24] According to this approach, the primary purpose of the payments must be ascertained in all cases. Payments primarily intended as compensation are taxable, even though the work being compensated is required of all degree candidates. The exclusion is available only with respect to payments primarily intended to further the education and training of the recipient. Sums primarily intended as compensation are not scholarships; hence, the exception to the part-time employment limitation does not come into play.

There is considerable logic in this view.[25] But, in rejecting the view that the existence of a service obligation imposed on all degree candidates is sufficient to shield from tax any receipts in respect thereto, it is arguable that the Tax Court has embarked on an unnecessary search for the always elusive primary purpose. Simplicity would accept at face value the declaration by the degree-awarding

22. Rev. Rul. 64–54, 1964–1 C.B. 81. Amounts paid "student-trainees" by a school of medical technology for work done in the "training program" are excludable, but compensation for work done on week ends outside the program is taxable. Rev. Rul. 64–29, 1964–1 C.B. 79. Also see Rev. Rul. 63–250, 1963–2 C.B. 79.

23. Chander P. Bhalla, 35 T.C. 13 (1960) (A).

24. Elmer L. Reese, Jr., 45 T.C. 407 (1966).

25. See pp. 164–67 *infra*.

institution that the required work is substantially related to the recipient's educational program. As it is, simplicity and certainty suffer at the hand of logic.[26]

The second set of limitations is somewhat more detailed. In the first place, to be entitled to an exclusion the non-degree candidate must receive a grant from a tax-exempt organization [27] or certain other designated governmental or international organizations.[28] In this manner the danger of compensation masquerading as fellowships has been reduced by eliminating from the latter category grants by commercial concerns to their employees to enable them to obtain additional training not leading to a degree.[29] On top of this is a monetary and time limit to the exclusion available to non-degree candidates. Putting aside the details, such candidates may exclude only "an amount equal to $300 times the number of months for which the recipient received amounts under the scholarship or fellowship grant during such taxable year." In addition, no exclusion is available for a non-degree candidate after he "has been entitled to exclude under this section for a period of 36 months (whether or not consecutive) amounts received as a scholarship or fellowship. . . ." [30]

Both sets of limitations, however, do not adequately

26. The part-time employment limitation does apply where the grant is conditioned upon research being done by the degree candidate which is neither in fulfilment of a degree requirement nor required of other degree candidates. Alex L. Sweet, 40 T.C. 403 (1963).

27. That is, "an organization described in section 501 (c)(3) which is exempt from tax under 501 (a)." Int. Rev. Code of 1954, § 117 (b)(2)(A)(i).

28. Int. Rev. Code of 1954, § 117 (b)(2)(A).

29. Rev. Rul. 57–484, 1957–2 C.B. 113.

30. Int. Rev. Code of 1954, § 117 (b)(2)(B). The regulations deal with such troublesome details as fractional months, grants received from two fellowships in a single month, lump-sum payments, etc. Treas. Reg. § 1.117–2 (b)(2) (1956).

distinguish between scholarships and fellowships on the one hand and compensation on the other. A more expertly drafted section 117 would have contained a definition, albeit a general one, of these excludable grants. Instead the definitional burden, which is not an easy one, has had to be shouldered exclusively by the regulations and court decisions. Fundamentally, this is because the task requires a definition which includes not only those grants which under the 1939 Code fell within the gift exclusion but also some which previously were treated as compensation.[31] This new classification, reaching as it does to some extent into the category of compensation, then must be distinguished from the balance of that category. Put more succinctly, the task involves separation of both gift and compensatory scholarships and fellowships from *ordinary* compensation.

The existing regulations go about the task in a somewhat circuitous manner.[32] In essence, they provide that

31. Frank Thomas Bachmura, 32 T.C. 1117, 1125 (1959), put it this way: "We agree that amounts received as a fellowship grant may be compensatory in character, and that with the enactment of section 117 of the 1954 Code it no longer follows that such amounts are to be included in gross income merely because they were in the nature of compensation for services rendered."

32. Treas. Reg. § 1.117-3 (a) (1956) defines a scholarship as follows: "A scholarship generally means an amount paid or allowed to, or for the benefit of, a student, whether an undergraduate or a graduate, to aid the individual in pursuing his studies." In Treas. Reg. § 1.117-3 (c) (1956) a fellowship is defined as follows: "A fellowship grant generally means an amount paid, or allowed to, or for the benefit of, an individual to aid him in the pursuit of study or research." In Treas. Reg. § 1.117-4 (c) (1956) these definitions are further qualified to provide that the exclusion does not apply to amounts which represent "either compensation for past, present, or future employment services or represents payment for services which are subject to the direction or supervision of the grantor" nor to any amount which enables the recipient "to pursue studies or research primarily for the benefit of the grantor." Then, finally, it is said: "However, amounts paid or allowed to, or on behalf of, an individual to enable him to pursue studies or research are considered to be amounts received as a scholarship or fellowship grant for the purpose of section 117 if the

scholarships and fellowships do not include compensation for past, present, or future services, payments for services subject to the direction or supervision of the grantor, or amounts which enable the recipient to pursue studies primarily for the benefit of the grantor. Affirmatively speaking, they include within the meaning of scholarships and fellowships amounts paid to aid in study and research when the primary purpose of the studies or research is to further the education and training of the recipient in his individual capacity.[33] The test is the primary purpose of the grant.[34] Determination of primary purpose requires, of course, the articulation, identification, and evaluation of various factors. Thus far, such factors as the past and contemplated future employment status of the recipient,[35]

---

primary purpose of the studies or research is to further the education and training of the recipient in his individual capacity and the amount provided by the grantor for such purpose does not represent compensation or payment for the services described in subparagraph (1) of this paragraph." (Italics added.)

33. Woddail v. Comm'r, 321 F.2d 721 (10th Cir. 1963); Ussery v. United States, 296 F.2d 582 (5th Cir. 1961); Howard Littman, 42 T.C. 503 (1964). The latter case states the substance of these regulations as follows: "Under these regulations the test is whether amounts paid or allowed to an individual are amounts paid or allowed *primarily* to aid the individual in the pursuit of study or research or whether such amounts represent compensation for services *primarily* for the benefit of the grantor." *Id.* at 509.

34. Certain educational and training allowances to veterans and educational allowances to members of the Armed Forces of the United States are not considered as scholarships or fellowships under the regulations. Treas. Reg. §§ 1.117–4 (a) and (b) (1956).

35. *E.g.*, Stewart v. United States, 66–2 U.S.T.C. 91 9519 (6th Cir. 1966) (includable, employment before and after educational leave by granting authority together with maintenance of civil service and retirement status during leave); Ussery v. United States, 296 F.2d 582 (5th Cir. 1961) (includable, employment before and after educational leave by granting authority); William Wells, 40 T.C. 40, 48 (1963) (excludable, no obligation to accept employment with granting authority after educational period); Aileene Evans, 34 T.C. 720, 726 (1960) (excludable, no obligation to accept employment after educational leave but if not so employed to return grant). The Service presently follows *Evans* in disposing of cases

166

the functional character of the institution within which the study or research is carried on,[36] the enunciated mission of the organization which is the source of funds,[37] the type of work done in fact by the grant recipient,[38] and, of course, the degree of supervision exercised over the grant recipient [39] have exerted significant influence. It is probable that the next phase of the development will consist of greater precision in both the articulation and evaluation of these factors. Thereafter, it is likely this precision will become a part of either the regulations, or both the Code and the regulations. In this manner tax law develops. At least within marginal limits, the scope of the exclusion depends upon the depth of national commitment to education and research. Since this microcriterion undoubtedly will not be disregarded in the future, some broaden-

---

having substantially similar facts. Rev. Rul. 65–146, 1965–1 C.B. 66. Similarly, the Service now will follow *Wells*, Rev. Rul. 65–59, 1965–1 C.B. 67.

36. *E.g.*, Howard Littman, 42 T.C. 503, 507 (1964) (includable, Argonna National Laboratory undertook research for AEC) ; Ethel M. Bonn, 34 T.C. 64, 73 (1960) (includable, Veterans Hospital was for care of patients and not training) ; Rev. Rul. 64–29, 1964–1 C.B. 79 (excludable, institution granting scholarship was a school of medical technology and grants given to each student in attendance, but includable to extent sums paid for week-end work) .

37. *E.g.*, Ussery v. United States, 296 F.2d 582 (5th Cir. 1961) (State Department of Welfare engaged in administering its programs and not education of welfare workers) ; William Wells, 40 T.C. 40, 48 (1963) (Veterans Administration had as one of its objectives the development of a continuing supply of psychological technicians) ; Clarence Peiss, 40 T.C. 78, 79 (1963) (foundation making grants sought "to improve medical research and education") ; Rev. Rul. 64–71, 1964–1 C.B. 82 (institute making grants sought to advance careers of promising public administrators) .

38. Where the work is of the type for which the payor usually must pay others to perform, the sum takes on compensatory characteristics. See Elmer L. Reese, Jr., 45 T.C. 407 (1966) ; Rev. Rul. 65–117, 1965–1 C.B. 67.

39. *E.g.*, Woddail v. Comm'r, 321 F.2d 721 (10th Cir. 1963) (includable, two-thirds of each day of grant recipient spent in performing clerical tasks) ; Rev. Rul. 65–117, 1965–1 C.B. 67.

ing of the exclusion is more probable than is the contraction thereof.

The relationship between the scholarship exclusion and that of prizes and awards and gifts is not entirely clear. Section 74, dealing with prizes and awards, provides that gross income includes prizes and awards except as provided "in section 117 (relating to scholarships and fellowship grants)." Presumably this means that a grant which qualifies as a scholarship or fellowship is governed exclusively by section 117.[40] This does not, however, contribute greatly to the task of distinguishing a prize or award from a scholarship or fellowship. The probable mutual exclusiveness of the two categories makes this task a significant one. A possible key to the distinction is that a prize or award is predominantly in recognition of past activities or accomplishments while the fellowship or scholarship seeks to promote future education and research.[41] The first faces the past, the second the future.

The distinction between these two categories on the one hand and excludable gifts on the other is also difficult to articulate. Presumably, it is possible for the dominant reason that explains the grantor's action to be that of "detached and disinterested generosity," even when the recipient is expected to use the funds for education or research.[42] Thus, an individual may make a gift to a university professor for the purpose of advancing either his education or research.[43] It is difficult to determine whether the gift exclusion is available when the grantor is not an

40. Max Isenbergh, 31 T.C. 1046, 1053 (1959); Clarence Peiss, 40 T.C. 78, 80 (1963).

41. *Cf.* Helmut Mueller, 41 T.C. 639, 643 (1964); Rev. Rul. 65–58, 1965–1 C.B. 37.

42. *Cf.* Rev. Rul. 61–66, 1961–1 C.B. 19.

43. *Ibid.*

individual. It seems unlikely that more can be found in the "minds and hearts" of most grantor organizations than a general desire to advance the ends of education and research. This should not be considered sufficient to remove the grant from the limitations of section 117. There exists "the business of philanthropy" which is permeated with a state of mind different from that which prompts the occasional manifestation of affection, respect, or admiration by an individual for which the gift exclusion is primarily designed. This certainly appears to be the intent of the regulations.[44]

44. Treas. Reg. § 1.117–1 (a) (1956) contains the following: "The exclusion from gross income of an amount which is a scholarship or fellowship is controlled solely by section 117. Accordingly, to the extent that a scholarship or a fellowship grant exceeds the limitations of section 117 (b) and § 1.117–2, it is includable in the gross income of the recipient notwithstanding the provisions of section 102 relating to exclusion from gross income of gifts, or section 74 (b) relating to exclusion from gross income of certain prizes and awards."

XI. Problems of Receipts from within the Family

1. Income-splitting; Disguised Gifts; and Part-gift, Part-sale Transactions

THE GIFT EXCLUSION performs its primary function in respect to *inter vivos* intrafamily transfers. These transfers, usually an integral part of the plan governing the disposition of family wealth, constitute the archetype upon which the policy of the exclusion is based. For this reason the problems springing from these transfers are not ordinarily the same as those considered in the preceding discussion.[1] A gratuitous transfer from a parent to his child, for example, does not usually necessitate a search for the "dominant reason that explains his action in making the transfer." "Detached generosity," within the tax meaning of that phrase, is generally assumed to exist.

Nonetheless, problems do exist. The most difficult and pervasive of these arises from a clash between the common reluctance of donors to part with control of family assets and the necessity inherent in a progressive income tax to devise means for taxing the income of the "family group" in a manner consistent with Equity and in harmony with the desired scope of Reduced Economic Inequality. The

---

1. On occasion, however, efforts are made to clothe taxable gain in the dress of a gift. See Canton v. United States, 226 F.2d 313 (8th Cir. 1955) (cancellation of loan treated as income and not gift) ; Bert M. Wuliger, 16 B.T.A. 1220 (1929) (hostility within family and arms-length character of dealings indicated receipt was not a gift) .

reluctance of donors leads to multifarious arrangements designed to vest in the donee certain rights in respect to the gift property while retaining substantial control of management, beneficial enjoyment, or both, in the donor. These range from simple escrow arrangements [2] to highly complicated trusts.[3] The pressure of Equity and Reduced Economic Inequality bring into being an elaborate set of principles and rules designed to prevent the donor's escape from liability for tax on the income of property which he has transferred subject to a retention of substantial control. These "attribution" problems, as they are sometimes designated, are sufficiently complex to merit a more complete treatment than is possible within the scope of this work. No more is attempted here than to point out that the problems in this area range from simple attempts to shift income by assignments of gain due to accrue shortly [4] to elaborate efforts to design trusts to mesh precisely with the degree of retained control permitted by the Code.[5]

Before passing from "attribution" problems, it should be emphasized that their roots are not in the gift exclusion. Even if it did not exist, the necessity would remain to determine what transfers were sufficient to insulate the donor from tax liability in respect to income from the donated property. That is, the problem of "income-

2. *Cf.* Zipp v. Comm'r, 259 F.2d 119 (6th Cir. 1958); Estate of Thomas W. Tebb, 27 T.C. 671 (1957).

3. Int. Rev. Code of 1954, §§ 671–78, are devoted to an elaboration of rules to determine whether a grantor under a trust has surrendered sufficient control to justify taxation of the income to the trust or beneficiaries as the case may be.

4. Helvering v. Horst, 311 U.S. 112 (1940).

5. *Cf.* Treas. Reg. § 1.674 (b) –6 (1956), where the circumstances under which a grantor or a non-adverse party, or both, may retain a power to accumulate income of a trust without taxation of the income to the grantor are carefully described.

splitting" would not disappear even if gifts were taxed as income. Under a system without a gift exclusion, presumably both donor and donee would be taxable on the income from gift property when the donor's retained control imposed liability on him. The donee, of course, also would be required to include the value of the gift property in his income.

Another type of problem which is unique to the intra-family transfer area is that of disguised gifts. Donors with some frequency attempt to conceal gifts within the folds of transactions of a different character. Thus, a transfer, the dominant reason of which is affection, may appear as a payment of salary from the closely held family corporation.[6] Or it may be made in the guise of interest,[7] an exchange of property for stock of a newly organized corporation,[8] a distributive share of partnership earnings,[9] or some other unusual garb. Usually, the purpose of this concealment is to attain a tax advantage more attractive than that offered by the exclusion. This may be an ordinary and necessary expense deduction, avoidance of the gift tax, the advantages of income-splitting, or some other highly valued benefit.[10] It is particularly painful, therefore, when not only is the sought advantage not obtained

6. *E.g.*, Snyder & Berman, Inc. v. Comm'r, 116 F.2d 165 (4th Cir. 1940); Sohmer & Co., Inc. v. United States, 86 F. Supp. 670 (S.D.N.Y. 1949); Driekorn's Bakery, Inc. 7 T.C.M. 276 (1948).

7. I.T. 1793, II–2 C.B. 110 (1923).

8. *Cf.* Treas. Reg. § 1.351–1 (b) (1955), which recognizes that stock which is issued in amounts disproportionate to contributions may be a gift or compensation.

9. *Cf.* Int. Rev. Code of 1954, § 707 (e)(2), for limitations on computation of distributive shares of certain family partnerships.

10. The donor may find, with the benefit of hindsight, that a short-term capital loss is preferable to gift treatment. See Ben Perlmutter, 44 T.C. 382 (1965).

but, in addition, the gift exclusion is lost.[11] The taxpayer is not infrequently required to abide by the consequences of the form of a transaction which he has chosen from among several others equally available.

One final problem area should be mentioned which, although not restricted to intrafamily transfers, does arise most frequently there. It concerns the proper tax treatment of transactions which partake of the qualities of both a sale and a gift. It is not unusual for a parent, for example, to sell to his child property at a price below its fair market value. The issues spawned by this arrangement are discernible immediately. First, is it to be regarded as a bargain purchase only? The consequences of doing so are that the parent has gain or loss [12] computed in the usual fashion, while the child is deemed to have made an investment in which his basis is the purchase price paid.[13]

If the transaction is both a sale and a gift, additional difficulties emerge. One of these has to do with the manner in which the parent's gain is to be computed and another with the fixing of the child's basis in the acquired property. The nub of both is whether the sales price is to be considered to the full extent possible a return of the capital invested by the parent in the property. If so treated, the sale of property which cost $90, but which is now worth $200, for $100 results in gain of only $10. If not, the

11. See Smith v. Manning, 189 F.2d 345 (3d Cir. 1951) (salary payments to children not deductible expenses but nonetheless taxable as income to children).

12. The loss would be disallowed, however, under Int. Rev. Code of 1954, § 267 (a)(1).

13. See Valleskey v. Nelson, 271 F.2d 6 (7th Cir. 1959) (basis of property acquired by exercise of option to purchase from an estate at a price below fair market value is amount paid under option); Mack v. Comm'r, 148 F.2d 62 (3d Cir. 1945) (basis of acquired property equal to amount paid).

parent must be viewed as having given away a part of his investment and sold the balance. Thus in the example just given, the parent would be considered as having sold one-half the property having a basis of $45 for $100 and made a gift of the other half which had a basis in the parent's hands of $45. It follows that the approach which results in gain of only $10 dictates that the child's basis be $100, while that which burdens the parent with $55 in gain requires that basis to be $145. The interpersonal consequence of regarding the purchase price as a return of capital to the full extent possible is to shift from the parent to the child a greater portion of the potential liability for tax on the appreciation in value which occurred while the property was held by the parent than otherwise would be the case. The Government presently appears to permit this shifting.[14]

When the purchase price is less than the parent's basis, the Government's present position suggests that the entire purchase price be treated as a return of capital. The unrecovered cost then should be regarded as constituting a part of the child's basis. Thus, to return to the above example, a sale for $80 would permit the child to have a basis of $90, $80 derived from the purchase price and $10 from the parent's unrecovered investment.[15] Where some of the par-

14. Treas. Reg. §§ 1.1001–1 (e)(1) and 1.105–4 (a) (1957) provide that the seller-donor has gain to the extent "the amount realized by him exceeds his adjusted basis in the property" and that the basis of the buyer-donee is the greater of the amount paid by him for the property or the seller-donor's adjusted basis at the time of the transfer. Its earlier position was opposed to such shifting. I.T. 2681, XII-1 C.B. 93 (1933). See also Reginald Fincke, 39 B.T.A. 510 (1939) (A). *Cf.* Kaufman's, Inc., 28 T.C. 1179 (1957).

15. Treas. Reg. § 1.1001–1 (e)(1) (1957) provides: "However, no loss is sustained on such a transfer if the amount realized is less than the adjusted basis."

ent's basis is allocated to the gift, a sale for $80 would still yield a gain to the parent and, correlatively, permit the child to have a larger basis.[16]

2. *What Constitutes a Bequest, Devise, or Inheritance*

The Code excludes from gross income not only gifts but also bequests, devises, or inheritances. Although the volume of litigation concerning the meaning of the latter is smaller than that pertaining to gifts, a number of problems common to both exist. One of these is that of distinguishing an excluded bequest or devise from taxable compensation for services.

Understanding of this problem may be aided by pointing out that taxable compensation results when an outstanding claim for compensation for personal services rendered by the claimant to the decedent is presented to the estate and discharged by payment from the assets of the estate.[17] Such a payment is no different from any other payment given in exchange for personal services. Difficulties are encountered when payment is made in settlement of a claim based on an unperformed promise by the decedent to include a bequest or devise in his will as compensation for personal services rendered to the decedent. Al-

16. A sale at $80 would be viewed as a sale of 2/5 of the property and a gift of 3/5. These portions have a basis in the hands of the parent of $36 and $54 respectively. Thus, a sale of 2/5 for $80 results in gain to the parent of $44. In the hands of the child the basis of 3/5 is $54 and that of the 2/5 is $80. The child's basis in the entire property is, therefore, $134. These computations regarding the basis in the hands of the child ignore any possible effect of Int. Rev. Code of 1954, § 1015 (d) , which deals with increasing the basis of gift property because of the gift tax paid.

17. The amount paid may constitute a deduction for estate tax purposes. When founded on a promise or agreement, claims are deductible "to the extent that they were contracted bona fide and for an adequate and full consideration in money or money's worth." Int. Rev. Code of 1954, § 2053 (c)(1)(A) . Personal service constitutes consideration "in money or money's worth."

though the claim is contractual, or quasi-contractual, in nature, the essence of the position of the taxpayer-recipient is (1) that the amount received is in lieu of a bequest or devise which, had it been made, would have been immune from tax and (2) that the receipt should be treated in the same manner as would have been the bequest or devise. The cases uniformly reject this position and tax the receipts as income.[18] This rejection is clearly justified if the first point of the taxpayer-recipient's position is unsound. Strangely enough, existing case law does not establish this conclusively.[19] Nonetheless, it is clear that compensation paid by means of a bequest or devise should be taxable.

Perhaps the existing remnant of uncertainty about this matter is attributable to an early Supreme Court decision, *United States* v. *Merriam*.[20] The issue in the case was the taxability of a bequest made to one designated to serve as executor when the will provided that the bequest was "in lieu of all compensation or commissions" to which he

18. Cotnam v. Comm'r, 263 F.2d 119 (5th Cir. 1959); John Davies, 23 T.C. 524 (1954); Cohen v. United States, 241 F. Supp. 740 (E.D. Mich. 1965); Cole L. Blease, 16 B.T.A. 972 (1929); Wilbur D. Jones, 17 T.C.M. 952 (1958); Hugh Coyne, 12 T.C.M. 1383 (1953). See Schenck, *Tax Effects of Will Contests and Compromises,* TUL. 1961 TAX INST. 214, 217.

19. Performance of the promise to include in the will a bequest in payment of personal services was perhaps involved to some degree in Mildred E. McDonald, 2 T.C. 840 (1943) (A). However, the Tax Court held that the property was acquired by bequest within the meaning of the exclusion. It emphasized that under the wording of the testament the bequest was made "in appreciation of the many years of loyal service and faithful care" and not as payment "in exchange for such service and care." *Id.* at 849. In any event, the case cannot be said to stand for the proposition that compensation for services can escape tax by being cast in the form of a bequest. Dictum in Cotnam v. Comm'r, 263 F.2d 119, 124 (5th Cir. 1959), strongly supports the view that a bequest or devise designed to compensate the beneficiary for services rendered to the decedent is taxable. The court observed: "The law does not stop at the form of a transaction, it goes to the substance. Thus, income received is taxable or nontaxable according to what it represents."

20. 263 U.S. 179 (1923).

would be entitled as executor or trustee. In holding the bequest not taxable, the Court expressly refrained from deciding whether "an amount expressly left as compensation for service actually performed" was also within the exclusion.[21] Instead, the Court seized upon a distinction derived from the common law of wills between a provision in the will fixing the compensation of an executor and a *bequest* to an executor on the implied condition that he "clothe himself with the character of [an] executor."[22] The Court then supplied the major premise of its syllogism by observing that Congress presumably used the term "bequest" in accordance with its "judicially settled meaning."[23] The conclusion that the "bequest" before the court was within the exclusion followed smoothly. Not only has the application of this common law distinction proved troublesome,[24] but its existence also permits the bequest exclusion to shelter compensation income to some degree.[25]

A second frequently litigated problem concerning the meaning of the exclusion for bequests, devises, or inheritances is that of distinguishing such receipts from other non-compensatory accessions to wealth which are related in some manner to the devolution of a decedent's property. At stake is the taxability of sums received by one whose vigorously manifested disappointment with the initial plan for distribution of a decedent's estate has induced

21. *Id.* at 185.

22. *Id.* at 187.

23. *Ibid.*

24. See Banks of New York v. Helvering, 132 F.2d 773 (2d Cir. 1943).

25. The shelter also may be availed of through waiver of statutory fees and commissions by an executor who is also a residuary legatee. Rev. Rul. 66–167, 1966 Int. Rev. Bull. No. 25 at 7 (waiver seasonably manifesting an intent to serve gratuitously insulates executor from income tax liability on fees even though he is a residuary legatee).

a compromise settlement with those more contented with their share. On the whole, tax law has tended to treat the satisfied and the dissatisfied with equal favor. Thus, amounts received in a compromise settlement by (1) an heir contesting the validity of a will,[26] (2) an alleged pretermitted heir,[27] (3) a legatee under an earlier will contesting the validity of a later one,[28] (4) and a surviving spouse who elected to take against the will [29] have been treated as excluded bequests. Apparently, the test is whether the receipt would have been within the exclusion had the claim upon which it is based been pursued to judgment against the estate.[30] Under this test the particular status of the taxpayer, except in so far as it would have affected the character of the proceeds derived from a judgment against the estate, is immaterial. The source of the funds used to liquidate the compromise settlement also should be immaterial, except to the extent reference to such source is necessary to determine the extent to which the amount received is attributable to income from property acquired from bequest or inheritance.

Finally, there is little indication that there exists a part-bequest and part-sale transaction similar to that previously mentioned in connection with gifts. Where a bifur-

26. Lyeth v. Hoey, 305 U.S. 188 (1938) .

27. United States v. Gavin, 159 F.2d 613 (9th Cir. 1947) .

28. Charlotte Keller, 41 B.T.A. 478 (1940) (A) .

29. Eugene C. Delmar, 25 T.C. 1015 (1956) ; Hale v. Anglim, 140 F.2d 235 (9th Cir. 1944) (assertion of community property interest in property passed by decedent's will) .

30. *Cf.* Housman v. Comm'r, 105 F.2d 973, 976 (2d Cir. 1939) . See Schenck, *Tax Effects of Will Contests and Compromises,* TUL. 1961 TAX INST., 214, 225. *But see* Lydia Hopkins, 13 T.C. 952 (1949) , where amount obtained in compromise of claim against father's estate was not treated as property acquired by inheritance when paid by mother from assets other than those in father's estate.

cation of the transaction has appeared possible, the courts have treated it as merely a bargain purchase.[31]

3. *Treatment of Basis of Property Acquired by Gift, Bequest, Devise, or Inheritance*

In Chapter II it was pointed out that one who acquires property by means of gift, bequest, devise or inheritance obtains a basis therein. Donees, generally speaking, take the basis of the donor as their own, and those whose gains are derived from transfers at death are entitled to a new basis equal to the fair market value of the property. Each acquires a basis, although neither has incurred an expenditure which resembles an investment.

No particular problem arises when the beneficiary of a donative transfer obtains the property outright. Receipts derived from such property are taxed to the beneficiary in the same manner they would have been had the property been acquired by purchase. Thus, to the extent that such receipts are properly allocated to a return of capital, or reduced by an allowance for depreciation, they escape tax. Any excess, however, constitutes gain subject to tax. The gift exclusion does not extend to this portion of the receipts; its protection is limited to the basis acquired by the beneficiary. This position is set forth in the Code by excluding from the gift characterization "income from any property" acquired by gift, bequest, devise, or inheritance.[32] The same principles, of course, are controlling when several beneficiaries obtain undivided interests in fee in the gift property.

31. Valleskey v. Nelson, 271 F.2d 6 (7th Cir. 1959) ; Mack v. Comm'r, 148 F.2d 62 (3d Cir. 1945) . See n. 13 *supra*.

32. Int. Rev. Code of 1954, § 102 (b)(1) .

Complex problems arise, however, when several beneficiaries have acquired rights to beneficial enjoyment during different intervals of time. The kernel of these problems is the manner in which the tax benefit of the basis of the gift property is to be apportioned between these beneficiaries. To illustrate, assume an *inter vivos* gift of a tract of unimproved land, which had a basis in the hands of the donor of $100 and a fair market value at the time of the gift of $200, to X for life with remainder to Y. At the time of the gift neither X nor Y is regarded as having received taxable gain. Each is protected by the gift exclusion. The fair market value of their respective interests depends upon the life expectancy of X. The basis of the tract in the hands of X and Y is $100. Had the gift been by reason of death, the basis under present law would have been $200. X, of course, is entitled to the entire income from the tract during his life. It is determination of the proper tax treatment of this income which opens the issues.

If X is taxed on the entire income, it appears that he is deprived of any use of any portion of the basis of $100 or $200, as the case may be. On the other hand, if he is not so taxed, income from the tract appears to escape tax unless Y is required to report what X does not. It is obvious, however, that to tax Y on income he does not receive is difficult. It can be justified by pointing to the fact that as X reduces his taxable income by amortization of his proper share of the aggregate basis, Y's interest in the property increases because of the passage of time. That is, X's interest wanes while Y's waxes.

Several alternative approaches are available to meet the situation. The first is the most simple and the one which presently is in use. It is to ignore any possible injustice to

X and tax the entire income of the tract to him.[33] In this respect X is treated as if he had been given the tract in fee.

The second is to permit X to amortize a portion of the basis of the tract against the annual income flow and to charge Y with income each year equal in amount to that portion of the basis amortized by X. In this way the burden of tax on the income from the tract is divided between X and Y. The amount of the total basis of the tract which X can amortize should be that portion which bears the same ratio to the total basis as the fair market value of X's life interest at the time of its acquisition bears to the fair market value of the tract at that time. Division of this portion by the life expectancy of X yields the amount of the income of the tract on which Y, the remainderman, should be taxed annually rather than X.[34]

A third alternative is identical to the second except to permit Y to defer taxation on the basis amortizable by X until X's death. In the year in which this occurs, Y is required to report as gain the aggregate amount of basis

33. Int. Rev. Code of 1954, § 102 (b)(2) . As put in this subsection, the gift exclusion does not apply "where the gift, bequest, devise, or inheritance is of income from property." Such income is taxable. This is based upon Irwin v. Gavit, 268 U.S. 161 (1925) . The Court observed: "Apart from technicalities we can perceive no distinction relevant to the question before us between a gift of the fund for life and a gift of income from it. The fund is appropriated to the production of the same result whichever form the gift takes. Neither are we troubled by the question where to draw the line. . . . But the distinction between the cases put of a gift from the corpus of the estate payable in instalments and the present seems to us not hard to draw, assuming that the gift supposed would not be income." *Id.* at 167–68.

34. Should X not survive his life expectancy, Y should be regarded as realizing gain in the year of X's death to the extent of that portion of the total basis which remained to be amortized by X at his death. Should X live beyond his life expectancy, all income from the tract should be taxable to him. Y should no longer be responsible for any portion thereof. Observe that the amortization process under this and the succeeding two alternatives should occur even when the income from the property is less than the amounts properly subject to amortization. In such a case X would suffer a loss. Y would continue to report gain.

available for amortization by X at the commencement of his life interest.[35]

The discussion to this point has assumed gift property which was non-depreciable. Additional complications arise when it is assumed that the property is subject to an allowance for depreciation. Under present law, which treats X as if he were the full owner of the property, the entire allowance should be, and is, available to X.[36] Under alternatives two and three, the entire depreciation allowance should be made available to the remainderman. To permit the life tenant, X, amortization fixed by the basis of the property as of the time of the transfer, undiminished by subsequent depreciation, plus all, or any portion, of the depreciation allowance deprives the remainderman, Y, of an allowance necessary to reflect accurately the net gain accruing because of the passage of time.[37] Y's basis on the termination of X's intervening interest should equal the original total basis diminished by depreciation properly attributable to the period during which Y's interest was outstanding. To achieve this, allocation of the entire allowance to him is necessary.

35. This accounts for any gain because of X's premature death. *Ibid.*

36. Treas. Reg. § 1.167 (h) –1 (a) (1956). In case of non-trust arrangements, the life tenant is treated as the absolute owner.

37. This suggestion should be compared with the present rules governing the determination of gain or loss on sale or other disposition of life and remainder interests in property acquired from a decedent. Treas. Reg. § 1.1014–5 (a) (1957). Under these rules determination of the so-called adjusted uniform basis requires that the "uniform basis" (the unadjusted basis of the entire property determined immediately after the decedent's death) be reduced by the depreciation allowed. This "adjusted uniform basis" is then apportioned to the life interest and remaindermen on the basis of mortality tables. The appropriate factor under such tables is fixed by the age of the life tenant at the time of the sale or other disposition of the interest. See the example in Treas. Reg. § 1.1014–5 (a) (2) (1957). Under such an approach the allowance affects the basis of both the life estate and the remainder. This is appropriate where the migration of basis from life tenant to remainderman does not affect the income tax payable by either.

Although the discussion to this point has involved only legal interests, the foregoing analysis is not altered by assuming that the gift is made in trust, providing the trustee is required to distribute all the income computed without regard to depreciation to the life beneficiary.[38] Where income distributable to the life beneficiary is computed with regard to depreciation, the situation is more complex. Under present law the allowance for depreciation is available to the trustee, rather than the life tenant, to the extent income is set aside as a reserve.[39] To a degree this further prejudices the position of the life tenant because not only is he not permitted to share in the gift exclusion (i.e., amortize the basis of his interest against the income flow) but, also, the amount of income is reduced to protect the remainderman. Under the two alternative approaches suggested above, the present rule would work quite well since it merely provides a mechanism by which the depreciation deduction is given to the remainderman. The existence of mandatory accumulations for a depreciation reserve would, by reducing the original value of the life interest, diminish the amortizable basis available to X and taxable to Y.

Consideration of trusts opens up many other exceedingly complex problems. Frequently, a grantor or testator directs that the trustee or executor make a series of payments to a particular beneficiary. The governing instrument may require that the amount be paid solely either

38. The problem of adjusting the basis of the interests of the life beneficiary and remainderman remains the same. Also, no difference exists so far as depreciation is concerned. Under present rules the depreciation deduction is available to the life beneficiary when "under the trust instrument or local law the income of a trust is to be computed without regard to depreciation" and is to be distributed to such beneficiary. Treas. Reg. § 1.167 (h) –1 (b) (1) (1956).

39. Treas. Reg. § 1.167 (h) –1 (b) (2) (1956).

from income or corpus, or it may permit payment from corpus to the extent income is insufficient. Under present law, payments "to be made at intervals" are taxable to the recipient to the extent paid or credited from income.[40] To this extent, no gift exclusion is available. Lump-sum payments payable, in any event, out of income or corpus, however, are not taxable to the recipient even if paid from income.[41] Under these circumstances, a full gift exclusion is available. It is plain that the line between these two types of payments is somewhat arbitrary. Obviously, this arbitrariness is the consequence of providing an income beneficiary no basis for amortization against the income receipts. Were such a basis provided to distributees of both "payments made at intervals" and lump sums, the need for arbitrary lines would disappear.

The difficulty in providing such a basis in all cases is that in discretionary trusts it would frequently be impossible to determine either the amount of basis which should be amortized by the income recipients or the identity of remaindermen who should be taxable on the sums amortized by the recipients. Those entitled to take on distributions by trusts and estates may not be known for many years. Some may be unborn until shortly before this distribution. Moreover, the magnitude of their interests may not be fixed until the last moment. One should not be

40. Int. Rev. Code of 1954, § 102. Prior to 1942, the rule was that such payments were not taxable when payable from surplus if necessary. Burnet v. Whitehouse, 283 U.S. 148 (1931), considered such payments as within the exclusion for gifts.

41. Miriam C. Lindau, 21 T.C. 911 (1954) observed that the rule of Burnet v. Whitehouse, n. 40 *supra*, remains applicable to such. Int. Rev. Code of 1954, § 663 (a)(1) somewhat expands the scope of the "lump sum payment" rule to amounts which are paid or credited "on a gift or bequest of a specific sum of money or of specific property and which is paid or credited all at once or in not more than three instalments." This rule is inapplicable to payments which can be paid or credited only from income. See Treas. Reg. § 1.663 (a) –1 (1956) .

required to report income not reported by an income beneficiary unless it is certain his interest is to become possessory. Furthermore, it still remains true that it is difficult to collect taxes from unborn taxpayers.

A not altogether satisfactory solution to the remainder-man problem would be to impose upon the trust itself the burden of tax on the basis amortized by the income recipients. This solution, however, does nothing to eliminate the difficulty in determining the amount of basis properly subject to amortization. Where income interests are discretionary, there exists no benchmark—such as the fair market value of the distributee's interest—to follow in apportioning aggregate basis.

In sum, present law traced out in this discussion of basis of property acquired by gift, bequest, devise, or inheritance fares rather well when measured against Practicality. It fails when examined from the standpoint of Equity because income distributees carry a portion of the tax burden which properly belongs to remaindermen. While it is feasible to design a structure which will correctly apportion this burden where income is required to be distributed for a fixed or determinable period of time and the remaindermen have interests certain to become possessory, such a structure is likely to be neither fair nor practical when applied to trusts or estates under which distributions are discretionary. It is not obvious that application of a redesigned structure to the former and not the latter is a step forward.

B. Life Insurance, Death Benefits,
and Annuities

XII. Life Insurance Proceeds

THE PRESENT INCOME TAXATION of life insurance proceeds paid by reason of the death of the insured also earns high marks when graded according to the criterion of Practicality. Such proceeds are excluded from gross income except where the recipient is a transferee for value.[1] Although this approach does not avoid all problems, it does bypass certain difficulties which would attend any effort to be guided by Equity and Free Market Compatibility.

1. Proceeds Not Paid at a Date Later than Death

To understand these difficulties, it is necessary to recall that life insurance proceeds may consist of three elements: savings previously invested in the policy, interest earned thereon, and an amount of "pure" insurance.[2] Generally

1. Int. Rev. Code of 1954, § 101 (a). To be entitled to the exclusion, the amounts received must be "insurance." The Service follows Helvering v. Le Gierse, 312 U.S. 531 (1941), in determining what constitutes "insurance." Under *Le Gierse,* an estate tax case, the Court held that "insurance" involves an undertaking to shift the risk of premature death from the insured and to distribute the risk to other policyholders. Thus, the Service has ruled that proceeds paid under a life insurance–annuity combination arrangement which eliminated the risk of premature death were not entitled to the exclusion of § 101 (a). Rev. Rul. 65–57, 1965–1 C.B. 56. See chap. xiii *infra.*

2. VICKREY, AGENDA FOR PROGRESSIVE TAXATION 65 (1947). Premiums also consist of three elements: the savings invested, the amount paid for current insurance protection, and amounts paid to cover expenses and provide a profit to the stockholders.

speaking, the two last-mentioned criteria indicate that at least the interest should be subject to tax either before or after the death of the insured.[3] Previously invested savings and "pure" insurance present more debatable issues. The former obviously represent an investment of capital by someone, although infrequently by the recipient of the proceeds. Whether such portion of the proceeds should be considered a return of capital depends upon whether this investment should be attributed to the recipient. Without such attribution, the receipt of previously invested savings is an accretion to the wealth of the beneficiary to the extent these savings are not derived from premiums paid by him. Inasmuch as those who acquire property from decedents are considered to have made an investment,[4] although they have made none in fact, it is reasonable to regard the receipt by insurance beneficiaries of previously invested savings as equivalent to that of a bequest.[5]

This leaves the "pure insurance" portion for consideration. Viewed narrowly, its receipt also enhances the wealth of the beneficiary. Furthermore, if this portion is regarded as indemnity for a loss of *income* caused by the untimely death of the insured, the case for taxation of this portion as received by the beneficiary is strengthened.[6] However, it

---

3. See GOODE, THE INDIVIDUAL INCOME TAX 132–139 ('1964).

4. See pp. 22–33 *supra.*

5. GOODE, *op. cit.* n.3 *supra,* at 131.

6. Inclusion of the "pure insurance" portion of the proceeds in the income of the beneficiary impels a deduction for that part of the premium which was paid for this protection. See VICKREY, AGENDA FOR PROGRESSIVE TAXATION 66 (1947). Computation of this amount may be difficult because in some instances a portion of the investment in the policy may be drawn upon to provide part of the insurance protection. *But cf.* Swihart, *Federal Taxation of Life Insurance Wealth,* 37 IND. L.J. 167, 171–76 (1962), where analysis of insurance as an investment led to inclusion of the pure insurance portion of the proceeds in the income of the beneficiary under certain circumstances without any deduction for a corresponding part of

is also possible to view this portion of the proceeds as being in lieu of certain gains from status [7] or gifts and bequests which would have been received had the insured survived. This view is particularly appealing when the beneficiary is a spouse or minor child of the insured.[8] Exclusion is dictated when this view prevails. The essence of the difficulty in fixing the proper treatment of "pure insurance" is that it is impossible to assert that one view or the other is appropriate in all instances. At one extreme stands the corporate beneficiary under a "key-man" policy while at the other is the young widow with several minor children. Income replacement is rather obviously the correct analysis of the first, but not of the second. The point is that no single rule can avoid the taint of arbitrariness.[9]

---

the premiums. Use and occupancy insurance proceeds when received in lieu of profits the taxpayer otherwise would have made are taxable income. *Cf.* Cappel House Furnishing Co. v. United States, 244 F.2d 525 (6th Cir. 1957); Treas. Reg. § 1.1033 (a) –2 (c)(8) (1957).

7. See chap. vi, *supra.*

8. See GOODE, *op. cit.* n. 3 *supra,* at 131.

9. The Supreme Court has never passed directly on whether insurance proceeds paid by reason of death constitute income. In United States v. Supplee-Biddle Hardware Co., 265 U.S. 189, 194–95 (1924), the Court observed: "It is earnestly pressed upon us that proceeds of life insurance paid on the death of the insured are in fact capital and cannot be taxed as income under the Sixteenth Amendment [citations omitted]. We are not required to meet this question. It is enough to sustain our construction of the Act to say that proceeds of a life insurance policy paid on the death of the insured are not usually classed as income. . . .

"The benefit to be gained by death has no periodicity. It is a substitution of money value for something permanently lost either in a house, a ship, or a life. Assuming without deciding that Congress could call the proceeds of such indemnity, income, and validly tax it as such, we think that in view of the popular conception of the life insurance as resulting in a single addition of a total sum to the resources of the beneficiary, and not in a periodical return, such a purpose on its part should be express, as it certainly is not here." To the extent that the Court relied on the notion of periodicity in suggesting that insurance proceeds are not within the reach of gross income, its position has been destroyed by Comm'r v. Glenshaw Glass Co., 348 U.S. 426 (1955). It has been suggested that Congress once assumed that proceeds paid by reason of death were not within the constitutional concept of gross income. Rapp, *Some Recent Developments*

Thus, only with respect to the interest element of life insurance proceeds is the present exclusion clearly unjustified when measured against Equity and Free Market Compatibility.[10] There is nothing in the institution of life insurance which displaces the condemnation of tax-exempt interest[11] that these two criteria always evoke. Nevertheless, it is difficult to determine with respect to each policy the amount of the interest which properly should be subject to tax. In addition, that portion of the premiums paid which constitutes expenses incurred to earn this interest should be accounted for in computing the net return of the taxpayer's investment in life insurance. It is alleged, however, that, difficult though these tasks may be, they are feasible ones which can be performed by the

---

in the Concept of Taxable Income, 11 TAX L. REV. 329, 340 (1956). Nonetheless, viewing life insurance as somewhat equivalent to property insurance is consistent with treating the proceeds as being received in lieu of non-taxable accretions to wealth which the beneficiary would have enjoyed had the insured survived. *Cf.* VICKREY, AGENDA FOR PROGRESSIVE TAXATION 72 (1947), where treatment of proceeds as property insurance proceeds is analyzed. It is there pointed out that loss of a deduction for premiums paid for pure insurance and exclusion of that portion of the proceeds (the treatment under present law) may impose a greater tax burden than would be the case under an income-insurance point of view where a deduction for such premiums and an inclusion of proceeds is provided.

10. The relevance of other macrocriteria is much more attenuated. Of course, the criterion of Reduced Economic Inequality suggests inclusion of the interest element unless it is demonstrated that the major portion of this element is enjoyed by lower income groups. This is not likely, however. See GOODE, *op. cit.* n.3 *supra,* at 136. The criteria of Stabilization and Political Order are not significantly involved, but Adequacy also suggests inclusion.

11. It has been estimated that in 1956 interest earned on sums invested in insurance policies amounted to $1.1 billion. See Pechman, *Erosion of the Individual Income Tax,* 10 NAT'L TAX J. 1, 17 (1957). Goode's estimate is higher. He asserts that the net interest earnings on life insurance reserves in 1957 was $2.0 billion. GOODE, *op. cit.* n. 3 *supra,* at 135. Some of the abuse of this exclusion has been eliminated by the enactment of subsections 264 (a)(3) and (c) of the Int. Rev. Code of 1954 by the Revenue Act of 1964.

insurer.[12] Furthermore, withholding either as the interest accrues or at the time the proceeds are paid could be instituted.[13] Even so, the practical problems remain substantial; but they may yield to solutions in the future. Should this occur, the additional problem of determining the proper taxpayer should be tractable.[14] With these solutions, only an explicit desire to encourage investment in life insurance will prevent the withdrawal of immunity from taxation now enjoyed by the interest element of the proceeds. It is possible to believe that such a desire has existed for some time [15] and has been nourished by the vast resources of the insurance industry.[16]

12. Swihart, *Federal Taxation of Life Insurance Wealth*, 37 IND. L.J. 167, 172 (1962); Surrey, *The Federal Income Tax Base for Individuals* in *Tax Revision Compendium, House Ways and Means Committee*, 86th Cong., 1st Sess. pt. 1, at 1–6 (1959); VICKREY, AGENDA FOR PROGRESSIVE TAXATION 71–73 (1947). Goode is somewhat more cautious. GOODE, *op. cit.* n. 3 *supra*, at 138–39.

13. *Ibid.* Where interest is taxed as it accrues, it should be added to the savings invested in the policy since inclusion in the income of the owner of the policy constitutes an additional investment. Where taxation of interest is deferred until the proceeds are paid, there is some possibility of bunching. However, the general averaging provisions of the Code may be adequate to avoid any unusual hardship. See Int. Rev. Code of 1954, § 1301–5. Such deferral also raises an issue concerning the proper taxpayer to report such income. It by no means follows that the beneficiary is the proper one. An insured who owned the policy to the moment of death is a more appropriate taxpayer than the beneficiary. Where the owner of the policy is other than the insured or beneficiary thereunder, accrued interest should continue to be taxed to him although not reportable until the proceeds become payable to the beneficiary.

14. Taxation to the holder of the policy's "incidents of ownership," as that term is used in § 2042 of the Estate Tax, would be satisfactory except when the "incidents" with respect to a single policy were held by two or more persons. Under those circumstances, some additional rules would have to be developed.

15. See BOWE, LIFE INSURANCE AND ESTATE TAX PLANNING 19 (1952 ed.).

16. Presumably, the purpose is to encourage the thoughtless breadwinner to make adequate provision for his untimely death. If so, the inducement is singularly sophisticated for one unmindful of such obvious responsibilities.

2. *Proceeds Paid at a Date Later than Death*

If the case for exclusion of predeath interest income is not a strong one, that for exclusion of postdeath interest is even weaker. To the extent that proceeds are paid at a date later than death, there is an interest element in each such deferred payment. Nonetheless, this postdeath interest has been excluded from gross income during much of the time since 1913. The Revenue Act of that year provided "that the proceeds of life insurance policies paid upon the death of the person insured . . . shall not be included in income." [17] Apparently, some doubt existed about the scope of this exclusion as applied to proceeds payable in instalments subsequent to the death of the insured. In 1926 the language was refined to exclude ". . . amounts received under a life insurance contract paid by reason of the death of the insured, whether in a single sum or in instalments (but if such amounts are held by the insurer under an agreement to pay interest thereon, the interest payments shall be included in gross income)." [18] In 1934 the words "or otherwise" [19] were substituted for "or in instalments." While these changes made it clear that the amount otherwise payable at the death of the insured was not stripped of its exclusion because in fact paid later in instalments or as an annuity, they did not explicitly require that amounts greater than this sum be excluded when not designated as interest and paid either in instalments or as an annuity.[20] Indeed, shortly after the Revenue Act of 1934, the Bureau of Internal Revenue ruled that

17. Revenue Act of 1913, ch. 16, § II.B., 38 Stat. 167.

18. Revenue Act of 1926, ch. 27, § 213 (b)(1), 44 Stat. 24.

19. Revenue Act of 1934, ch. 277, § 22 (b)(1), 48 Stat. 687.

20. Neither were the Committee Reports explicit. See H. R. REP., No. 1, 69th Cong. 1st Sess. 33 (1926) (conference report); S. REP. No. 558, 73d Cong., 2d Sess. 23 (1934) (Senate Finance Committee).

these provisions "exclude from gross income only the principal sum of the capital value of a life insurance policy as of the time of the insured's death, and do not exclude any amounts which are added to such principal sum (when it is paid in instalments) by reason of the running of time." [21] The sole problem was the familiar one of apportioning receipts between a return of capital and interest.[22]

Six years later, the Bureau's interpretation was rejected in *Commissioner* v. *Winslow*.[23] The court was convinced that Congress did not intend to bring within gross income "amounts which are added to . . . principal . . . by reason of the running of time." Amounts paid in instalments, or as annuities, were within the exclusion to the extent of both the amount payable at death as well as the interest element in these deferred payments.[24] In 1943 the Treasury accepted the interpretation of *Winslow* but restricted it to instances where the instalment option was elected by the insured.[25] The restriction fared no better than the 1934 interpretation. In *Commissioner* v. *Pierce* [26] it was rejected as an effort to insert the word "only" between the

21. G.C.M. 13796, XIII-2 C.B. 41 (1934). The ruling, however, was made prospective only.

22. See pp. 29–37 *supra*.

23. 113 F.2d 413 (1st Cir. 1940).

24. The court put it this way: "Congress has been consistent in all its acts in exempting from taxation amounts received in settlement of death claims. It draws no distinction whether such amounts are paid in instalments or as annuities. Accepting the analysis of the Commissioner that the policy in question is a life insurance policy for $53,000 principal value payable as an annuity, rather than one for $100,000 payable in 50 instalments, it still falls precisely within the language of Section 22 (b)(1) of the Revenue Act of 1934 according to the legislative intention as set forth in the reports by the Congressional committees." 113 F.2d 413, 423 (1st Cir. 1940). A similar view was adopted by other circuits: Comm'r v. Bartlett, 113 F.2d 766 (2d Cir. 1940); Allis v. La Budde, 128 F.2d 838 (7th Cir. 1942); Kaufman v. United States, 131 F.2d 854 (4th Cir. 1942).

25. Treas. Reg. 103 § 19.22 (b) (1)–1 (1940), as amended by T.D. 5231, 1943 C.B. 89. See also G.C.M. 23523, 1943 C.B. 91.

26. 146 F.2d 388 (2d Cir. 1944).

words "paid" and "by" and thus make the code provision read, "Amounts received under a life insurance paid *only* by reason of the death of the insured. . . ." Finally, in 1946 the Treasury abandoned its effort to distinguish between an option exercised by the insured and one by the beneficiary.[27] Postdeath interest became taxable only when "the proceeds are held by the insurer under an agreement to pay interest thereon." [28]

In 1954 the Treasury, however, was not to be denied—at least, not completely. In addition to continuing the inclusion of interest payments when the proceeds are held pursuant to an agreement to pay such interest,[29] the 1954 Code adopted the principle that the postdeath interest element in insurance proceeds paid at a date later than death constitutes a part of gross income.[30] This was done by, first, determining the value of the agreement at the date of death of the insured by use of the interest rate and mortality tables used by the insurer in calculating the payments to be made thereunder [31] and, second, limiting

27. Treas. Reg. 111 § 29.22 (b) (1)–1 (1941), as amended by T.D. 5515, 1946–1 C.B. 26.

28. *Ibid.* See United States v. Heilbroner, 100 F.2d 379 (2d Cir. 1938) (interest payments included in income although described as "annuity" payments).

29. Int. Rev. Code of 1954, § 101 (c).

30. Int. Rev. Code of 1954, § 101 (d).

31. Int. Rev. Code of 1954, § 101 (d)(2). The value of the agreement is designated in the statute as "an amount held by an insurer." Treas. Reg. § 1.101–4 (b)(1) (1957) contains the general statement describing the manner in which the "amount held by an insurer" is computed. "The present value of such agreement is to be computed as if the agreement under the life insurance policy had been entered into on the date of the death of the insured, except that such value shall be determined by the use of the mortality table and interest rate used by the insurer in calculating payments to be made to the beneficiary under such agreement. Where an insurance policy provides an option for the payment of a specific amount upon the death of the insured in full discharge of the contract, such lump sum is the amount held by the insurer with respect to all beneficiaries (or their beneficiaries) under the contract."

the exclusion in a taxable year to that portion of the value of the agreement properly prorated to such period.[32] Any amount received in excess of this exclusion constitutes income, except that a surviving spouse is given each year an additional $1,000 exclusion.[33] Thus, each payment is apportioned between interest income and a return of capital. In this setting, however, capital may consist not only of an investment made by one other than the beneficiary but also predeath interest income and "pure insurance" proceeds which, only in a refined sense, can be said to represent an investment by anyone. To some extent, therefore, the "capital" being "returned" is derived from a "constructive" investment.[34] On top of this, as pointed out, the surviving spouse is given tax-exempt interest income to the extent of $1,000 per annum. It remains true that widows, orphans, and insurance companies, when bolstered by Practicality, are an almost irresistible combination. Only ascendancy of an attitude inimical to private arrangements to provide security for dependents and great public devotion to Reduced Economic Inequality is likely to be stronger.

32. Proper proration becomes somewhat difficult when payments are to be made to two or more beneficiaries and when guaranteed payments, in the event a primary beneficiary dies before a certain number of payments have been made, are provided under the policy. The regulations deal with such matters. Treas. Reg. § 1.101–4 (1957), as amended by T.D. 6577, 1961–2 C.B. 17.

33. This exclusion is not applicable to interest payments governed by Int. Rev. Code of 1954, § 101 (c). This is made explicit by Int. Rev. Code of 1954, § 101 (d)(4). In some instances, as, for example, policies which have a family income rider, both sections 101 (c) and 101 (d) may be applicable to different portions of payments made at a date later than death. Treas. Reg. § 1.101–4 (h) (1957) as amended by T.D. 6577, 1961–2 C.B. 17. An election to receive interest payments only does not ban a subsequent election to receive the proceeds in instalments which will qualify for the $1000 exclusion of section 101 (d)(1)(B). Rev. Rul. 65–284, 1965–2 C.B. 28.

34. See pp. 21–23 *supra*.

3. *Proceeds Paid to Transferees for Value*

Despite the potency of this combination of sympathy and financial power, there exists a puzzling and often irritating limitation of the exclusions available with respect to insurance proceeds paid by reason of death of the insured. In general, this limitation provides that such proceeds received by a transferee for valuable consideration of the policy are excludable only to the extent of "the sum of the actual value of such consideration and the premiums and other amounts subsequently paid by the transferee." [35] The limitation does not reach a transfer which is not for a valuable consideration.[36] However, a gratuitous transferee, who acquired the policy from one who obtained it for a valuable consideration, stands in the shoes of his transferor and, accordingly, is considered a transferee for valuable consideration.[37]

Light is cast upon the function of this limitation by referring to some rudimentary principles of insurance law.

35. Int. Rev. Code of 1954, § 101 (a)(2).

36. Haverty Realty & Inv. Co., 3 T.C. 161 (1944) (parol evidence showing no consideration permitted to rebut recital of consideration given for policies). Payment of debts secured by the policies by the beneficiary has been held to make beneficiary a transferee for a valuable consideration. See Grace R. Maxson Hall, 12 T.C. 419 (1949). In certain such instances it may be difficult to distinguish between purchasing an annuity and acquiring a life insurance policy for valuable consideration. *Ibid.* There must be an effective transfer before the limitation is applicable. Myra H. Pritchard, 3 T.C.M. 1125 (1944) (transfer held ineffective because previously determined to have been in contemplation of death for estate tax purposes). *But see* Bourne Bean, 14 T.C.M. 786 (1955) (transfer effective even though transfer previously treated by executors as in contemplation of death for estate tax purposes as result of revenue agent audit).

37. *Cf.* James F. Waters, Inc. v. Comm'r, 160 F.2d 596 (9th Cir. 1957). Treas. Reg. §§ 1.101–1 (b)(2) and (5), example 6 (1957). If the gratuitous transferee is within the limited class described in section 101 (a)(2)(b) (*i.e.*, the insured, a partner of the insured, etc.), he is entitled to the full exclusion of § 101 (a)(1) and is not required to stand in the shoes of his transferor.

Without pausing to consider the purpose of the doctrine of insurable interest, it is generally recognized that the doctrine does not prevent the gift, or an assignment for value, of a validly issued insurance policy to one who has no insurable interest in the life of the insured.[38] Moreover, one who has obtained a valid policy of insurance on his own life can designate as beneficiary one who has no insurable interest.[39] In short, the doctrine of insurable interest does sometimes permit those not having an insurable interest to obtain enforceable rights under life insurance contracts.

This presents a serious problem to the designers of an income tax. Proceeds derived from contracts deemed to be wagers, because of the absence of an insurable interest, should not be, and are not, accorded an exclusion for either the accumulated interest or "pure insurance" portion thereof.[40] Such proceeds are not "received under a life insurance contract." However, the insurable interest rules just described make it possible to classify for tax purposes certain sums received by those not having an insurable interest as proceeds "received under a life insurance contract." For tax law to condition its exclusion entirely on the ability of the beneficiary to meet the tests of the local insurable interest doctrine would result in questionable

38. Grigsby v. Russell, 222 U.S. 149 (1911); Lyman v. Jacobsen, 128 Ore. 567, 275 P. 612 (1929); Curtis v. Aetna Life Ins. Co., 90 Cal. 245, 27 P. 211 (1919); Annot., 30 A.L.R. 2d 1310 (1953). Of course, a transfer intended to evade the policy of the insurable-interest requirement will not be effective.

39. Aetna Life Ins. Co. v. Patton, 176 F. Supp. 368 (S.D. Ill. 1959); Penn Mut. Life Ins. Co. v. Slade, 47 F. Supp. 219 (E.D. Ky. 1942). The transaction must be in good faith and not for the purpose of circumventing the policy against wagering or gambling insurance contracts. See PATTERSON & YOUNG, CASES ON INSURANCE 250 (4th ed. 1961).

40. *Cf.* Ducross v. Comm'r, 272 F.2d 79 (6th Cir. 1959) (by implication); Atlantic Oil Co. v. Patterson, 63–1 U.S.T.C. ¶ 9445 (N.D. Ala. 1963).

differentiations between those not having an insurable interest, as well as some lack of national uniformity. An alternative is to devise explicit limitations on the type of beneficiaries entitled to the exclusion. This alternative, for example, might seek to restrict the exclusion to the surviving spouse and minor children, these being situations in which the death of the insured clearly has deprived the beneficiary of non-taxable benefits of status.

No such alternative, however, has been developed. The nearest thing to it is the transfer-for-valuable-consideration rule. How wide of the mark it is becomes apparent when its history is considered. It came into the law in 1926 [41] under circumstances which throw little light on the intention of Congress. Strangely enough, the available record suggests that the major thrust of the change was to provide an *exclusion* to those other than the insured who received sums upon the *maturity* of policies during the life of the insured.[42] Nonetheless, the provisions were made applica-

41. Int. Rev. Act of 1926, § 213 (b)(2) 44 Stat. 9. The complete subsection reads as follows: " (b) The term 'gross income' does not include the following items, which shall be exempt from taxation under this title: . . . (2) Amounts received (other than amounts paid by reason of the death of the insured and interest payments on such amounts) under a life insurance, endowment, or annuity contract, but if such amounts received before the taxable year under such contract exceed the aggregate premiums or consideration paid (whether or not paid during the taxable year) then the excess shall be included in gross income. In the case of a transfer for a valuable consideration, by assignment or otherwise, of a life insurance, endowment, or annuity contract, or any interest therein, only the actual value of such consideration and the amount of the premiums and other sums subsequently paid by the transferee shall be exempt from taxation under paragraph (1) or this paragraph. . . ." Paragraph (1) deals with the payment of proceeds by reason of the death of the insured.

42. See Brown, *Transfers of Life Insurance for Valuable Consideration*, 28 TAXES 907 (1950), where the committee reports and the *Congressional Record* are analyzed. These sources suggest that prior to the 1926 Act only the insured upon maturity of a policy during his life was entitled to exclude a return of premiums paid. It is a fact that under the Revenue Act of 1924 gross income did not include the "amount received by the *insured* as a return of premium or premiums paid by him under life

ble both to receipts paid by reason of death as well as those upon maturity of the policy. Perhaps it was only a desire for symmetry which caused this. Clearly, there is nothing to suggest that Congress was concerned with depriving those who "speculated" in life insurance policies of an exclusion which the local law of insurable interest would not otherwise preclude.[43]

In any event, a major difficulty with this extension to death-generated proceeds was that certain recipients were deprived of the full exclusion even though the death of the insured may have destroyed a source of gains derived from family status which they had enjoyed prior to such death without tax. Thus, purchase of a policy by the insured or his spouse from a third person and designation of their child as the beneficiary opened the possibility that receipts of the proceeds would be taxed under the transfer-for-value rules. This possibility became the accepted view when the purchase was by the spouse of the insured,[44] but not when by the insured.[45]

---

insurance, endowment, or annuity contracts, either during the term or at the maturity of the term mentioned in the contract or upon surrender of the contract." (Italics added). The 1926 Act thus extended the exclusion to others and limited it in the case of transferees for valuable consideration. It should be noted that the provisions in the 1926 Act were also applicable to endowment and annuity contracts as well as life insurance contracts.

43. An intent of this sort was manifested by Congress in its enactment of the 1954 Code. See n. 53 *infra*.

44. Alcy Siver Hacker, 36 B.T.A. 659 (1937) (purchase by spouse of insured from insured and gift by purchasing spouse to child made receipts taxable under transferee-for-value rules) ; Treas. Reg. § 1.101 (b)(5) , example (6) .

45. I.T. 3213, 1938–2 C.B. 65 (purchase by insured and designation of his spouse as beneficiary did not make receipts taxable under transferee-for-value rules. It is not easy to grasp the basis for excluding from the operation of the transferee-for-value rule cases where the acquisition is by the insured. The ruling simply asserts that where the insured acquired the policy from his employer "for its then cash surrender value," the transaction was "not a transfer within the contemplation" of the transferee-

Another source of difficulty was that the rule operated to reduce the exclusion in situations where the transfer, although for valuable consideration, was pursuant to good faith adjustments of business interests in which investment in insurance policies was incidental to the major purposes of the transactions. In these instances the recipients were no less deserving of the full exclusion than were those from whom they acquired the policies. Nonetheless, the acquisition of a policy by way of a tax-free corporate reorganization, in which the acquiring corporation exchanged its stock for all the assets of another corporation, resulted in the acquiring corporation being classified as a transferee for valuable consideration.[46] Also, transfers between shareholders and their corporations,[47] partners and their partnerships,[48] and shareholders or partners [49] presented a similar difficulty. Limited relief was provided in this area in 1942 when the 1939 Code was amended to make the transfer-for-valuable-consideration rule inapplicable if the contract has a basis in the hands of the transferee determined in whole or in part by reference to its

for-value provisions. Hacker, n. 44 *supra,* was said not to apply when the insured is the transferee. This position was made a part of the express language of the Code in 1954. Int. Rev. Code of 1954, § 101 (a)(2)(B) .

46. King Plow Co. v. Comm'r., 110 F. 2d 659 (5th Cir. 1940) ; Stroud & Company, Inc., 45 B.T.A. 862 (1941) .

47. James F. Waters, Inc. v. Comm'r. 196 F.2d 596 (9th Cir. 1947) (transferee from corporation which acquired policy from its employee deemed a transferee for value even though acquisition by transferee from employer of insured was by way of merger in which gain or loss was not recognized.)

48. I.T. 2591, X-2 C.B. 123 (1931) (transferee partnership is a transferee for valuable consideration) . *But see* Rev. Rul. 72, 1953–1 C.B. 23, where transfer to partnership as part of capital contribution did not result in partnership being a transferee for valuable consideration. See n. 51 *infra.*

49. *Cf.* Monroe v. Patterson, 197 F. Supp. 146, 149 (N.D. Ala. 1961) .

basis in the hands of the transferor.[50] This permitted the acquisition of policies through tax-free reorganizations without adverse tax consequences.[51]

In 1954 Congress, after being urged to discard completely the transfer-for-valuable-consideration rule,[52] further broadened its exceptions.[53] Under the 1954 Code transfers for valuable consideration "to the insured, to a partner of the insured, to a partnership in which the insured is a partner, or to a corporation in which the insured is a shareholder or officer" [54] were removed from the scope of the rule. Nonetheless, present provisions still do not exclude all legitimate business-motivated transfers of policies.[55]

The result is that there exists neither a limitation which confines the exclusion to instances where the recipient is being compensated for the loss of satisfactions flowing

50. Int. Rev. Code of 1939, § 22 (b)(2)(A).

51. "Thus, where a corporation transfers an insurance policy to a successor corporation in a tax-free reorganization, the proceeds received under the policy will be exempt from taxation when received by the transferee if they would have been exempt if received by the transferor," S. Rep. No. 1631, 77th Cong. 2d Sess. 69 (1942). Observe that this provision did not suffice to remove from the operation of the transferee-for-valuable-consideration rule the proceeds involved in James F. Waters, Inc. v. Comm'r., n. 47 *supra.* However, it is the justification for the position taken in Rev. Rul. 72, n. 48 *supra.*

52. H. R. Rep. No. 1337, 83d Cong., 2d Sess (1954). The House version of the 1964 Code did abolish completely the transferee-for-valuable-consideration rule. See S. Rep. No. 1622, 83d Cong. 2d Sess. 14 (1954).

53. The intent, apparently, was to distinguish between transfers for legitimate business reasons and those for speculation purposes. See S. Rep. No. 1622, 83d Cong., 2d Sess. 14 (1954).

54. Int. Rev. Code of 1954, § 101 (a)(2)(B).

55. *E.g.,* transfers between shareholders of a closely held corporation pursuant to a cross-purchase stock agreement between such shareholders. For other possibly similar situations see McNeill, *Transfers for Value— Contingent Ownership,* 18 J. Am. Soc'y. 342, 343 (1964).

from his family relationship with the insured, nor one which makes the exclusion available to all legitimate transfers made in the ordinary course of business and not for speculative purposes. In this manner, a provision born under circumstances which obscure its purpose is shaped by a mindless destiny.

XIII. Employee Death Benefits

THE LIMITATIONS IMPOSED by the transferee-for-value rules only come into play when the receipts are properly designated for tax purposes as "amounts received . . . under a life insurance contract . . . paid by reason of the death of the insured." In many situations such designation presents no problem; but this is not always true. Aside from the already mentioned situation where the doctrine of insurable interest forces classification of the receipts as wagering gains, it is clear that proceeds received by a creditor who has taken an assignment of policies on the life of the debtor as collateral security for the debt do not come within the exclusion.[1] The right of the creditor to these proceeds is limited to the amount of the undischarged debt, and any excess is payable to the appropriate beneficiary under the policy.[2]

Moreover, the arrangement pursuant to which payments are made must possess the basic characteristics of life insurance; that is, a number of individuals must have made payments into a common fund from which, upon the death of a particular insured, a designated beneficiary will be paid a certain amount without regard to the amount paid into the fund by the payor in respect to the

1. St. Louis Refrigerating & Cold Storage Co. v. United States, 162 F.2d 394 (8th Cir. 1947).
2. *Ibid. Cf.* Federal Nat'l Bank of Shawnee, 16 T.C. 54, 59 (1951); T. O. McCamant, 32 T.C. 824 (1959).

deceased.[3] In the words of the Court in *Helvering* v. *Le Gierse,* "Historically and commonly, insurance involves risk-shifting and risk-distributing."[4] Thus, payments made by a surviving partner to the spouse of a deceased partner out of profits arising from a continuation of the business do not constitute the proceeds of life insurance.[5] The extent to which the risk of premature death is shifted and distributed under such an agreement is too conjectural to warrant classification of the arrangement as insurance.

Another area out of which arises the issue whether particular receipts constitute life insurance proceeds is that of employee death benefits. Previously, the uncertainty surrounding their classification as gifts by the employer was discussed.[6] However, for many years the Government's position was that such benefits constituted gifts when "paid by an organization to which the recipient has rendered no service."[7] In 1950 this position was reversed.[8] In holding that the benefits constituted gross income, emphasis was placed upon the fact that the employer had received services, even though not performed by the recipient. Following this reversal, Congress in 1951 enacted section

3. In this manner the risk to the beneficiary of premature death of the insured is shifted and distributed to the others making contributions to the fund.

4. 312 U.S. 531, 539 (1941). The Court proceeded to find that no such shifting and distributing occurred when an eighty-year-old woman purchased for two single premiums an insurance policy and an annuity policy covering her life. "The fact remains that annuity and insurance are opposites; in this combination the one neutralizes the risk customarily inherent in the other." (541). *Cf.* Comm'r v. Treganowan, 183 F.2d 288 (2d Cir. 1950); Rev. Rul. 65–57, 1965–1 C.B. 56, n. 1, chap. xii *supra.*

5. Mary Tighe, 33 T.C. 557, 564 (1959). *Cf.* Int. Rev. Code of 1954, § 736.

6. See pp. 143–46 *supra.*

7. I.T. 3329, 1939–2 C.B. 153.

8. I.T 4027, 1950–2 C.B. 9.

22 (b) (1) (B) of the 1939 Code, which excluded from gross income amounts received "under a contract of an employer providing for the payment of such amounts to the beneficiaries of an employee, paid by reason of the death of the employee." [9] This exclusion could not exceed, however, $5,000 per employer. The Senate Report indicated that the provision was intended to remove the hardship caused by the fact that employer-paid death benefits did not constitute life insurance payments. [10] This appears an understandable generalization, although in 1957 the Supreme Court employed a definitional approach to the issue of what constitutes "accident and health insurance" which, if applied to death benefits, might have resulted in their classification as life insurance proceeds. [11] In any

9. Rev. Act of 1951, § 302 (a) .

10. S. REP. No. 781, 82d Cong., 1st Sess. 50 (1951) . *Cf.* Hess v. Comm'r, 271 F.2d 104 (3d Cir. 1959) , for a discussion of the legislative history.

11. Haynes v. United States, 353 U.S. 81 (1957). The Court determined that amounts received pursuant to a "plan" of an employer to provide, *inter alia*, "sickness disability benefits" when an employee missed work because of illness constituted "amounts received, through accident or health insurance . . . as compensation for personal injuries or sickness." *Id.* at 83. After stating that the crucial issue was whether the "plan" should be treated as health insurance, Mr. Justice Black, speaking for the Court, said: "Broadly speaking, health insurance is an undertaking by one person for reasons satisfactory to him to indemnify another for losses caused by illness. We believe that the Southern Bell disability plan comes within this meaning of health insurance." *Ibid.* Were the word "health" preceding "insurance" in the first sentence of this quotation changed to "life" and the word "illness" in the same sentence to "death," a definition of life insurance sufficiently broad to cover employee death benefits would emerge. It is doubtful, however, that such a definition would be consistent with the Court's emphasis on risk-shifting and risk-distributing in Helvering v. Le Gierse, 312 U.S. 531 (1941) . Nonetheless, an employee death benefit plan administered by a large corporate employer probably does involve a substantial degree of shifting and distributing. It is interesting to note that the plan involved in *Haynes* was labeled "Plan for Employees' Pensions, Disability Benefits and Death Benefits."
Prior to *Haynes,* the authorities were divided on whether an agreement to pay wages during sickness was health insurance. See Moholy v. United States, 235 F.2d 562 (9th Cir. 1956) . In *Moholy* it was held that it was not health insurance. In support the court cited the congressional action in 1951 in the death benefit area and observed that if such benefits were

event, the 1951 amendment substantially reduced the scope of the importance of the distinction between life insurance proceeds paid by reason of the death of the insured and employer-paid death benefits. Furthermore, the legislative history accompanying the amendment has made it difficult to urge successfully that death benefits be excluded as life insurance proceeds. This difficulty, together with the $5,000 limitation, accounts for the great pressure on the gift exclusion.[12]

Interpretation of the 1951 amendment proved difficult, however. For example, under what circumstances did a "contract" of the proper sort exist? How was the exclusion to be apportioned when death benefits were paid to several beneficiaries of an employee? And, most important of all, to what extent was the exclusion available in respect to sums paid subsequent to death of an employee which he could have received during his life had he chosen to do so, or which he would have received had he lived? Locked within this last general inquiry were such concrete issues as whether death benefits included items such as uncollected salary, unused leave, payments to the surviving spouse under a joint-survivor annuity, retirement plan payment which the deceased employee had the power to enjoy during his life had he elected to do so, and payments, also pursuant to a retirement plan, which the deceased employee might have enjoyed during his life had he survived beyond retirement age.

The regulations temporarily filled some of the gaps in

"insurance" no such action was necessary. At present, the accident and health insurance area is governed by specific provisions of the Code. Int. Rev. Code of 1954; §§ 104, 105, 106. See pp. 229–39 *infra*.

12. See pp. 143–46 *supra*.

the fragmentary language of the 1951 amendment.[13] Under these the term "contract" was construed to include, under certain circumstances, an "established plan" making provision for employees generally or a class of employees; [14] the exclusion was apportioned to beneficiaries of employees in the same proportion as the amount payable to, or received by, each bears to the total death benefit; [15] uncollected salary, payments for unused leave, and payments to a survivor of a deceased employee under a survivor's annuity were excluded from the scope of death benefits; [16] and the exclusion was made inapplicable "to amounts with respect to which the deceased employee possessed, immediately prior to his death, a non-forfeitable right to receive the amounts while living." [17]

In 1954 Congress eliminated the requirement that payments be made "under a contract" and further restricted the exclusion by limiting it to $5,000 "with respect to any employee." [18] In addition, the inapplicability of the exclusion to amounts in respect to which the employee had a non-forfeitable right was made an express part of the

13. Treas. Reg. § 39.22 (b) (1)–2 (1953).

14. Treas. Reg. § 39.22 (b) (1)–2 (c) (1953).

15. Treas. Reg. § 39.22 (b) (1)–2 (a) (1) (1953).

16. Treas. Reg. § 39.22 (b) (1)–2 (d) (1) (1953).

17. *Ibid.* The validity of the regulations in respect to this last point was sustained in Hess v. Comm'r, 271 F.2d 104 (3d Cir. 1959). The theory of these regulations was that the exclusion was limited to sums paid only by reason of the death of the employee. In this manner death benefits were analogized to the "pure insurance" portion of insurance proceeds. However, the resemblance between the two becomes less marked as "forfeitability" becomes an easier requirement to satisfy. For an indication of the ease with which it may be satisfied see Hazel W. Pollnow, 35 T.C. 715 (1961).

18. When death benefits are received in two or more taxable years, the exclusion must be applied against the first such benefits received and not apportioned to each payment. John C. Nordt Co., 46 T.C. 40 (1966).

Code, subject to an exception for lump-sum distributions by a qualified pension, profit-sharing, or stock bonus plan.[19] Congressional explicitness was also reflected by enactment of the provision in the regulations just described which excluded amounts received by a surviving annuitant.[20]

Obviously, this specificity did not eliminate all problems. For example, even though the requirement of forfeitability is now a part of the statute, determination of the existence of this characteristic remains troublesome. In general, rights of the employee are considered non-forfeitable when there is no contingency under the plan which may cause him to lose such rights.[21] Despite the resemblance of excludable death benefits to life insurance proceeds which results from this requirement of forfeitability, the $5,000 limitation makes it necessary to maintain a

19. Int. Rev. Code of 1954, § 101 (b)(2)(B).

20. Int. Rev. Code of 1954, § 101 (b)(2)(C). In addition, where taxation of amounts received is governed by § 72, which pertains to annuities, the amount excluded is determined by reference to the value of such amount on the date of death. The amount excluded constitutes additional consideration paid by the employee for the annuity. Int. Rev. Code of 1954, § 101 (b)(2)(D). See p. 221 *infra*.

21. Rev. Rul. 59–255, 1959–2 C.B. 36. The regulations contain an elaborate definition of non-forfeitability. Treas. Reg. § 1.101–2 (d)(1) (1957). Under it an employee has a non-forfeitable right with respect to any amount which he would have been entitled to receive either upon demand, or at the time of termination, by death or otherwise, of his employment. Thus, if a plan provides that termination of employment prior to retirement results in loss of rights to contributions by the employer, the interest of the employee in such contributions is forfeitable. Rev. Rul. 59–255, *supra*. If the plan provides that these contributions are payable to another upon the death of the employee prior to retirement, the recipient of the contributions under such circumstances has received a death benefit within the meaning of the exclusion. In other situations where death of the employee generates benefits payable to a beneficiary having a greater value than those to which the employee was entitled immediately before his death, similar reasoning prevails. See examples (2), (3), (4), (5) in Treas. Reg. § 1.101–2 (d)(2) (1957).

distinction between the two. This is not always easy.[22] In addition to these problems, it is necessary to distinguish death benefits from both (1) amounts received by a surviving annuitant under a joint and survivor's annuity contract [23] and (2) sums received under annuity contracts purchased by an employee with his own funds.[24]

The precision in definitions required for solution of these problems, the somewhat untidy manner in which the present statutory structure has developed, and the existing uncertainty about the scope of the gift exclusion make it difficult to ponder the employees' death benefit area without a sense of discomfort. Indeed, it forces to the level of consciousness the question whether the special statutory provisions of section 101 (b) are needed. Had no such provisions been enacted, the task would have been to classify death benefits as either compensation, gifts, insurance

22. *E.g.*, Rev. Rul. 63–76, 1963–1 C.B. 23 (sums received under life insurance policies distributed to employee by qualified pension plan upon termination of employment treated as life insurance and not employee death benefits). Compare Essenfeld v. Comm'r, 311 F.2d 208 (2d Cir. 1963), where amounts paid pursuant to employment contract on death of employee prior to retirement derived from life insurance policies taken out on life of employee by employer were held to be employee death benefits and not proceeds of life insurance. *Accord* Laura V. Lilly, 45 T.C. 168 (1965).

23. Treas. Reg. § 1.101–2 (e) (1957) is devoted to elaborating this distinction. § 1.101–2 (e)(1)(ii) provides: "Under section 101 (b)(2)(C), no exclusion is allowable for amounts received by a surviving annuitant under a joint and survivor's annuity contract if the annuity starting date (as defined in section 72 (c)(4) and paragraph (b) of § 1.72–4) occurs before the death of the employee." Where amounts being received by a disabled employee prior to his death are other than annuity payments within the meaning of § 72 of the 1954 Code, payments received by the surviving spouse following the employee's death prior to normal retirement age are not deprived of the exclusion by reason of § 101 (b)(2)(C) of the 1954 Code. Rev. Rul. 61–161, 1961–2 C.B. 15.

24. See Rev. Rul. 54.144, 1954–1 C.B. 15 (annuities acquired by members of uniformed services under Uniform Services Contingency Option Act of 1953 with own funds for benefit of surviving spouse, child or children not entitled to exclusion); Rev. Rul. 59–254, 1959–2 C.B. 33.

proceeds, or annuities. Probably, most would have found their way into the categories of compensation and annuities. Assuming this is an accurate prediction,[25] the consequence would have been to include in the income of the beneficiaries a greater amount than presently is the case.

The case for doing this is not overwhelming, however. To the extent that death benefits resemble the "pure insurance" portion of such proceeds, death's destruction of non-taxable gains from family status precludes unequivocal condemnation of the exclusion in the name of Equity. Undoubtedly, Free Market Compatibility suggests elimination of the exclusion for much the same reason as it did in the instance of insurance proceeds; that is, the exclusion encourages the investment of earnings from personal service in a manner, and in an amount, other than what would be the case in a free market. Also, the exclusion probably has some tendency to impair labor mobility; on the other hand, it does permit employers to provide the equivalent of insurance protection without the necessity of purchasing the product of insurance companies. In this manner, perhaps, a market distortion was slightly diminished. Elimination of the death benefit exclusion also would reduce somewhat the scope of the present taxonomic task; but it is doubtful that this would represent a significant advance.

Also, it is likely that Reduced Economic Inequality is advanced by the exclusion. Certainly, the combined effect of progressive rates and the fairly low ceiling of the exclusion is that the rate of tax on the entire death benefit tends to increase as the amount of the benefit increases. Furthermore, a limited exclusion of this type perhaps introduces a mild additional element of progression in the tax struc-

25. *But cf.* n. 11 *supra.*

ture when, as is the case here, the item is one frequently received by low- and middle-income taxpayers. Finally, sympathy for the bereaved and affection for any measure which appears to enhance financial security also exert an influence in this area.

On balance, exclusion of death benefits can be tolerated, providing it can be restricted to modest sums which bear a functional resemblance to life insurance proceeds.[26] It remains true that even when so restricted, the employee acquires the protection without the payment of tax on the necessary "premiums." [27]

26. See n. 17 *supra*.
27. See p. 82, n. 7 *supra*.

XIV. Annuities

THE UNCERTAINTIES which beset theoretical analysis of life insurance proceeds and death benefits diminish significantly when annuities are considered. The central issue in the annuity area is the manner in which receipts should be allocated between the return of capital and gain in the form of interest or other taxable returns on an investment. The general outline of this aspect of the return of capital problem was described earlier; [1] here, analysis of the problem is continued in a particularized setting.

The taxation of annuities has moved through at least three phases. Prior to 1934, amounts received by annuitants were excluded from gross income until the entire investment of capital was recovered.[2] This "recovery of

1. See pp. 33–34 *supra*.

2. There is some indication that for a period prior to 1926 each amount received as an annuity was apportioned between a return of capital and income. *Hearings on Revenue Revision before the House Ways and Means Committee*, 73d Cong., 2d Sess. 554 (1934). It is clear that the language of the 1926 Revenue Act, § 213 (b) (2), required that all amounts be excluded until the "aggregate premiums or consideration paid" is recovered. Its language was that gross income did not include "amounts received (other than amounts paid by reason of the death of the insured and interest payments on such amounts) under a life insurance, endowment, or annuity contract, but if such amounts (when added to amounts received before the taxable year under such contract) exceed the aggregate premiums or consideration paid (whether or not paid during the taxable year) then the excess shall be included in gross income."
The language of previous revenue acts was less explicit. *E.g.*, the 1916 Revenue Act, § 4, provided that exempt income included "the amount received by the insured, as a return of premium or premiums paid by him under life insurance, endowment, or annuity contracts, either *during the*

215

cost" approach was not only simple to apply but also quite favorable to annuitants. In 1934 the law was altered to require that an amount received as an annuity during a taxable year be included in the gross income of the annuitant to the extent it did not exceed 3 per cent of the aggregate premiums or consideration paid for the annuity. Under this rule 3 per cent of the total consideration was considered to be the income element in the annuity payment and the balance a return of capital. When the amount excluded equaled the total consideration paid, all receipts thereafter constituted taxable gain.

The 1934 change appears to have been in response to the views (1) that each amount received as an annuity contained an interest, or income, element,[3] and (2) that failure to subject such element to tax discriminated in favor of wealthy taxpayers who could afford to risk some loss of capital in exchange for long deferral of tax on this type of investment income. The difficulty was that although annuitants were never permitted to recover tax-

---

term or at the maturity of the term mentioned in the contract or under the surrender of the contract." (Italics added.) The 1913 Revenue Act was even more obscure. The pertinent provision was: "That the proceeds of life insurance policies paid upon the death of the person insured or payments made by or credited to the insured, on life insurance, endowment, or annuity contracts, upon the return thereof to the insured at the maturity of the term mentioned in the contract, or upon surrender of contract, shall not be included as income." It is possible to read the language of the 1916 Revenue Act (language which appeared in succeeding Acts until that of 1926) as requiring an apportionment between capital and income. See Florence L. Klein, 6 B.T.A. 617 (1927), and Guaranty Trust Co., 15 B.T.A. 20 (1929), where the language was so read. This construction was approved in MAGILL, TAXABLE INCOME 428 (rev. ed. 1945).

3. See H.R. REP. No. 704, 73d Cong., 2d Sess. 21 (1934). There is also a "premium paid by the life insurance company, in return for the escheat to the company of the balance of the capital should the annuitant die during the year." VICKREY, AGENDA FOR PROGRESSIVE TAXATION 75 (1947). This should not be considered a taxable element unless losses on capital invested in annuities because of premature death be made deductible.

free more than their invested capital, only a small portion of them were permitted to recover that much.[4] The reason for this was that 3 per cent of the consideration substantially overstated the interest element in each payment.[5] Only the long-lived excluded from gross income an amount equal to their investment; all others perished before this was achieved. Equity and Free Market Compatibility plainly suggested that this method was undesirable.[6] Like an erratic parent, the Government during this period indulged those who received insurance proceeds and unjustly punished annuitants.

After an unsuccessful attempt in 1948[7] to alter the taxation of annuities, Congress enacted the present scheme as a part of the 1954 Code. The underlying premise of this third phase of annuity taxation is that capital invested by the annuitant should be recovered over a period of time measured by the expected duration of payments received as an annuity. Thus, to each year of this period should be apportioned a part of the total consideration paid for the annuity.[8] Amounts received as an an-

---

4. VICKREY, AGENDA FOR PROGRESSIVE TAXATION 76 (1947).

5. *Cf.* Egtvedt v. United States, 112 Ct. Cl. 80 (1948). Despite this overstatement, the court in *Egtvedt* refused to hold the 3 per cent rule unconstitutional.

6. Simons departed from the logic of his definition of income to suggest that consumption be treated as the "lower limit in the calculation of taxable income." PERSONAL INCOME TAXATION 107 n. 7 (1938). Thus, the consumption of capital involved when an annuitant lives on amounts received as an annuity would justify inclusion of the entire amount in taxable income. The 3 per cent rule somewhat approached this fusion of expenditure tax principles with those of an income tax advocated by Simons.

7. H.R. 6712, 80th Cong., 2d Sess. (1948).

8. Where part of the cost of the annuity has been contributed by the employer and during the first three years the employee annuitant will receive a sum in excess of his contributions thereto, the entire amount of employee-contributed capital will be recovered free of tax within the three years. Int. Rev. Code of 1954, § 72 (d)(1). This simplifies the reporting of such annuities.

nuity in each such year in excess of this portion of the entire investment constitute the income element and are subject to tax.

Although the technical structure by which this is accomplished is complex, its main posts and beams are readily discernible. To begin with, the portion of an amount received as an annuity under an annuity, endowment, or life insurance contract which is excluded from gross income as a return of capital is fixed by means of an "exclusion ratio." [9] This ratio is that which the "investment in the contract" bears to the "expected return under the contract." The excludable portion of an amount received as an annuity bears the same ratio to the total of such amount as the investment in the contract bears to the expected return. Thus, if $80 is invested in an annuity which has an expected return of $100, four-fifths of an amount received as an annuity is excluded from gross income. This exclusion ratio remains applicable to all amounts received as an annuity without regard to the extent the annuitant has previously recovered his capital. Amounts not received as an annuity (such as dividends, a return of premiums, a refund of consideration upon full discharge of the contract, or amounts received on surrender, redemption, or maturity of the contract) [10] receive different treatment.[11] Dividends or similar payments received before the annuity starting date are includable in gross income only to the extent they, together with other payments previously treated as a return of capital, exceed

9. Int. Rev. Code of 1954, § 72 (b) .

10. Treas. Reg. § 1.72–11 (1956) , as amended by T.D. 6676, 1963–2 C.B. 41, describes payments which, for the purposes of § 72 of the 1954 Code, are classified as amounts received as an annuity.

11. Int. Rev. Code of 1954, § 72 (e) .

the aggregate consideration paid for the contract;[12] that is, a "cost recovery" approach is applied to these payments. The same approach is used when the amounts are a refund of consideration or an amount received upon the surrender, redemption, or maturity of a contract.[13] When, however, a dividend, or similar payment, is received after an annuity starting date, it is treated as income.[14] Interest payments are treated similarly.[15]

The fact that the foregoing description fairly bristles with terms needing precise definitions makes clear that the two major sources of complexity in the annuity taxation structure are, first, the formulation of such definitions and, second, their application to a given state of facts.

At the threshold is the issue of the scope of this structure. The statutory language which marks its outer limits directs that the payments to which the structure relates be made "under an annuity, endowment, or life insurance contract." [16] No definition of such contracts appears in the Code, and the regulations merely observe that the structure embraces those contracts which are considered annuity, endowment, or life insurance contracts under "the customary practices of life insurance companies." [17] This is immediately followed by a denial that the structure is limited to contracts made by insurance companies.[18] Thus, section 72 of the 1954 Code encompasses, as did section

12. Int. Rev. Code of 1954, § 72 (e)(1)(B) .

13. Int. Rev. Code of 1954, § 72 (e)(2) .

14. Int. Rev. Code of 1954, § 72 (e)(1)(A) .

15. Int. Rev. Code of 1954, § 72 (j) .

16. Int. Rev. Code of 1954, § 72 (a) .

17. Treas. Reg. § 1.72–2 (a)(1) (1956) , as amended by T.D. 6497, 1960–2 C.B. 19.

18. *Ibid.*

22 (b) (2) of the 1939 Code, so-called private annuity contracts not involving an insurance company.[19] In addition, both sections are inapplicable to "gratuitous annuities" established under trusts or estates.[20] Less certainty exists about the line between a sale of property for deferred payments and an exchange of property for a "private annuity." Since section 72 covers instalment annuities pay-

19. See Ware v. Comm'r, 159 F.2d 542 (5th Cir. 1947); Gillespie v. Comm'r, 128 F.2d 140 (9th Cir. 1942); Jane J. de Canizares, 32 T.C. 345 (1959); Rev. Rul. 239, 1953–2 C.B. 53; Rev. Rul. 62–136, 1962–2 C.B. 12. There are several cases which have held that when an annuitant has transferred appreciated property to one not engaged in writing annuity contracts in exchange for an undertaking to pay an annuity, no gain or loss is realized in the year of transfer because the undertaking has no "fair market value." Comm'r v. Kann's Estate, 174 F.2d 357 (3d Cir. 1949); Frank C. Deering, 40 B.T.A. 984 (1939); J. Darsie Lloyd, 33 B.T.A. 903 (1936). Rev. Rul. 239, 1953–2 C.B. 53 points out that these decisions do not mean that gain is never taxed even though the amount received under the annuity contract is in excess of the adjusted basis of the property transferred. It proceeds to state that under the 1939 Code that part of annuity payments not subject to tax under the 3 per cent rule was to be excluded from gross income until it equaled the adjusted basis of the property; thereafter, it was taxed as gain until the aggregate amount excluded by the 3 per cent rule equaled the fair market value of the property at the time of the transfer. Hill's Estate v. Maloney, 58 F. Supp. 164 (D.N.J. 1944), relied on in this ruling, reached a similar result. Presumably, the ruling is applicable under the 1954 Code, except that the exclusion ratio (fixed by reference to the fair market value at the time of the transfer of property) is applicable even after the annuitant has received amounts subject to exclusion thereunder in excess of the fair market value at the time of transfer. Is Rev. Rul. 239, *supra,* undercut in any way by United States v. Davis, 370 U.S. 65 (1962)?

This deferral of gain on the disposition of property until the capital invested therein has been recovered through annuity payments is not permitted when the transferree is "an organization, such as a corporation, trust, fund, or foundation (other than a commercial insurance company) which, from time to time, issues annuity contracts." Rev. Rul. 62–136, *supra,* provides that there is taxable gain in the year of the transfer in such cases measured by the difference between the transferor's adjusted basis and the present value of payments to be made under the contract. Appropriate tables for computing present values are set forth in Rev. Rul. 62–137, 1962–2 C.B. 28. Transfers to charitable organizations in exchange for annuities is both an old—see Raymond v. Comm'r, 114 F.2d 140, 142 n. 3 (7th Cir.), *cert. denied,* 311 U.S. 710 (1940)—and a troublesome problem. See VICKREY, AGENDA FOR PROGRESSIVE TAXATION 78–80 (1947).

20. *Cf.* Frank H. Mason Trust v. Comm'r, 136 F.2d 335 (6th Cir. 1943).

able for a term certain,[21] it is not possible to assert confidently that only where payments are computed with regard for life expectancy do "private annuities" exist.[22] Perhaps the phrase "customary practices of life insurance companies" supplies the touchstone here; but, be that as it may, the existence of section 483, which treats as interest a portion of the payments under a contract of sale that provides inadequate interest,[23] has substantially reduced the importance of the distinction.

Once within the walls of section 72, a fairly impressive array of technical structures confronts one. First, there is the "investment in the contract" which must be computed. Adjustment must be made for any "refund feature" [24] and any previous return of capital.[25] Allocations must be made where several annuity elements were acquired for a single consideration [26] and, where distributions under the employee's plans are involved, the extent to which interrelated contributions and benefits are considered separate contracts as well as the investment therein, must be determined.[27]

21. Int. Rev. Code of 1954, § 72 (c)(3)(B) .

22. Such a view was possible under the 1939 Code because payments not computed with regard for life expectancy did not constitute amounts received as an annuity. George H. Thornley, 2 T.C. 220 (1943) , *rev'd on other grounds*, 147 F.2d 416 (3d Cir. 1944) . See Int. Rev. Code of 1954, § 72 (h) , for manner in which the problem of *Thornley* is approached presently. See also Treas. Reg. §§ 1.72–11 (d) , (e) (1956) , as amended by T.D. 6676, 1963–2 C.B. 41.

23. Int. Rev. Code of 1954, § 483.

24. Int. Rev. Code of 1954, § 72 (c)(2) .

25. Treas. Reg. § 1.72–6 (a) (1956) , as amended by T.D. 6676, 1963–2 C.B. 41.

26. Treas. Reg. § 1.72–6 (b) (1956) .

27. Treas. Reg. §§ 1.72–2 (a)(3) , –8 (1956) . Computation of the investment made by employees illustrates two previously mentioned means by which an investment can be made. First, contributions by an employer to a plan which were includable in the gross income of the employee are

Next is the determination of the "expected return." In only the simplest of cases is this an uncomplicated task. Where, for example, monthly payments are to be received for a period measured by a single life, the annual amount is multiplied times the appropriate multiple set forth in the regulations.[28] Even more simple is the computation where the contract provides for specific periodic payments to be paid for a term certain. Multiplication of the former by the latter is the only step required.[29] However, complexity mounts when one determines the "expected return" of joint and survivor annuities,[30] contracts which provide for termination of payments at death or some earlier contingency,[31] and "variable" annuities.[32]

Then, of course, "amounts received as an annuity" (to which the exclusion ratio is applicable) must be distinguished from amounts not so received;[33] and to accom-

---

considered an investment made by the employee in the contract. Thus, an investment is made by inclusion of an item in gross income. See p. 21 *supra*. Contributions includable in the gross income of an employee include those made pursuant to a trust or plan which fails to qualify under section 401 (a) and to which the employee has a non-forfeitable right at the time it is made. Treas. Reg. § 1.72–8 (a)(1) . Second, although the general rule is that contributions by an employer not includable in the gross income of the employee are not considered a part of the employee's investment, amounts which qualify as death benefits under section 101 (b) are deemed contributions by an employee. Treas. Reg. 1.72–8 (b) , 1.101–2 (e)(2) , example 1 (1956) . This is another example of "constructive" investment. See p. 21 *supra*. Generally, contributions by an employer under a qualified trust or plan are not includable in the employee's gross income.

28. Int. Rev. Code of 1954, § 72 (c)(3)(A) ; Treas. Reg. § 1.72–5 (a) (1956) .

29. Int. Rev. Code of 1954, § 72 (c)(3)(B) ; Treas. Reg. § 1.72–5 (c) (1956) .

30. Treas. Reg. § 1.72–5 (b) (1956) .

31. Treas. Reg. § 1.72–5 (a)(3) (1956) .

32. Treas. Reg. § 1.72–5 (f) (1956) .

33. The regulations set forth three tests which must be met if sums are to be considered "amounts received as an annuity": (1) the amount must

plish this, as well as for other purposes, the "annuity starting date" must be fixed.[34] To bring this quite skimpy list of complex issues to a close, interest payments must be distinguished from annuities,[35] both, from dividends,[36] and all three from amounts received upon surrender, redemption, or maturity of a contract.[37]

---

be received after the "annuity starting date"; (2) amounts must be payable in periodic instalments over a period of more than one year from the starting date; and (3) except in the case of "variable annuities," total amounts payable must be determinable at the starting date. Treas. Reg. § 1.72–2 (b)(2) (1956).

34. To a degree, the "annuity starting date" and "amounts received as an annuity" are defined by reference to one another. See n. 33 *supra* for the manner in which "amounts received as an annuity" relies on the meaning of the "annuity starting date." The last-mentioned term is then described as the later of the date the contract's obligations became fixed or the first day of the period (which may be a year or a smaller unit of time, depending upon the period between payments) which ends on the date of the first annuity payment. Treas. Reg. § 1.72–4 (b) (1956).

35. See Igleheart v. Comm'r, 174 F.2d 605 (7th Cir. 1949) (where contract purchased from insurance company by payment of sum equal to principal value of contract, which sum is payable to purchaser on demand or to named beneficiaries at purchaser's death, annual payments of amount less than ordinary return on principal invested is not annuity payment regardless of label used in contract). Receipt of periodic payments under so-called combination life insurance–annuity contracts has proved troublesome. Comm'r v. Meyer, 139 F.2d 256 (6th Cir. 1943) (periodic payments treated as annuity); G.C.M. 21716, 1940–1 C.B. 82 (periodic payments treated as interest only).

36. See Florence M. Shelley, 10 T.C. 44 (1948) (amount designated "dividend" treated as either interest or annuity payment rather than dividend properly speaking).

37. A particularly difficult problem arises when the contract permits an election between a lump-sum payment in full discharge and payments over a period of time. Since a "cost recovery" approach is used in respect to payments in full discharge while the investment is apportioned over the payment period in the case of an annuity, it is necessary to determine whether the periodic payments constitute an annuity. *Cf.* George H. Thornley, 2 T.C. 220 (1943), *rev'd on other grounds*, 147 F.2d 416 (3d Cir. 1944). Under the 1954 Code it appears they do. See nn. 33 & 34 *supra*. This then raises the issue of whether the election to take an annuity amounts to a surrender and discharge of the original contract upon which gain may be recognized and investment of the "constructively received" proceeds in a new annuity contract. The 1954 Code has a special provision which permits exercise of the option to receive an annuity in lieu of a lump-sum settlement "within 60 days after the day on which such lump

Annuities

It is clear that the present rules cannot be described as simple. At the same time, none can gainsay that the 1954 changes represent an improvement in Equity. Under present rules all annuitants whose contracts provide payments measured in duration by their life and who die at a time other than that predicted by mortality tables recover either more or less than their invested capital free of tax. This means the probabilities of a full recovery of capital are substantially better than under the 3 per cent rule. The extent to which the present structure conflicts with the end of Reduced Economic Inequality depends upon the distribution of annuitants within the wealth groups and the public's attitude toward those who consume capital. Probably, most annuitants have adjusted gross income

---

sum first became payable" without constructive receipt of the lump sum. Int. Rev. Code of 1954, § 72 (h). The status of elections prior to the day the lump sum became payable is uncertain. However, such an exercise of an option by the holder of an endowment policy did not result in constructive receipt under the 1939 Code. Estate of Snider, 31 T.C. 1064 (1959) (A); Rev. Rul. 56–77, 1956–1 C.B. 620; I.T. 3963, 1949–2 C.B. 36. Presumably, a similar rule is applicable under the 1954 Code.

Elections after maturity appear to result in constructive receipt except to the extent the result is qualified by § 72 (h). Thus, an election at or after maturity to receive *interest* on the amount payable at maturity may result in constructive receipt, at least where withdrawals of principal thereafter are not restricted. See Blum v. Higgins, 150 F.2d 471 (2d Cir. 1945) (election made "a few days before the maturity date"); Constance C. Frackelton, 46 B.T.A. 883 (1942) (second policy there involved).

Another difficulty related to elections to receive payments other than in full discharge of the contract arises when, after amounts are received as an annuity, the terms of the contract are modified to permit the payments to be received for a different term. The regulations appear to treat the modification as an exchange of an old contract for a new one. Treas. Reg. §§ 1.72–11 (d), (e) (1956). The exclusion ratio applicable to the annuity payments as modified is computed on the basis of the new contract. The exchange of contracts normally would not result in recognized gain or loss. Int. Rev. Code of 1954, § 1035. Accordingly, the investment in the new contract is that in the old, adjusted for previous returns of capital. Where the modification merely involves a reduction in the amount of annuity payments, and not a change in the term of the annuity, following a lump-sum payment, a somewhat different approach is used. Treas. Reg. § 1.72–11 (f) (1956).

of under $5,000,[38] and they do not appear to be a promising group at which to strike in an effort to reach those who avoid the income tax by the expedient of consuming their large stocks of capital. Should Reduced Economic Inequality suggest the elimination of this group, a broader approach is required than merely taxing as income all amounts received as an annuity.

In addition, the existing rules accomplish the removal of an artificial impediment to the investment in annuity contracts at a clearly tolerable revenue cost.[39] The balance is in favor of the present structure.

38. This is based on the facts (1) that in 1957 80 per cent of the taxpayers age 65 and over had under $5,000 adjusted gross income and (2) that the large majority of annuitants are over 65. See Andrus, *Taxation of the Aged* in *Tax Revision Compendium, House Committee on Ways and Means,* 86th Cong., 1st Sess. pt. 1, at 563, 565 (1959). Of course, those who consume capital may have a very low adjusted gross income. However, the large number of annuitants who use the three-year rule for recovering their cost suggests that many annuitants are former employees who do not have large accumulations of capital. See Andrus, *supra,* at 569. Nonetheless, consumption of capital by living on annuity payments does occur within groups where large capital accumulations frequently exist.

39. *Cf.* H.R. Rep. No. 1337, 83d Cong., 2d Sess. 10–11 (1954).

C. *Status and Compensation Again Distinguished:*
From Damages for Personal Injury
to Meals on the Job

XV. Compensation for Injuries and Sickness, Including Amounts Received under Accident and Health Insurance

THE PRESENT CODE excludes from gross income amounts received (1) under workmen's compensation acts as compensation for personal injuries or sickness, (2) as damages (whether by suit or agreement) on account of personal injuries or sickness, and (3) through accident or health insurance for personal injuries or sickness.[1] Although these exclusions have existed for many years, somewhat different views prevailed during the infancy of the present income tax. Thus, an early Treasury Decision [2] took the position that "money paid to the person insured by an accident insurance policy on account of accidents sustained is returnable as gross income by the insured person." Early regulations took the same position in respect to amounts received as a result of a suit or compromise for personal injury.[3] These rulings were put aside,[4] however, following the decision by the Supreme Court in *Doyle* v. *Mitchell.*[5] It was reasoned that both the proceeds of an accident insurance policy and amounts received as a result of a suit or compromise for personal injuries sustained through accident are but a "substitute, so far as they go,

1. Int. Rev. Code of 1954, § 104 (a)(1), (2), (3).
2. T.D. 2135, 17 TREAS. DEC. INT. REV. 39 (1915).
3. Treas. Reg. 33, Rulings under Article 4 as to Income (1918).
4. T.D. 2747, 20 TREAS. DEC. INT. REV. 457 (1918).
5. 247 U.S. 179 (1918). See pp. 13–14 *supra*.

[for] capital which is the source of *future* periodical income." [6]

While perhaps a sounder theoretical basis for exclusion of certain of these sums exists, Congress, in the Revenue Act of 1918,[7] determined that the matter should be put to rest by enactment of a specific exclusion. The exclusion embraced "amounts received, through accident or health insurance or under workmen's compensation acts, as compensation for personal injuries or sickness, plus the amount of any damages received whether by suit or agreement on account of such injuries or sickness." Thus began the evolution of a statutory structure which at present appears in sections 104 through 106.[8]

The theoretical difficulty in fixing the proper treatment of accident insurance proceeds and compensation for personal injuries is traceable to the diversity of purposes intended to be accomplished through the receipt of such sums. To the extent that these amounts are to cover medical and hospital expenses, their receipt is but an adjustment of the cost of certain personal expenditures and, hence, not included in income.[9] In addition, an exclusion

6. 31 Ops. Att'y Gen. 304, 308 (1918). This opinion which used the language quoted in the text led to the promulgation of T.D. 2747, n. 4 *supra,* which revoked earlier rulings and regulations. That is, they are "capital," not "income" receipts.

7. Revenue Act of 1918, § 213 (b)(6), 40 Stat. 1066 (1919). H.R. Rep. No. 767, 65th Cong., 2d Sess. 9–10 (1918), explains the change as follows: "Under the present law it is doubtful whether amounts received through accident or health insurance, or under workmen's compensation acts, as compensation for personal injuries or sickness, and damages received on account of such injuries or sickness, are required to be included in gross income. The proposed bill provides that such amounts shall not be included in gross income."

8. Int. Rev. Code of 1954, §§ 104–6.

9. *Cf.* Vickrey, Agenda for Progressive Taxation 63 (1947). This assumes the premiums of insurance, as well as the medical expenses themselves, are not deductible and that the receipt of insurance proceeds simply fixes the accurate cost to the insured of the illness. In the case of

is justified if a segment of such amounts is viewed as received in lieu of the tax-free enjoyment of the status of health and an unimpaired body.[10] However, to the extent that these sums replace income of the past or future, the case for exclusion rests more on Practicality than on Equity.[11] Apportionment between the income replacement element and other possible elements always would be difficult and in some instances impossible. It has been suggested in respect to accident and health insurance proceeds that apportionment could be avoided and a result more in conformity with Equity could be achieved by permitting full deduction of the premiums and requiring inclusion of the proceeds.[12] While this is true,[13] a similar technique is not available in respect to damages for personal injuries or workmen's compensation awards.

No changes in the statutory structure occurred after 1918 until 1942, at which time the exclusion was narrowed in one respect and expanded in another. It was narrowed by removing from the exclusion "amounts attributable to (and not in excess of) deductions allowed" for medical

---

damages for personal injuries, their receipt either eliminates or reduces such cost. In both instances the receipt, to the extent it does not exceed the aggregate medical and hospital expenses, can be viewed as a return of capital. See p. 20, n. 20 *supra*.

10. *Cf.* chap. vi *supra*.

11. Perhaps, a vague "humanitarian" microcriterion can be discerned also. *Cf.* KLEIN, FEDERAL INCOME TAXATION, 160 (1929); Epmeier v. United States, 199 F.2d 508, 511 (7th Cir. 1952).

12. VICKREY, AGENDA FOR PROGRESSIVE TAXATION 63 (1947).

13. *But see* GOODE, THE INDIVIDUAL INCOME TAX 112 (1964). Of Vickrey's proposal he says: "While that approach has a certain appeal, it would have the questionable result of increasing insured persons' income tax liability in years in which they were sick or injured relative to tax in other years. The total tax base would be decreased, since aggregate insurance benefits fall short of premiums by a wide margin representing company expenses, taxes, and profits." Humanitarian and paternalistic impulses, as well as perhaps concern with the political acceptability of the income tax, may be reflected by these views.

expenses.[14] The purpose was to eliminate the possibility of certain events generating both an exclusion and a deduction of the same, or equivalent, funds. The section was expanded to include, "amounts received as a pension, annuity, or similar allowance for personal injuries or sickness resulting from active service in the armed forces of any country."[15] The result was to bring within the exclusion certain retirement pensions not previously afforded exempt status.[16]

No further change took place until 1954.[17] During the period between 1942 and 1954, the issue whether payment of sick leave benefits by an employer pursuant to a self-insured plan constituted "amounts received, through accident or health insurance" proved very troublesome. Despite some vacillation, the Government's position was that the exclusion did not extend to a payment of that type.[18]

14. Revenue Act of 1942, § 127 (d) 56 Stat. 826. Medical and other expenses are now governed by Int. Rev. Code of 1954, § 213.

15. Revenue Act of 1942, § 113, 56 Stat. 811.

16. Thus, retirement pay of Regular Army officers retired because of personal injuries or sickness resulting from active service became exempt. See I.T. 3641, 1944 C.B. 70. Prior to that date, they did not fall within the protection afforded some by P.L. 262, 74th Cong., 49 Stat. 607 (1935), relating to exemption from tax of veteran benefits. Further refinements in this area occurred in 1944. P.L. 314, 78th Cong., 2d Sess., 58 Stat. 230, and in 1949, Career Compensation Act of 1949, 63 Stat. 820. See I.T. 3739, 1945 C.B. 61; I.T. 4017, 1950–2 C.B. 12; Rev. Rul. 55–88, 1955–1 C.B. 241; Espenshade v. United States, 66–1 U.S.T.C. ¶ 9120 (Ct. Cl. 1965). For some nice distinctions see Elmer D. Pangburn, 13 T.C. 169 (1949) and Prince v. United States, 119 F. Supp. 421 (Ct. Cl. 1954).
In addition, disability pensions paid by foreign governments were excluded by the 1942 Act. See H. N. Henry, 47 B.T.A. 149 (1942) and the mention of this problem in the Senate discussion of the 1942 Act, 88 CONG. REC. 7805–6 (1942).

17. In 1948 an effort was made to limit the scope of the exclusion for disability pensions as it applied to certain retired military personnel who engaged in gainful employment after retirement. See H.R. 6712, § 106, 80th Cong., 2d Sess. (1948). The measure did not gain Senate approval.

18. *Cf.* I.T. 4107, 1952–2 C.B. 73; I.T. 3738, 1945 C.B. 90; G.C.M. 23511, 1943 C.B. 86, 88. *But see* I.T. 4000, 1950–1 C.B. 21; I.T. 4015, 1950–1 C.B. 23; I.T. 4060, 1951–2 C.B. 11. All modified I.T. 4107, *supra.*

The judicial viewpoint, ultimately endorsed by the Supreme Court,[19] was to the contrary.[20]

In 1954 the statutory structure was extensively revised. First, the *exclusion* for amounts received under policies of accident and health insurance was made *inapplicable* to proceeds attributable to employer contributions not taxable to the employee recipient.[21] Next, a new section was added which fixed the general rule that these amounts were includable in gross income.[22] Then followed three major exceptions to this general rule: (1) amounts paid to reimburse the taxpayer for medical expenses for care of himself and his spouse and dependents; [23] (2) payments for permanent loss of a member or function of the body (including permanent disfigurement) of taxpayer, his spouse, and dependents, computed without regard to the period employee is absent from work; [24] and, within certain limitations, payments (as wages or in lieu of wages) for a period during which the employee is absent from work on account of personal injuries or sickness.[25] These amounts were *excluded* from gross income. Next came the heart of this new structure—the setting aside of the Gov-

19. Haynes v. United States, 353 U.S. 81, 83 (1957). The Court observed: "Broadly speaking, health insurance is an undertaking by one person for reasons satisfactory to him to indemnify another for losses caused by illness." A somewhat similar problem arose in connection with employee death benefits. See chap xiii, pp. 206–8 *supra*.

20. Epmeier v. United States, 199 F.2d 508 (7th Cir. 1952). The Court meticulously examined the characteristics of the plan which provided sick benefits and concluded they conformed to those of "accident and health" insurance.

21. Int. Rev. Code of 1954, § 104 (a)(3).

22. Int. Rev. Code of 1954, § 105 (a). The general rule was applied in William E. Conroy, 41 T.C. 685 (1964), *aff'd*, 341 F.2d 290 (4th Cir. 1965).

23. Int. Rev. Code of 1954, § 105 (b).

24. Int. Rev. Code of 1954, § 105 (c).

25. Int. Rev. Code of 1954, § 105 (d).

ernment's position on self-insured plans. This was done by defining "accident and health insurance" to include both (1) amounts received under an accident and health plan for employees, as well as (2) payments under state sickness and disability funds.[26] Finally, contributions by employers to accident and health plans (through insurance or otherwise) were excluded from gross income of employees.[27]

Conformity of the structure with Equity and Free Market Compatibility was reduced by these changes. Not only did the exclusion of wage-continuation payments further expand the scope of compensation income omitted from the tax base under these provisions, but also the exclusion of employer contributions to accident and health plans discriminates against those not covered by such plans who must pay accident and health insurance premiums with after-tax dollars.[28] In addition, economic waste in the form of malingering is encouraged somewhat, despite the tightening up in the wage-continuation area accomplished by the 1964 Revenue Act.[29]

From a technical standpoint the administration of these sections encounters many complex issues. To recount them in full detail would extend this chapter beyond a reasonable length. Awareness of their rich variety, however, may be imparted by briefly sketching certain major problem areas under each section.

26. Int. Rev. Code of 1954, § 105 (e) .

27. Int. Rev. Code of 1954, § 106.

28. See Rev. Rul. 58–90, 1958–1 C.B. 88, where the treatment by a corporate employee and sole proprietor for tax purposes of premiums on, and amounts as benefits under, sickness and disability policies is compared. The premiums paid by the corporate employer are excluded from the employee's gross income while those paid by the sole proprietor are not deductible. *Cf.* Int. Rev. Code of 1954, §§ 104 (a) , 105 (g) as they relate to self-employed individuals.

29. Several additional limitations relating to waiting periods and amounts excludable under Int. Rev. Code of 1954, § 105 (d) were added by the 1964 Revenue Act. See § 205, P.L. 88–272.

Section 104 (a) (1), for example, by excluding "amounts received under workmen's compensation acts as compensation for personal injuries or sickness," requires close examination to determine whether sums are being paid pursuant to statutes "in the nature of a workmen's compensation act" [30] and to compensate for personal injuries and sickness incurred in the performance of the taxpayer's duties.[31] The scope of "damages received . . . on account of personal injuries or sickness" [32] is somewhat less complex. The regulations extend its scope to amounts received in settlement of claims based "upon tort or tort type rights"; [33] but it is by no means certain that settlements in advance of anticipated injury [34] are entitled to the protection of this portion of section 104.

The exclusion of accident and health insurance proceeds not attributable to contributions paid directly by an

---

30. Treas. Reg. § 1.104–1 (b) (1956). William L. Neill, 17 T.C. 1015 (1951) (A).

31. Lottie Robinson, 42 T.C. 403, 408 (1964); Charles F. Brown, 25 T.C. 220 (1955). The issue is put clearly in *Brown*: "Even in those cases where exemption has been allowed on the theory that the disability payments were in the nature of 'amounts received . . . under workmen's compensation acts,' it has been universally recognized that the mere fact that the taxpayer was incapacitated at the time of retirement is not sufficient to bring the exemption into play. [Citation omitted.] Rather it must be shown, consistent with such theory, that the injury or sickness which caused such disability arose out of and was incurred in the taxpayer's regular performance of his duties. Normally, retirement pay is not exempt, whether or not the retirement is the result of disability, if such disability merely occurred during the period of employment." *Id.* at 222. Even when a disability incurred in the line of duty exists, retirement on account of age may deprive the taxpayer of this exclusion from gross income. See Simms v. Comm'r, 196 F.2d 238 (D.C. Cir. 1952). *But cf.* Prince v. United States, 119 F. Supp. 421 (Ct. Cl. 1954).

32. Int. Rev. Code of 1954, § 104 (a)(2).

33. Treas. Reg. 1.104–1 (e) (1956). The pertinent language is as follows: "The term 'damages received (whether by suit or agreement)' means an amount received (other than workmen's compensation) through prosecution of a legal suit or action based upon tort or tort type rights, or through a settlement agreement entered into in lieu of such prosecution."

34. See Starrels v. Comm'r, 304 F.2d 574 (9th Cir. 1962); chap. vi n. 37 *supra.*

employer also presents its share of issues. Thus, questions have arisen concerning its application to (1) amounts received under a matured endowment life insurance contract subsequent to the total disability of the insured and the resulting waiver of premiums due thereafter,[35] (2) sums representing replacement of lost income received under insurance contracts,[36] and (3) amounts to reimburse the taxpayer for certain overhead expenses incurred during prolonged disability due to injury or sickness.[37] In addition, somewhat complex regulations have been promulgated to assist the determination whether accident and health insurance proceeds are attributable to contributions by the employer.[38]

The range of problems under section 105 is even greater. The exclusion under subsection (b) of amounts intended to reimburse the taxpayer for medical expenses even when attributable to employer contributions may permit exclusion of multiple reimbursements of certain medical expenses.[39] The exclusion in subsection (c) of certain payments unrelated to absence from work requires determination of what constitutes a permanent loss of

35. Estate of Wong Wing Non, 18 T.C. 205 (1952) (litigants and Tax Court assumed that amount equal to face value of policy was within exclusion).

36. Rev. Rul. 58–90, 1958–1 C.B. 88 (income insurance proceeds excludable). To the same effect is Rev. Rule. 55–331, 1955–1 C.B. 271.

37. Rev. Rul. 55–264, 1955–1 C.B. 11 (overhead expense reimbursement includable in gross income).

38. Treas. Reg. § 1.105–1 (1956).

39. See H.R. Rep. No. 749, 88th Cong., 1st Sess. 43 (1963). The Revenue Act of 1964, as passed by the House, contained a provision to eliminate this possibility of double exclusion. This provision was deleted by the Senate and not restored in the Conference Committee. Exclusion of multiple reimbursement of medical expenses derived from insurance attributable to contributions by the employer appears contrary to the regulations which limit the exclusion under § 105 (b) to amounts not in excess of the actual expenses for medical care. Treas. Reg. § 1.105–2 (1956).

function of the body [40] or disfigurement.[41] Furthermore, the manner in which the amount of the payment is computed must be examined to ascertain whether it is "unrelated to absence from work." [42]

These issues, however, are relatively simple when contrasted with those spawned by section 105 (d). The pertinent statutory language excludes amounts which "constitute wages or payments in lieu of wages for a period during which the employee is absent from work on account of personal injuries or sickness." Thus, not only is it necessary to determine what constitutes "personal injuries or sickness," [43] but it is also necessary to fix the point in time after which continued employee absence can not be attributed to "personal injuries or sickness." [44] Moreover,

40. See Rev. Rul. 63–181, 1963–2 C.B. 74 (acute cancerous condition resulting in total and permanent disability constitutes a permanent loss of function of the body).

41. Treas. Reg. § 1.105–3 (1956) provides: "The term 'disfigurement' shall be given a reasonable interpretation in the light of all the particular facts and circumstances."

42. If the amount is fixed by reference to the period of absence from work, rather than the extent of bodily impairment, the exclusion of § 105 (c) is not available. Treas. Reg. § 1.105–3.

43. Brave efforts to distinguish absences due solely to pregnancy from those due to sickness attributable to pregnancy were made in two Revenue Rulings. See Rev. Rul. 55–263, 1955–1 C.B. 16; Rev. Rul. 59–170, 1959–1 C.B. 36.

44. Absence from work due to retirement because of age is not attributable to personal injuries or sickness even though during the retirement period the former employee endures personal injuries or sickness the origins of which are traceable to a point in time prior to retirement. Treas. Reg. § 1.105–4 (a)(3)(i) (1956). However, amounts received prior to retirement age attributable to absences caused by such personal injuries or sickness are excludable. Comm'r v. Winter, 303 F.2d 150 (3d Cir. 1962). This makes necessary a determination of the appropriate retirement age. Numerous rulings and cases have struggled with this problem. *E.g.*, Rev. Rul. 61–6, 1961–1 C.B. 15, modifying Rev. Rul. 57–76, 1957–1 C.B. 66; Rev. Rul. 58–544, 1958–2 C.B. 43; Comm'r v. Winter, *supra;* Corkum v. United States, 204 F. Supp. 471 (D. Mass. 1962). Bigley v. United States, 252 F. Supp. 757 (E.D. Mo. 1966), recently the Service announced that pending a re-examination of the area, cases similar to *Winter* would be disposed of in

(1) the limitation of the exclusion to the amount which does not exceed the weekly rate of $100; (2) the inapplicability of the exclusion (where the amounts paid exceed 75 per cent of the regular weekly wage rate) to the first 30 days of the period of sickness; and (3) the restricted applicability of the exclusion (where the amounts paid do not exceed the 75 per cent figure) during the first thirty-day period to amounts which do not exceed a weekly rate of $75 and which are not attributable to the first seven calendar days of the period unless the employee is hospitalized for at least one day of such seven-day period, suggest numerous additional problems. Thus, the applicability of the seven-day waiting period depends, in part, on the meaning of "hospitalization," [45] the necessity of the thirty-day waiting period on calculation of the "regular weekly rate of wages," [46] and the operative effect of the $100 limitation on the "weekly rate" of wage continuation payments. Finally, the availability of the exclusions under section 105 may turn on the existence of an "accident and health plan." [47]

---

accordance with that opinion. T.I.R. No. 822, May 31, 1966. It appears some never retire.

Similarly, absences during vacation periods can not be attributed to personal injuries or sickness even though the employee would have been forced to be absent from work because of these maladies had the vacation period not intervened. Harry Cohen, 41 T.C. 181 (1963); Edward I. Weinroth, 33 T.C. 58 (1959). This principle has been relaxed somewhat to permit the exclusion of pay attributable to a legal holiday when the taxpayer was absent from work on account of personal injuries or sickness on the day immediately preceding such legal holiday and on the next normal working day following such holiday. Rev. Rul. 63–219, 1963–2 C.B. 76.

45. See Treas. Reg. § 1.105–4 (e)(4) (1956).

46. See Treas. Reg. § 1.105–4 (e)(5) (1956).

47. Treas. Reg. § 1.105–5 (1956). Mere *"ad hoc"* benefit payments do not constitute a "plan." Estate of Kaufman v. Comm'r, 300 F.2d 128 (6th Cir. 1962). "A plan presupposes a predetermined course of action under prescribed circumstances, and a plan, for purposes of section 105 (d), must

The case for the fairly elaborate structure of sections
104 (a) (3) , 105, and 106 primarily rests not on Practicality, Equity, or Free Market Compatibility but rather on a
desire to encourage a greater allocation of resources to sick
care and injury reimbursement than would otherwise be
the case in order to provide employees, in particular, with
more security against the hazards of injury and illness.
Viewed in this manner, and on the assumption that the
tax system is the proper instrumentality to accomplish
this, the crucial issues become, first, the scope of the security which should be afforded, and, second, the means
which must be used to prevent abuse.[48] The legislative,
judicial, and administrative history from 1954 onward
reflect an increasing degree of involvement with these issues. The future is not likely to be different, except that
co-ordination of these provisions with sickness benefits
made available by governments will emerge as a problem.

---

do more than anticipate the favorable exercise of discretion by the
employer when sickness arises; it must be identified by more than an
occasional *ad hoc* benefit." John C. Lang, 41 T.C. 352, 356–57 (1963) . Also
see Estate of Chism v. Comm'r, 322 F.2d 956, 961 (9th Cir. 1963) .

48. It has been suggested that the 1964 Revenue Act provisions intended to reduce malingering may result in expanded medical insurance
programs. Costelloe, *A Sophisticated View of Fringe Benefits,* 43 Taxes 36,
45 (1965) . See n. 29 *supra.*

XVI. Selected "Fringe Benefits"

IN CHAPTER VI "working conditions" were distinguished from compensation paid in kind, and it was pointed out that the line between the two is often difficult to trace. In this chapter, two vexatious "fringe benefits," both governed by specific sections of the Code, will be examined. Because the general setting of the problems with which these sections are concerned was discussed in Chapter VI, present attention will be focused on the specific structure of the sections.

1. Group Term Life Insurance

In 1920 it was ruled that the gross income of employees did not include any amount in respect of premiums paid by employers on group term life insurance.[1] This view prevailed until 1964, at which time it was significantly qualified by legislation. During the intervening forty-four years, it was necessary on several occasions to distinguish between group term insurance and other forms of employ-

---

1. L.O. 1014, 2 C.B. 88 (1920); Treas. Reg. 45, art. 33 (1920). The exclusion appeared in all subsequent corresponding articles of the regulations. Its most recent appearance was in Treas. Reg. § 1.61–2 (d) (2) (1956), where it was provided: "Generally, life insurance premiums paid by an employer on the lives of his employees, where the proceeds of such insurance are payable to the beneficiaries of such employees, are part of the gross income of the employees. However, premiums paid by an employer on policies of group term life insurance covering the lives of his employees are not gross income to the employees, even if they designate the beneficiaries."

er-financed life insurance whose premiums were taxable to the employees.[2] Moreover, a distinction was drawn between those who were employees and those who were not. Only the former were entitled to the exclusion.[3] The originally stated justification for the exclusion was that the premium payment was an investment in increased efficiency rather than compensation.[4] Obviously, the difficulty in computing the portion of the premium properly attributable to any specific employee and the insignificant revenue involved also suggested an exclusion.

In 1963 it was estimated that the volume of group term insurance premiums had reached $840 million per year.[5] President Kennedy, in requesting that Congress alter the long-standing practice, explicitly described employer-paid premiums of group term insurance as a form of compensation.[6] Reduced Economic Inequality was marshaled in support by revealing that high-income executives sometimes obtained large coverage through so-called jumbo group term policies.[7]

Congress responded, but not precisely in the manner

2. G.C.M. 16069, XV–1 C.B. 84 (1936) (premiums on the ordinary type of life insurance taxable to employees); Mim. 6477, 1950–1 C.B. 16 (premiums on group-permanent life insurance policies taxable to employees except when employee's rights to permanent insurance, or equivalent benefits, other than current term insurance, is forfeitable in case of subsequent separation from service); Rev. Rul. 54–165, 1954–1 C.B. 17 (premiums paid by employer within exclusion where costs of any permanent or non-forfeitable features of policy are borne by employee).

3. Rev. Rul. 56–400, 1956–2 C.B. 116 (group hospitalization and life insurance premiums paid as compensation by others on behalf of salesmen who are neither common law employees nor employees defined in section 7701 (a) (20) of the Code includable in salesmen's income). Also see Edward P. Clay, 46 T.C. 48 (1966).

4. L.O. 1014, 2 C.B. 88, 89 (1920).

5. *President's 1963 Tax Message, Hearings Before the House Committee on Ways and Means*, 88th Cong., 1st Sess. 108 (1963).

6. *Id.* at 20.

7. *Id.* at 51.

requested by the President. His suggestion was that the annual value of employer-financed group term life insurance protection in excess of the first $5,000 of coverage be included in gross income.[8] The House broadened the $5,000 exclusion to $30,000,[9] the Senate to $70,000,[10] and in conference it was reduced to $50,000.[11] Thus, section 79 of the Code requires inclusion in gross income of the cost of group term life insurance provided by the insured's employer to the extent such cost exceeds the cost of $50,000 of such insurance plus any amount paid by the insured toward the purchase of such insurance.[12] It does not, however, attempt to define "group term life insurance"; presumably the distinctions developed during the 1920–64 period between such insurance and other types of employer-financed coverage will continue to have force.[13] In any event, the regulations do attempt a fairly comprehensive definition of the term.[14] In addition, the meaning of the term "policy" must be fixed inasmuch as section 79

8. *Id.* at 20.

9. H.R. REP. No. 749, 88th Cong., 1st Sess. 40 (1963).

10. S. REP. No. 830, 88th Cong., 2d Sess. 46 (1964).

11. H.R. REP. No. 1149, 88th Cong., 2d Sess. 21 (1964).

12. Int. Rev. Code of 1954, § 79 (a). For an illustration of the manner in which the contribution of the insured employee reduces the amount included in gross income, see S. REP. No. 830, 88th Cong., 2d Sess. 48–49 (1964). The point of the illustration is that the cost of group-term insurance in excess of $50,000 coverage is reduced by the employee contribution to determine the amount of such cost included in the gross income of the insured employee.

13. Certain of these distinctions have been carried forward in the Regulations under § 79. See Treas. Reg. 1.79–1 (b)(1)(ii) (1966) which states that permitting an employee to convert (or continue) term insurance protection after the employer ceases to provide it does not constitute "permanent insurance." See n. 2 *supra.*

14. Treas. Reg. § 1.79–1 (b)(1) (1966). Observe that this regulation requires that in order to constitute "a plan of group insurance" it must include a group of employees selected "on the basis of factors which preclude individual selection." § 1.79–1 (b)(1)(iii)(b).

reaches only group term life insurance made available under "a policy (or policies) ." [15]

The previously mentioned difficulty in determining the extent to which premium costs should be attributed to individual employees was dealt with by granting authority to prescribe by regulations uniform premiums computed on the basis of five-year age brackets.[16] These uniform premiums are favorable to the employee taxpayers, and at present they appear not to reflect loading charges.[17] If

15. Int. Rev. Code of 1954, § 79 (a). Proposed Treas. Reg. 1.79–1 (b)(1)(ii)(b), 29 Fed. Reg. 10517 (1964), provided that the term did not include a "contract, or portion of a contract, to the extent it is a contract of travel insurance or accident and health insurance which does not provide general death benefits." Moreover, the term did not embrace "a double indemnity clause or rider, since under such portion of a contract only an accident benefit is payable." This position appears to have been derived from the Conference Committee Report, which stated: "In providing for the inclusion, to the extent specified, in a taxpayer's income of certain amounts representing the cost of group-term life insurance, it is not intended that such insurance include the death benefits in so-called travel insurance or accident and health policies where such policies do not provide general death benefits." H.R. REP. No. 1149, 88th Cong., 2d Sess. 21 (1964). Also see *President's 1963 Tax Message, Hearings Before the House Committee on Ways and Means,* 88th Cong., 1st Sess. 109 (1963). The final regulations reach the same result but eliminate the stress on the term "policy (or policies)." Rather, it is said § 79 "only applies to insurance which provides general death benefits." Treas. Reg. 1.79–1 (b)(1)(i) (1966).

16. Int. Rev. Code of 1954, § 79 (c). In the House version of § 79 the employer was permitted to elect between the uniform premium table method and an actual average-premium-cost method. See H.R. REP. No. 749, 88th Cong., 1st Sess. 41 (1963). The latter method was eliminated by the Senate on the grounds that the computations required were difficult and that, since no loading charges were reflected in the uniform premium table method, such method in any event would result in a cost lower than actual average premium cost. See S. REP. No. 830, 88th Cong., 2d Sess. 48 (1964). The Conference Committee accepted the Senate version. See Treas. Reg. § 1.79–3 (d) (1966).

17. See Treas. Reg. § 1.79–3 (d) (1966). In rejecting the actual average-premium-cost method, the Senate Finance Committee set forth a uniform premium table computed on the basis of five-year age brackets which was to govern "until provided otherwise by regulation" and which did not include loading charges. See S. REP. No. 830, 88th Cong., 2d Sess. 47, 48 (1964). The Conference Committee expressed the hope that the uniform premium table set forth as indicated would be reviewed to determine whether it reflects recent mortality experience and whether

sufficiently favorable, significant pressure toward expanding the scope of the terms "group term life insurance" and "policy" will be exerted.[18] The use of uniform premium tables does not eliminate all practical problems, however. It remains necessary to fix the employee's contribution and to ascertain the group term life insurance costs under employer-financed arrangements providing benefits other than such insurance.[19]

In addition to the tenfold increase in the amount of employer-financed coverage which results in no inclusion in the gross income of employees, Congress also limited the Administration's suggestions by creating several exceptions to the general rule of inclusion. The first makes inapplicable the rule of inclusion in respect of retired or disabled employees.[20] Apparently the desire is to avoid any possible hardship which might arise from the necessity of paying tax on a form of compensation not reducible to cash.[21] Practicality and the desire to give aid and comfort to the aged prevailed. To come within this exception, the employee must have "terminated" his employment and either have reached "retirement age" or be "disabled." All three terms present their share of minor problems.[22] The

---

some allowance for expenses should be made. A somewhat different and more favorable table is set forth in the Treasury Regulations, § 1.79–3 (d)(2) (1966). There is no indication that this table includes loading charges. It is said that the Treasury table uses figures below actual group term insurance costs to employers.

18. Treas. Reg. § 1.79–3 (d)(3) (1966) states that the table does not apply to "group-term life insurance" not within the scope of § 79 (a) of the Code. Also see Proposed Treas. Reg. § 1.79–3 (b), 29 Fed. Reg. 10519 (1964).

19. See Treas. Reg. § 1.79–3 (e)(3) (1966).

20. Int. Rev. Code of 1954, § 79 (b)(1).

21. See H.R. Rep. No. 749, 88th Cong., 1st Sess. 40 (1963); S. Rep. No. 830, 88th Cong., 2d Sess. 46–47 (1964).

22. "Termination" refers to cessation of the rendition of services as an employee. Treas. Reg. § 1.79–2 (b)(2) (1966). "Retirement age" presents a

second exception removes from the reach of section 79 those instances where the employer is the beneficiary of the insurance. Under these circumstances the premiums bear little resemblance to compensation.[23]

The third exception also turns on the identity of the beneficiary. Section 79 does not require inclusion of any amount when the beneficiary is a charitable organization.[24] The committee reports indicate that the exception is based upon a difficulty which besets many efforts to tax as income compensation paid in kind—the inappropriateness of including the receipt at its full value when it was neither sought after nor desired by the employee.[25] They point out that designation of a charity suggests employee disinterest in receiving the coverage and, hence, the inclusion rules should not be invoked.[26] In view of tax law's deep involvement in the promotion of philanthropic objectives, this bit of motivational analysis may be somewhat incomplete. In any event, these exceptions make necessary an allocation of amounts paid by the employee between insurance coverage within the rule of inclusion and that which is not.[27]

---

problem similar to that encountered in distinguishing sick pay from disability pensions. See chap. xv n. 44 *supra.* A definition somewhat similar to that used in the sick-pay area is set forth in Treas. Reg. § 1.79–2 (b) (3) (1966). "Disabled" is defined by tying it to the meaning given the term in section 213 (g)(3), after disregarding paragraph (4) of section 213 (g).

23. See H.R. REP. No. 749, 88th Cong., 1st Sess. 40 (1963); S. REP. No. 830, 88th Cong., 2d Sess. 47 (1964).

24. Int. Rev. Code of 1954, § 79 (b)(2)(B). Of course, no charitable deduction is available to the employee in such instances. H.R. REP. No. 749, 88th Cong., 1st Sess. 41 (1963); S. REP. No. 830, 88th Cong., 2d Sess. 47 (1964).

25. See n. 23 *supra.*

26. See H.R. REP. No. 749, 88th Cong., 1st Sess. 41 (1963); S. REP. No. 830, 88th Cong., 2d Sess. 47 (1964).

27. See Treas. Reg. § 1.79–2 (a)(2) (1966).

The last exception is a technical one. It co-ordinates section 79 with the pre-existing treatment of life insurance contracts purchased under qualified employee plans.[28] Generally, the cost of this insurance protection is included in the gross income of the employee, and section 79 in no way alters this treatment.

The future developments in this area are difficult to foresee. Perhaps some of the problems here mentioned will generate statutory solutions; or perhaps the Administration will renew its efforts to reduce the death benefit exclusion by any amount of insurance proceeds received by reason of group term life insurance coverage.[29] Another possibility is a reduction of the present $50,000 limit on tax-free coverage. It is clear, however, that present provisions, while representing an improvement over the 1920–64 rules, still fall short when measured by Equity and Free Market Compatibility. To the extent there has been improvement, it has been at the expense of Practicality (section 79 is more complicated than the old rules), but without significant sacrifice of the particularized objectives of family security and vigorous philanthropy.

2. *Meals and Lodging Furnished for the Convenience of the Employer*

While the problems of group term life insurance only recently have come to the forefront, those pertaining to meals and lodging furnished for the convenience of the employer have long occupied the attention of tax men. As

28. Int. Rev. Code of 1954, § 72 (m)(3).

29. President Kennedy's message explicitly requested that group term life insurance proceeds reduce the $5,000 exclusion of death benefits now provided by section 101 (b). See chap. xiii *supra*. This was thought necessary to prevent a double benefit. *President's 1963 Tax Message, Hearings Before the House Committee on Ways and Means*, 88th Cong., 1st Sess. 108 (1963).

pointed out in Chapter VI, the problem has been to distinguish meals and lodging which amount to compensation from those more appropriately classified as "working conditions." Because of the shadowy nature of this distinction and the frequency with which employees are furnished meals and lodging, it became necessary very early in income tax history to face the difficulties of this area.

It has been said that in 1914 the Treasury first indicated that quarters furnished for the convenience of the employer were not taxable.[30] It appears that this view was expressed as a qualification, applicable to quarters furnished to officers in *excess* of those required by law, to a ruling which included in gross income commutation of quarters (or their value if furnished in kind) to the extent such commutation was allowed by law. *Excess* quarters were presumed to be for convenience of the employer and not taxable. It is difficult to condemn this initial effort. Assuming a rational military organization, additional quarters must serve predominantly an employer purpose other than that of providing compensation. Nonetheless, a phrase, "for convenience of the employer," was introduced which has yet to cease confounding both the doctors and the students of tax law.

Almost five years later, it appeared in the regulations issued under the Revenue Act of 1918. Its function then was to exclude from gross income "living quarters such as camps [which are] furnished to employees for the convenience of the employer." [31] This appears to have opened a

30. Comment, *Tax Treatment of Compensation in Kind,* 37 CALIF. L. REV. 628, 632 (1949). The author cites T.D. 2079, 16 TREAS. DEC. INT. REV. 249 (1914).

31. T.D. 2831, 21 TREAS. DEC. INT. REV. 170, 180 (1919). The complete statement is as follows: "When living quarters such as camps are furnished to employees for the convenience of the employer, the ratable value need not be added to the cash compensation of the employee, but where a

door. The distinction between "camps" and board and lodging furnished seamen is by no means obvious. Hence, the latter was also excluded by an Office Decision.[32] Again, "convenience of the employer" was employed by the ruling. "Supper money" given to an employee who voluntarily performs after-hours work,[33] and quarters and meals furnished hospital employees subject to call on a twenty-four hour basis were also excluded by reason of the beguiling phrase.[34] Similarly, "lodging and sustenance" furnished fishing and canning employees because of the location and nature of their work were not included in gross income.[35]

The Commissioner, however, did not permit the phrase to divert his entire attention from the compensatory aspect of meals and lodgings. The value of lodgings furnished Indian Service employees was taxable when the Department of Interior treated it as compensation.[36] When not so treated, it was assumed quarters were furnished for the convenience of the employer. When it subsequently appeared that the Department normally regarded quarters furnished as a part of the compensation without regard to the manner in which the internal accounting for them was done, the Commissioner obliged by requiring inclusion in gross income.[37] Hospital employees

---

person receives as compensation for services rendered a salary and in addition thereto living quarters, the value to such person of the quarters furnished constitutes income subject to tax."

32. O.D. 265, 1 C.B. 71 (1919).

33. O.D. 514, 2 C.B. 90 (1920).

34. O.D. 915, 4 C.B. 85 (1921).

35. O.D. 814, 4 C.B. 84 (1921).

36. O.D. 914, 4 C.B. 85 (1921).

37. I.T. 2051, III–2 C.B. 55 (1924). Quarters furnished officers and employees of the Public Health Service also were treated as compensation. O.D. 1098, 5 C.B. 85 (1921).

whose duties made it possible to obtain meals and lodging elsewhere were considered to have received additional compensation when they availed themselves of employer-furnished meals and lodging.[38] Board and lodging furnished a domestic servant "as part of his compensation" were also included.[39]

This dichotomy set the stage for the initial court test in the area. In *Jones* v. *United States* [40] the taxpayer, an army officer, contended that the value of public quarters and the sum of commutation of quarters furnished to him not in excess of that allowed by law were not taxable. The Government asserted the contrary. The issue, as framed by the court, was whether these items were "compensation." In holding that they were not, it was pointed out that the taxpayer was "paid a salary to live in the quarters furnished" and not furnished housing and cash as compensation for his services.[41] The quarters, as well as the commutation, were regarded as necessary to proper rendition of the duties required of the taxpayer and the successful accomplishment of the employer's enterprise.[42]

Thus, the scope of "working conditions" was significantly broadened while that of taxable compensation was narrowed. The contents of the periodic pay envelope, to

38. O.D. 915, 4 C.B. 85 (1921).

39. O.D. 874, 4 C.B. 348 (1921). Quarters furnished to missionaries who are not ordained ministers were taxable. I.T. 1306, I–1 C.B. 110 (1922).

40. 60 Ct. Cl. 552 (1925).

41. *Id.* at 570.

42. "If the nature of the services require the furnishing of a house for their proper performance, and without it the services may not properly be rendered, the house so furnished is part of the maintenance of the general enterprise, an overhead expense, so to speak, and forms no part of the individual income of the laborer." *Id.* at 575. The court relied on Tenant v. Smith, [1892] A.C. 150, which excluded from the income of a bank employee the accommodations within the bank which he was required to occupy.

the extent of base "pay," was compensation, but other receipts fell within the doubtful category. The Commissioner struggled to confine the *Jones* case within narrow limits,[43] but concessions had to be made.[44] However, the regulations remained substantially unchanged.

In *Benaglia* v. *Commissioner*,[45] the Government suffered another defeat. The taxpayer, general manager of two hotels, was permitted to exclude meals and lodging furnished by the employer "solely because he [the taxpayer] could not otherwise perform the services required of him." [46] Under these circumstances "occupation of the premises was imposed upon him for the convenience of the employer." [47] Three years later, the Government perhaps sought to improve its position by subtly shifting the emphasis of the regulations from the "convenience of the

43. In Ralph Kitchen, 11 B.T.A. 855 (1928), meals and lodging furnished the president of a corporation engaged in operating a hotel were taxable when evidence failed to show they were "solely for the convenience of his employer." Allowances for living quarters furnished employees of the United States stationed abroad taxable as compensation. G.C.M. 11453, XII–1 C.B. 26 (1933). Veterans Administration employees taxable on value of quarters, subsistence, heat and light furnished by employer when Act of Congress treated them as part of compensation. I.T. 2692, XII–1 C.B. 28 (1933).

44. Board and room furnished domestics "required to remain on duty and subject to call the entire time" not taxable. I.T. 2253, V–1 C.B. 32 (1926). *Jones* case extended to members of Coast Guard, Coast and Geodetic Survey, and Public Health Service, I.T. 2232, IV–2 C.B. 144 (1925). A similar extension took in rental allowances paid military chaplains, I.T. 2760, XIII–1 C.B. 35 (1934), revoking I.T. 1307, I–1 C.B. 110 (1922). Allowances for living quarters paid Foreign Service employees of State Department not taxable, but "cost of living" adjustments were taxable, G.C.M. 12300, XII–2 C.B. 30 (1933). Exclusion was also accorded allowance for living quarters furnished employees of the Foreign Commerce Service of the Bureau of Foreign and Domestic Commerce, G.C.M. 14710, XIV–1 C.B. 44 (1935), revoking G.C.M. 13442, XIII–2 C.B. 119 (1934), and to Treasury attachés and their subordinates, G.C.M. 14836, XIV–1 C.B. 45 (1935), revoking G.C.M. 11453, XII–1 C.B. 26 (1933).

45. 36 B.T.A. 838 (1937).

46. *Id.* at 839.

47. *Id.* at 840.

employer" test to the compensatory standard.[48] Exclusion was made to depend heavily upon whether acceptance of meals and lodging furnished by the employer was necessary in order to perform properly the duties of the position.[49]

In the following year, 1941, the Government won a significant victory. In *Martin* [50] the Board of Tax Appeals refused to permit a wireless operator, employed by the United States Army Engineers on its dredging vessels, to exclude from his gross income an amount which was deducted from his base pay to reimburse the Engineers for lodging and subsistence furnished him while on board the vessels. Although it was recognized that the exigencies of the situation required that the taxpayer obtain his meals and lodging on board ship, the required reimbursement

---

48. T.D. 4965, 1940–1 C.B. 13. The shift was accomplished in the following fashion. The old regulation read: "If living quarters such as camps are furnished to employees for the convenience of the employer, the ratable value need not be added to the cash compensation of the employees, but if a person receives as compensation for services rendered a salary and in addition thereto living quarters, the value to such person of the quarters furnished constitutes income subject to tax." As amended it read: "If a person receives as compensation for services rendered a salary and in addition thereto living quarters or meals, the value to such person of the quarters and meals so furnished constitutes income subject to tax. If, however, living quarters or meals are furnished to employees for the convenience of the employer, the value thereof need not be computed and added to the compensation otherwise received by the employees." This change was described in Mim. 5023, 1940–1 C.B. 14 as a "clarification." It was further stated: "Except as indicated below, if living quarters or meals are furnished to an employee, the value thereof to him constitutes income subject to tax and must, therefore, be included in his gross income as compensation. If, however, the living quarters or meals furnished are not compensatory or are furnished for the convenience of the employer, the value thereof need not be added to the compensation otherwise received by the employee."

49. Mim. 5023, 1940–1 C.B. 14, 15 observed: "As a general rule, the test of 'convenience of the employer' is satisfied if living quarters or meals are furnished to an employee who is required to accept such quarters and meals in order to perform properly his duties."

50. 44 B.T.A. 185 (1941).

stamped the items as compensation.[51] This was a position long espoused by the Government.[52] While the distinction between meals and lodging furnished without charge and those made available under an arrangement requiring reimbursement may in some instances appear more one of form than substance, it is true that requiring reimbursement at least suggests that the items were intended as compensation. Moreover, the acceptance in *Martin* as the touchstone of inclusion provided the Government with a guideline easy to administer.

Nonetheless, the cases continued to prove troublesome; [53] and in 1950 the Government moved once again to strengthen and clarify its position.[54] Citing *Martin,* the Commissioner made exclusion turn on whether the "circumstances involved" demonstrate that the quarters and meals do not represent "compensation for services rendered." The "convenience of the employer" test was said to be an administrative test, applicable only when "the com-

51. At 44 B.T.A. 189 the Board summarized its reasoning as follows: "In the present case, petitioner was required to receive his subsistence and occupy quarters on board ship by the exigencies of the situation, but meals and lodging furnished to petitioner was obviously not considered or treated by him or his employer as an allowance or gratuity. Petitioner received compensation of $2100 per year for his services, and paid to his employer $40 per month for his keep while on board ship. The entire amount of his compensation is taxable income to petitioner, without deduction or exclusion of his living expenses."

52. *Cf.* I.T. 2692, XII–1 C.B. 28 (1933).

53. Olin O. Ellis, 6 T.C. 138 (1946) (taxpayer, president of employer, permitted to exclude only a portion of rental value of apartment even though no charge made for the entire apartment); Lloyd N. Farnham, 6 T.C.M. 1049 (1947) (apartment occupied by janitor excluded notwithstanding employer requiring reimbursement when purpose of such reimbursement was to minimize danger of sit-down strike); Hazel W. Carmichael, 7 T.C.M. 278 (1948) (determination made with respect to various employees of Government housing project and in all instances some reliance placed on whether reimbursement for employee-occupied quarters required).

54. Mim. 6472, 1950–1 C.B. 15.

pensatory character of such benefits is not otherwise determinable." Thus, twenty-five years after the *Jones* decision, the Government sought to recover most of the ground lost thereby. The Tax Court accepted this position;[55] but it was rejected by the Second Circuit.[56]

Resolution of the issue was taken from the hands of the judiciary by congressional enactment of the 1954 Code. Section 119 rescued the "convenience of the employer" test from the exile imposed in 1950 and made it the basic test of exclusion;[57] that is, when it is determined that meals and lodging are furnished primarily for the convenience of the employer, it is unimportant that the surrounding circumstances also indicate that they were intended as compensation.[58] The exclusion remains available, provid-

55. Charles A. Brasher, 22 T.C. 637 (1954) (food and housing furnished for convenience of employer taxable when furnished to and received by taxpayers as compensation); Joseph L. Doran, 21 T.C. 374 (1953) (convenience of employer merely one test to determine whether meals and lodging are compensation). Also see Herman J. Romer, 28 T.C. 1228 (1957); Leslie Dietz, 25 T.C. 1255 (1956). *But cf.* William H. Kenner, 20 T.C.M. 185 (1961) (quarters furnished for convenience of employer excludable but evidence showed not so furnished); George I. Stone, 32 T.C. 1021 (1959) (living quarters and meals excluded when for convenience of employer; compensatory test not used).

56. Diamond v. Sturr, 221 F.2d 264 (2d Cir. 1955). This rejection was specifically applicable to the taxable year 1949. It is not entirely clear it reached beyond this period.

57. S. Rep. No. 1622, 83d Cong., 2d Sess. 19 (1954).

58. The statute is not as clear on this as it might be. After providing that meals and lodging furnished for the convenience of the employer are excluded, providing the explicit conditions are met, the section concludes with this sentence: "In determining whether meals or lodging are furnished for the convenience of the employer, the provisions of an employment contract or of a state statute fixing terms of employment shall not be determinative of whether the meals or lodging are intended as compensation." The importance of whether meals and lodging are intended as compensation is not made clear. However, the Senate Report observes: "Under section 119, as amended by your committee, there is excluded from the gross income of an employee the value of meals and lodging furnished to him for the convenience of his employer whether or not such meals or lodging are furnished as compensation." S. Rep. No. 1622, 83d Cong., 2d

ing, in the case of meals, that they "are furnished on the business premises of the employer" and, in the case of lodging, "the employee is required to accept such lodging on the business premises of his employer as a condition of his employment."

Restoration of the "convenience of the employer" standard perhaps broadens the scope of the exclusion, but it does not significantly diminish the difficulty of ascertaining whether a particular benefit should be excluded. Thus, in original regulations promulgated under the section, after pointing out that the exclusion applies only to meals and lodging furnished in kind, it was stated that meals and lodging for which the employee was required to reimburse the employer were included in gross income.[59] The Commissioner pressed the interpretation in *Boykin* v. *Commissioner*,[60] where the taxpayer, a physician employed by the Veterans Administration, was required to occupy assigned quarters in order properly to perform his duties. The Administration treated the fair rental value of the quarters as compensation and deducted this amount from the taxpayer's salary. Quite properly, the court rejected this somewhat circuitous effort to return compensatory intent to a paramount position in this limited class of cases and held that the fair rental value was correctly

---

Sess. 190 (1954). Nonetheless, it is by no means clear that the presence of an intent that meals and lodging be compensatory is irrelevant in determining whether such meals and lodging are furnished for the convenience of the employer. Perhaps the 1954 Code exchanged the functions of these two standards, *i.e.*, the compensatory-intent test became merely an "administrative test" to be applied only in cases when the convenience-of-the-employer character of such benefits is not otherwise determinable. If so, the concluding sentence of § 119 does not permit the establishment of such intent by exclusive reliance on "the provisions of an employment contract or of a state statute fixing terms of employment."

59. Treas. Reg. § 1.119-1 (c) (1956).

60. 260 F.2d 249 (8th Cir. 1958).

excluded from the taxpayer's gross income.[61] The Commissioner amended his regulations to conform to this view.[62]

The complexity of the "convenience of the employer" standard is not significantly reduced by the fact that in the case of lodging a large portion of its function is carried by the two explicit statutory requirements that lodging be furnished on the employer's business premises and the employee be required to accept it as a condition of his employment. This is true because, although compliance with these two requirements often assures that the "convenience of the employer" standard is met, it is difficult in many instances to determine whether the two requirements are satisfied.

The existing regulations state that an employee is required to accept lodging as a condition of employment

61. Building on the Congressional intent to restrict § 119 to meals and lodging furnished in kind, the Commissioner argued that this required that the benefits be furnished gratuitously. Otherwise, he reasoned, the employer was furnishing money, not meals and lodging in kind. *Id.* at 251–52. His regulations set forth this position by stating, "The exclusion provided by section 119 applies only to meals and lodging furnished in kind, without charge or cost to the employee." Treas. Reg. § 1.119–1 (c)(2) (1956). The Tax Court accepted the position of the Commissioner, interpreting the restriction of the statute to benefits furnished in kind as Congressional approval of their result reached in Herman Martin, 44 B.T.A. 185 (1941). See J. Melvin Boykin, 29 T.C. 813 (1958). In view of the manner in which *Martin* was employed by the Commissioner in Mim. 6472, 1950–1 C.B. 15, and the explicit purpose of the 1954 legislation to reject the Commissioner's position as therein stated, it would have been quite strange to have the case obtain renewed vitality in this manner. The circuit court's view in *Boykin*, n. 60, *supra*, was accepted in Powell v. White, 58–2 U.S.T.C. ¶ 9559 (S.D. Ill.) and Wolf v. Commissioner, 59–2 U.S.T.C. ¶ 9558 (4th Cir.).

62. After setting forth the three requirements essential to exclusion of lodging, *i.e.*, (1) convenience of the employer, (2) furnished on employer's business premises, and (3) acceptance of lodging a condition of employment, the amended regulations provide: "If the tests described in sub-paragraphs (1), (2), and (3) of this paragraph are met, the exclusion shall apply irrespective of whether a charge is made, or whether, under an employment contract or statute fixing the terms of employment, such lodging is furnished as compensation." Treas. Reg. § 1.119–1 (b) (1956), as amended by T.D. 6745, 1964–2 C.B. 42.

when acceptance is necessary in order to enable him properly to perform his duties.[63] But when, if ever, is it necessary that a corporate president and principal shareholder occupy lodging on the business premises properly to perform his duties? [64] Moreover, must it appear that performance of the duties is almost impossible in the absence of occupancy of the quarters,[65] or is it sufficient that the employer, for no apparent reason, made occupancy a condition of employment.[66]

The scope of the term "business premises" is also more troublesome, even as it relates to lodging, than might be expected. The "U.S. Jaycee White House," a residential structure located three miles from the headquarters of the United States Junior Chamber of Commerce and used by its president as his official residence, is not obviously located on the employer's business premises even though its situs was so determined by the Court of Claims.[67] Business premises to the court simply meant the premises of the employer on which the employee's duties were performed. Even this link with employer-owned estates in land has been broken in the case of meals. A highway patrolman,

63. Treas. Reg. § 1.119–1 (b) (1956) , as amended by T.D. 6745, 1964–2 C.B. 42.

64. Mary B. Heyward, 36 T.C. 739 (1961) (no necessity that quarters be occupied by president and principal shareholder properly to perform his duties) .

65. *Cf.* United States Junior Chamber of Commerce v. United States, 334 F. 2d 660 (Ct. Cl. 1964) , where virtual impossibility was rejected, and it was pointed out it should be sufficient if the employment required a certain type of residence which the employer would not normally have available for use of his employee.

66. The Tax Court insists that occupancy of the quarters be related to the employee's tasks and that this is an objective test. Thus, an employer's requirement that the quarters be occupied would not provide insulation from tax when the objective test is not met. See Mary B. Heyward, 36 T.C. 739 (1961) ; Gordon S. Dole, 43 T.C. 697, 706 (1965) .

67. United States Junior Chamber of Commerce v. United States, 334 F.2d 660 (Ct. Cl. 1964) .

employed by the state of Mississippi, has been permitted to exclude from income reimbursement of meals purchased by him in restaurants during his twelve-hour day of patrol duty on the highways.[68] On the other hand, the First Circuit accepts the view that business premises mean the place at which occurs the actual conduct of the employer's business.[69]

It is employee consumption of meals furnished by the employer on his business premises and unaccompanied by lodging which under section 119 forces the most direct confrontation with the meaning of the "convenience of the employer" standard. In most such instances an employer purpose of some sort is served while only those few employees with extremely fastidious tastes honestly can assert that the free meals do not convenience them. In short, the arrangement usually is mutually convenient. While it appears to be accepted that whether the "convenience of the employer" standard is met is primarily a question of fact,[70] this does not indicate the manner in

68. United States v. Barrett, 321 F.2d 911 (5th Cir. 1963). The same result was reached in United States v. Morelan, 356, F.2d 199 (8th Cir. 1966). The Service refuses to follow these decisions. T.I.R. No. 741 (June 21, 1957), in its view, highway patrolmen continue to be governed by 1939 Code decisions such as Charles H. Hyslope, 21 T.C. 131 (1953) and Saunders v. Comm'r, 215 F.2d 768 (3d Cir. 1954).

69. Dole v. Comm'r., 351 F.2d 308 (1st Cir. 1965). This per curiam decision adopted Judge Raum's concurring opinion in the Tax Court proceedings which denied that "on the business premises" meant some reasonably convenient place located nearby the premises on which the employer's business was conducted. See Gordon S. Dole, 43 T.C. 697, 708 (1965). Only the latter spot constitutes business premises as he saw it. Judge Dawson's opinion in *Dole* was more generous to the taxpayer. It contained the following sentence: "We think the phrase [business premises] should be construed to mean either (1) living quarters that constitute an integral part of the business property or (2) premises on which the company carries on some of its business activities." 43 T.C. at 707. *Cf.* Charles N. Anderson, 42 T.C. 410 (1964).

70. William I. Olkjer, 32 T.C. 464 (1959); George I. Stone, 32 T.C. 1021 (1959).

which employer and employee convenience are to be evaluated in applying the standard. Nor does it suggest what account, if any, is to be taken of a compensatory intent on the part of the employer in determining whether the meals are to be excluded.

The original regulations appeared to suggest that any employer business purpose, other than providing additional compensation, was sufficient to remove the meals from gross income.[71] The current regulations are much more restrictive. Presence of a "substantial non-compensatory business reason" is necessary to have the meals regarded as furnished for the convenience of the employer.[72] Any lesser "non-compensatory business reason" is subordinate to a compensatory reason. Thus, much depends on the scope of the term "substantial." Interpreted broadly and with a Government bias, it could give renewed vitality to the old 1954 Code compensatory intent test,[73] but this would not appear consistent with the intent

71. "Likewise, meals furnished immediately preceding or immediately following working hours of the employee will be deemed to be for the convenience of the employer if the furnishing of such meals serves a business purpose of the employer other than providing additional or indirect compensation to the employee." Treas. Reg. § 1.119–1 (a)(2) (1956), as amended by T.D. 6745, 1964–2 C.B. 42.

72. "Meals furnished by an employer without charge to the employee will be regarded as furnished for the convenience of the employer if such meals are furnished for a substantial noncompensatory business reason of the employer. If an employer furnishes meals as a means of providing additional compensation to his employee (and not for a substantial noncompensatory business reason of the employer), the meals so furnished will not be regarded as furnished for the convenience of the employer. Conversely, if the employer furnishes meals to his employee for a substantial noncompensatory business, the meals so furnished will be regarded as furnished for the convenience of the employer, even though such meals are also furnished for a compensatory reason." Treas. Reg. § 1.119–1 (a)(2), as amended by T.D. 6745, 1964–2 C.B. 42.

73. That is, a compensatory intent would overcome almost any non-compensatory reason on the ground of its lack of substantiality. Such a posture would be reminiscent of Ralph Kitchen, 11 B.T.A. 855 (1928), which made exclusion turn on whether meals and lodging were furnished

of Congress in enacting section 119.[74] In this area, however, the necessity to fight old battles over and over is characteristic. In any event, the existence of a compensatory intent cannot rest exclusively on "provisions of an employment contract or of a State statute fixing terms of employment." [75]

No prescience is required to assert that the end of the process of interpretation described here is not in sight. Moreover, it is probable that the use of meals and, to a lesser extent, lodging as a fringe benefit has increased in

---

"solely" for the employer's convenience. This interpretation was rejected under the 1939 Code, Olin O. Ellis, 6 T.C. 138 (1946), and also would be improper under the 1954 Code. *Cf.* Carlton R. Mabley, 34 T.C. Memo 1963 (1965).

74. The Senate Report gives little assistance to an effort to read "substantial" as the equivalent of "all-embracing," "exclusive," "heavily preponderant," or the like. In the general explanation the Committee said: "Your committee has provided that the basic test of exclusion is to be whether the meals are furnished primarily for the convenience of the employer (and thus excludable) or whether they were primarily for the convenience of the employee (and therefore taxable)." S. REP. No. 1622, 83d Cong., 2d Sess. 19 (1954). The technical explanation at 190 in the same report provides even less support. It states: "Under section 119 as amended by your committee, there is excluded from the gross income of an employee the value of meals or lodging furnished to him for the convenience of his employer whether or not such meals or lodging are furnished as compensation."

75. The last sentence of § 119 provides: "In determining whether meals or lodging are furnished for the convenience of the employer, the provisions of an employment contract or of a State statute fixing terms of employment shall not be determinative whether the meals or lodging are intended as compensation." The current regulations provide that if under its tests meals are furnished on the employer's business premises and for his convenience, "the exclusion shall apply irrespective of whether under an employment contract or a statute fixing the terms of employment such meals are furnished as compensation." Treas. Reg. § 1.119–1 (a) (1956), as amended by T.D. 6745, 1964–2 C.B. 42. In theory this leaves unsettled the situation where meals are furnished for an "insubstantial" non-compensatory business reason and the only evidence of a compensatory intent is such an employment contract or statute. The text takes the position that because of the last sentence of § 119 even an "insubstantial" non-compensatory business reason justifies exclusion under these circumstances. Usually, when non-compensatory business reasons are insubstantial, other evidence of a compensatory purpose will be available.

recent years.[76] Certainly, it is probable that meals furnished by employers are of better quality than would be purchased by the employees from compensation paid in money. Quality improvement is the price demanded by employees for their loss of choice.[77]

Equity, rigorously pursued, dictates the inclusion of meals and lodging at their fair market value, even though this value may be more or less than the employee would have been willing to pay had he received cash.[78] Free Market Compatibility points in the same direction.[79] The contribution which any possible increase in consumption may make to Stability is negligible. Perhaps section 119 contributes to employer paternalism, an attitude consistent with the political tenets of some. Finally, Reduced Economic Inequality and Adequacy furnish little guidance, although the first may faintly suggest approval (at least as long as the benefits are enjoyed by rank-and-file employees) and the latter, the contrary. On balance, the case for section 119 is not a strong one. Only the practical convenience of avoiding the problems of valuation which inclusion would create strongly supports it.

76. In 1963 it was reported that fringe benefits, including a large segment consisting of free lunches, have increased from $3.8 billion in 1946 to $20.6 billion in 1962. Wall St. Jour., May 14, 1963, p. 1, col. 6.

77. MACAULAY, FRINGE BENEFITS AND THEIR FEDERAL TAX TREATMENT, 163–64 (1959).

78. *Cf.* Reginald Turner, 13 T.C.M. 462 (1954) (prize consisting of an opportunity to enjoy a luxury beyond means of recipient valued at below its retail cost).

79. Macaulay, n. 77 *supra,* at 162, also suggests that fringe benefits such as meals and lodging tend to reduce employee incentive to work. However, this may depend upon the income level of the recipient. *Id.* at 48–50. Low-income taxpayers furnished meals for the convenience of the employer may offer fewer hours on the labor market than they would were the extra compensation paid in cash subject to tax. That is, the income effect of the tax is reduced when compensation is paid in a form not subject to tax. High-income taxpayers, however, may substitute work for leisure when the marginal return is not subject to tax. That is, the fringe benefit may have a significant substitution effect in part countering that of the tax on the balance of their income.

D. Special Areas: Alimony, Tax-exempt
Interest, and Cancellation
of Indebtedness

XVII. Alimony and Separate Maintenance Payments

1. From 1913 to 1942

ONLY FOUR YEARS after the enactment in 1913 of the income tax, the Supreme Court in *Gould* v. *Gould*[1] held that alimony payments received by a divorced wife were not "income arising or accruing to her within the enactment."[2] Although the opinion is quite cryptic, it appears based on the notion that ordinary alimony, because of its origin in the marriage relationship, represents a portion of the husband's earnings rather than income to the wife.[3] To her it was a non-taxable receipt derived from status.[4] The corollary, that the husband was entitled to no deduc-

1. 245 U.S. 151 (1917).

2. *Id.* at 154. The decision was not on constitutional grounds. Mahana v. United States, 88 F. Supp. 285 (Ct. Cl. 1950), *cert. denied,* 339 U.S. 978, *rehearing denied,* 340 U.S. 847 (1950).

3. The Court quoted from Audubon v. Shufeldt, 181 U.S. 575, 577–78 (1901), to support this characterization.

4. *Cf.* chap. vi, pp. 99–114. It has been pointed out that *Gould* v. *Gould* could have been decided the other way. See Paul, *Five Years With Douglas v. Willcuts,* 53 HARV. L. REV. 1, 3 n. 6 (1939). Paul asserted that, although the wife is not taxable on amounts expended for her support during marriage, it does not follow that a "pecuniary substitute" allowed upon divorce should be immune from tax. While Paul did not employ the "voluntary conversion of status" analysis suggested in Chapter VI, his result can be viewed in that manner. He analogized the permanent alimony situation to exclusion of one-half the earnings of a spouse in a community property state. In both instances, he reasoned, the non-earning recipient spouse is entitled to the sum because of operation of law. So, for that matter, is the spouse receiving support during marriage; hence, the principle which the analogy suggests carries one too far.

tion, was indicated explicitly.[5] Equity provides no clear guidance here because, as pointed out in Chapter VIII, it fails to come to grips adequately with the problem of the identity of the taxable person.[6] Practicality perhaps supported the result;[7] however, it is clear that *Gould* could impose upon the male victim of several ill-fated matrimonial ventures a tax burden in excess of his income after alimony. As long as the income tax was a burden of only the rich, this possibility contributed its bit to Reduced Economic Inequality. In essence, however, the solution of tax problems caused by dissolution of marriage should turn on, first, economic fairness between the former husband and wife and, second, the extent to which the burden of taxes should be adjusted to facilitate or impede divorce. Both fairness and facilitation of divorce require more particularized tax results than it was possible for *Gould* to provide.

Not long after *Gould*, the alimony trust emerged as the focal point of a host of problems. Were payments by such trusts to former wives to be treated as alimony? Did this depend upon whether the husband retained powers which would make him taxable in any event? Or did it turn on whether the creation of the trust discharged the grantor husband's duty of support and maintenance? If so, under

5. "The net income of the divorced husband subject to taxation was not decreased by payment of alimony under the court's order. . . ." 245 U.S. at 154.

6. Chap viii, p. 134. However, *Gould* did reduce the likelihood of transfers of capital being taxed as income. *Cf.* Daisy M. Twinam, 22 T.C. 83, 89 (1954), where the court found it unnecessary to determine whether the present code provisions taxing alimony payments to the recipient were constitutional when made from capital rather than earnings.

7. Many problems relating to the characteristics of alimony taxable to the wife which have arisen under Int. Rev. Code of 1954, § 71, were avoided by the *Gould* result. Dependency problems were also reduced. See pp. 268–88 *infra*. However, *Gould* created its own classification problems which impaired its practicality. See pp. 267–68 *infra*.

what law was the existence of a discharge to be determined? If local law, what if its answer is ambiguous? How are the provisions fixing the taxation of trusts and their beneficiaries to be fitted into this scheme? These and many other questions puzzled the public, the Treasury, and the lower courts for almost two decades.[8]

The Supreme Court assumed its responsibilities in this area in *Douglas* v. *Willcuts*,[9] commencing a line of decisions which culminated, seven years later, in *Pearce* v. *Commissioner*.[10] Trusts incident to divorce were divided into two categories, viz., those intended to discharge a continuing obligation, even though contingent and remote, of the husband having its origin in his contract or local law, and those whose execution discharged his obligation finally and completely. The husband remained taxable on the first, while the wife bore the burden in the second. Local law was presumed to make the husband's obligation a continuing one in the absence of clear and

8. The Treasury vacillated. First, it applied *Gould* to the income of a trust established to secure payment of an amount in lieu of alimony. O.D. 399, 2 C.B. 156 (1920). Then, it reversed itself on the same facts and imposed the tax burden on the recipient. Still later, it returned to its original position in a ruling concerning a trust established in consideration of the release by the wife of alimony and other marital rights under which the husband agreed to make up any income deficiencies by the transfer of additional securities and in which he retained a reversionary interest. I.T. 2628, XI-1 C.B. 34 (1932). The Board of Tax Appeals developed a distinction between trusts established to discharge obligations originating in the marital status and irrevocable indentures voluntarily established, even though incident to divorce, under which the husband has no control and a remote reversionary interest. *Compare* Mary R. Spencer, 20 B.T.A. 58 (1930) *with* S. A. Lynch, 23 B.T.A. 435 (1931). See Paul, *Five Years With Douglas v. Willcuts*, 53 HARV. L. REV. 1, 4 (1939), for a summary of this era. The circuit courts were also troubled. *Compare* Willcuts v. Douglas, 73 F.2d 130 (8th Cir. 1934), *with* Schweitzer v. Comm'r, 75 F.2d 702 (7th Cir. 1935).

9. 296 U.S. 1 (1935).

10. 315 U.S. 543 (1942). The intervening cases were Helvering v. Fitch, 309 U.S. 149 (1940); Helvering v. Fuller, 310 U.S. 69 (1940); Helvering v. Leonard, 310 U.S. 80 (1940).

convincing proof that both local law and his contract had given him full discharge.[11] A continuing obligation, even though remote and contingent, followed from either a power in the local divorce court to revise the decree or trust, a guarantee against deficiencies by the husband, or perhaps even the retention of a substantial interest in the property.[12] The necessity to dilate local law applicable to alimony trusts, the obscurity of such law even when dilated, a general dissatisfaction with the *Gould* result, and the increase in rates resulting from World War II induced Congress to intervene.

2. *The Revenue Act of 1942*

The Revenue Act of 1942 contained the provisions which in large measure are those in effect at the present time. The purpose of these provisions, as stated by the Committee on Ways and Means, was to treat "payments in the nature of or in lieu of alimony or an allowance for support as between divorced or legally separated spouses . . . as income to the spouse actually receiving or actually entitled to receive them and to relieve the other spouse from the tax burden upon whatever part of the amount of such payment is under present law includable in his gross

11. In Helvering v. Fitch, 309 U.S. 149, 156 (1940), the Court said: "For if such a result is to obtain, it must be bottomed on clear and convincing proof, and not on mere inferences and vague conjectures, that local law and the alimony trust have given the divorced husband a full discharge and leave no continuing obligation however contingent."

12. See Note, *Federal Income Taxation of Alimony Trusts*, 35 ILL. L. REV. 332, 336–7 (1940). In holding that a complete discharge had been achieved, the Court in Pearce v. Comm'r, 315 U.S. 543, 552 (1942) said: "But where, as here, the settlement appears to be absolute and outright, and on its face vests in the wife the indicia of complete ownership, it will be treated as that which it purports to be, in absence of evidence that it was only a security device for the husband's continuing obligation to support."

income." [13] In addition, uniformity was to be achieved by elimination of recourse to local law to determine the existence or continuance of an obligation to pay alimony.[14]

Accomplishment of these goals was sought through provisions which, although they did not appear to be extraordinarily complex at the time, have produced a considerable amount of litigation. Gross income was defined to include periodic payments, whether or not made at regular intervals, received by a wife who was divorced or legally separated under a decree of divorce or of separate maintenance, in discharge of, or attributable to, property transferred (in trust or otherwise) in discharge of a legal obligation which, because of the marital or family relationship, was imposed upon, or incurred by, the husband under such decree or under a written instrument incident to such divorce or separation.[15] The husband was not required to include in his income amounts taxable to the wife attributable to property transferred in discharge of his legal obligation,[16] and a deduction was available for amounts paid to the wife not so attributable to transferred property which were includable in her gross income.[17] Periodic payments were defined to exclude instalment payments *except* when the principal sum may be, or is to be,

13. H.R. REP. No. 2333, 77th Cong., 2d Sess., 71–72 (1942). A similar purpose was stated in S. REP. No. 1631, 77th Cong., 2d Sess., 83 (1942). This has been translated to mean giving tax relief to the husband. Ruth Borax, 40 T.C. 1001, 1004 (1963).

14. *Ibid.*

15. Section 22 (k). Int. Rev. Code of 1939, § 171 (a), dealt with trust income after divorce and separation to which § 22 (k) is not applicable. See pp. 290–92 *infra.*

16. Int. Rev. Code of 1939, § 22 (k).

17. Int. Rev. Code of 1939, § 23.

paid within a period ending more than ten years from the date of the decree or instrument. This exception, however, was limited in scope to that amount of instalment payments received within the taxable year of the wife not in excess of 10 per cent of the principal sum. Instalment payments in advance, but not those delinquent when received, were to be considered in determining whether payments received within the taxable year exceeded the 10 per cent ceiling.[18] Periodic payments fixed by the decree or written instrument as sums payable for the support of minor children remained taxable to the husband. Finally, amounts expended for support of minor children taxable to the wife because not specifically designated for this purpose could not be considered as contributions by the husband in determining whether the husband could claim the child as a dependent. Such amounts were contributions by the wife.

Thus, the essential characteristics of alimony were abstracted from the maze of local law rules which govern it and made the conditions with which the taxpayer must comply in order to be governed by Congress' rejection of both *Gould* and the nice distinctions developed by the alimony trust cases. The result is a structure which imposes fewer tax obstacles to divorce than did its predecessor and which is reasonably flexible. A wife, sufficiently powerful at the bargaining table, may, however, continue to obtain a significant portion of the benefits of *Gould* by insistence that relatively large sums be paid as either (1) instalment payments discharging a principal sum over a period of not more than ten years, (2) amounts for the support of minor children, or (3) both. In addition, she may insist upon periodic payments sufficient in amount

18. Int. Rev. Code of 1939, § 22 (k).

to give her the desired sum after taxes imposed on her are deducted.

Nonetheless, complete contractual freedom to fix the income tax consequences of divorce does not exist. While dogmatism in a matter of this kind is not possible, this partial contractual freedom requires that the question be asked why complete freedom should not exist. It is at least arguable that, to the extent the marriage relationship becomes more consensual by means of removal of legal impediments to divorce, so should the income tax consequences of the financial arrangements incident to divorce. As it is, the structure is a somewhat curious blend of status and contract—a blend, however, which is no more curious than that reflected by the local laws of divorce.

3. Validity of Decree of Divorce or Separate Maintenance

Whatever its other merits, the Revenue Act of 1942, as already indicated, did nothing to reduce tax litigation in the area. To begin with, the legislation required, as does the present section 71 (a) (1) of the 1954 Code, a divorce or legal separation "under a decree of divorce or of separate maintenance." Immediately two basic issues become apparent, viz., the extent to which the decree must be valid and immune from attack from any source, and the source of the law to be used in determining such validity as may be required. Both issues only recently have received careful attention. In several decisions [19] it has been held that a decree of divorce not declared invalid by the jurisdiction in which it was granted and which employs a

19. Borax v. Comm'r, 349 F.2d 666 (2d Cir. 1965), *cert. denied*, 383 U.S. 935 (1966). Wondsel v. Comm'r, 350 F.2d 339 (2d Cir. 1965). An earlier decision, Feinberg v. Comm'r, 198 F.2d 260 (3d Cir. 1952), reached a similar result.

concept of divorce not "totally alien" [20] to that employed by federal tax law satisfies the statutory requirement. Accordingly, its invalidity determined by an appropriate proceeding in, and under the law of, another jurisdiction, including that of the marital domicile, is disregarded. Both Practicality and Equity strongly influenced the result. It was reasoned that this "rule of validation" would promote certainty, because only seldom will a decree be declared invalid by the granting jurisdiction, and uniformity, because all obtaining decrees from a particular jurisdiction will receive similar treatment without regard to the view another jurisdiction might take of any such decree. Moreover, it was asserted that the holding accords with the policy of placing the tax burden of "general marriage settlement payments" [21] on the recipient.

Previous approaches to these two issues were much less informative. Despite quite frequent assertions that the existence and dissolution of marriage is a matter of local law,[22] less regularly discussed were the issues posed when the local laws of several jurisdictions affected the validity and scope of the decree.[23] At one time the Service appeared

20. Borax v. Comm'r, n. 19 *supra,* at 672.

21. *Id.* at 670.

22. Riddell v. Guggenheim, 281 F.2d 836, 842 (9th Cir. 1960) (taxability of payments to wife under an interlocutory decree of divorce prior to final decree not payments under a decree of divorce or separate maintenance because California law does not regard an interlocutory decree as being either) ; Comm'r v. Evans, 211 F.2d 378 (10th Cir. 1954) (similar result under Colorado law) ; Gersten v. Comm'r, 267 F.2d 195 (9th Cir. 1959) (eligibility to file a joint return dependent on validity of marriage under California law) ; Ruth Borax, 40 T.C. 1001, 1007 (1963) (status of divorce in part determined by reference to state law) ; John J. Untermann, 38 T.C. 93, 95 (1962) (eligibility to file joint return determined by state law) ; Kenneth T. Sullivan, 29 T.C. 71, 74 (1957) (eligibility to file joint return determined by state law) .

23. The ex parte divorce generates these issues. Thus, Williams v. North Carolina, 325 U.S. 225 (1945) (Williams II) permits relitigation of a finding of domicile by court granting the ex parte decree which, if

to require only that there be a publicly recorded decree of divorce or separate maintenance upon which the husband and wife relied in good faith.[24] Later rulings reflect some retreat from this position. Perhaps it is fair to say that prior to recent decisions the divorce decree must have been valid under the law of the jurisdiction where entered [25] and either (a) valid under the law of any other appropriate jurisdiction or (b) relied upon in good faith by both spouses.[26]

At the very least, it could have been said that the absence of either reliance or a favorable adjudication of validity by any other interested jurisdiction appeared to

---

successful, invalidates the decree. Estin v. Estin, 334 U.S. 541 (1948) created the doctrine that a support order obtained in, and by a domiciliary of, a jurisdiction other than that granting the divorce survives the granting of a valid ex parte decree. The doctrine was extended to support orders obtained subsequent to the divorce in Vanderbilt v. Vanderbilt, 354 U.S. 416 (1957). For a discussion of the issues raised by these and other cases, see Note, *Divisible Divorce*, 76 HARV. L. REV. 1233–52 (1963).

24. G.C.M. 25250, 1947–2 C.B. 32 (Mexican divorce probably invalid in domiciliary state but relied on in good faith sufficient to make payments incident to a decree of divorce). It was reasoned that this interpretation would not open the door to income-splitting between the husband and wife since few would clutter their lives with a Mexican divorce solely for purposes of tax avoidance.

25. *Cf.* Estate of Daniel Buckley, 37 T.C. 664, 670 (1962).

26. *Cf.* Ruth Borax, 40 T.C. 1001, 1006 (1963), *rev'd*, Borax v. Comm'r., 349 F.2d 666 (2d Cir. 1965), *cert. denied*, 383 U.S. 935 (1966). In acquiescence to Eccles v. Comm'r, 208 F.2d 796 (4th Cir. 1952) and Evans v. Comm'r, 211 F.2d 378 (10th Cir. 1954) the Service indicated that the existence of a decree of divorce or separate maintenance would be controlled by the applicable local law. Rev. Rul. 57–368, 1957–2 C.B. 896. This ruling revoked previous rulings (I.T. 3761, 1945 C.B. 76; I.T. 3934, 1949–1 C.B. 54; I.T. 3942, 1949–1 C.B. 69; I.T. 3944, 1949–1 C.B. 56; Rev. Rul. 55–178, 1955–1 C.B. 322) which permitted periodic payments pursuant to interlocutory decrees to be considered as incident to a decree of divorce or legal separation notwithstanding the fact that local law did not consider an interlocutory decree as one of either divorce or separate maintenance. In Gersten v. Comm'r., 267 F.2d 195 (9th Cir. 1959), the taxpayer, a resident of California at all material times, was not entitled to file a joint return with his second wife for the period of the second marriage which fell within a one-year period after the entry of the interlocutory decree. *But see* Feinberg v. Comm'r. 198 F.2d 260 (3d Cir. 1952).

make it possible for the decree to fail to satisfy the requirements of section 71 (a) (1).

Despite the decision in *Borax*, there is something to be said for looking beyond the absence of a declaration of invalidity by the issuing jurisdiction. Only by doing this can tax effect be given a status fixed by a jurisdiction whose legitimate interests surpass those of all others, including the issuing jurisdiction, and whose decrees may be entitled to full faith and credit. It is true that doing so requires determination of the jurisdiction whose law overrides that of the issuing jurisdiction. Moreover, under some imaginable alternatives to *Borax*, careful scrutiny of this law, often complex and fragmentary, might be necessary.

A note writer recently suggested the following approach as one superior to the *Borax* rule:

Where an invalidating decree has been rendered by the parties' domiciliary state, the invalidity of the divorce is clear. Where an invalidating decree has been rendered in another jurisdiction and is entitled to full faith and credit, the invalidity is also clear. Where there is no invalidating decree or there is one that is not entitled to full faith and credit (such as one rendered by a foreign jurisdiction), the Service could assume that the divorce was valid.[27]

Under this view, only in the last described situation would the decree of the issuing jurisdiction control.

In addition, the bargaining position of the stay-at-home spouse (usually the wife) is somewhat reduced by an approach which does not look beyond the issuing jurisdiction. Where the couple have lived under a pre–1954 separation agreement and contemplate a complete divorce in

27. 18 STAN. L. REV. 750 (1966).

the future, *Borax* gives the husband the power to shift a tax burden to the wife without her consent by obtaining an ex parte decree which he knows can be declared invalid. Moreover, a wife living apart from her husband may find her bargaining power, derived from her ability to withhold her signature on a joint return, diminished by the husband's ability to obtain a vulnerable ex parte decree. Of course, a subsequent determination of invalidity accompanied by an adjustment of the amount of support, or a valid divorce, initiated by the wife, normally would provide protection against the danger of inadequate support under the ex parte decree.

In any event, the Supreme Court, despite the denial of certiorari in *Borax,* may be forced to give guidance. An adoption of the recently enunciated validation rule will further enhance the efficacy of the foreign ex parte divorce—a trend which peaked in the first *Williams* case,[28] but from which the second *Williams,*[29] *Estin,*[30] and *Vanderbilt*[31] have departed.

4. The Required "Linkage" between Payments Taxable to the Wife and Divorce or Separate Maintenance

a. Under Section 71 (a) (1) of the 1954 Code

Mindful of the necessity at the time to preclude relatively free income-splitting between couples not put asunder by law and the continuing importance of distinguishing periodic gifts, loan repayments, and other property adjustments from alimony, Congress in the Revenue Act

28. 317 U.S. 287 (1942).
29. 325 U.S. 226 (1945).
30. 334 U.S. 541 (1948).
31. 354 U.S. 416 (1957).

of 1942 required, as does the present section 71 (a) of the 1954 Code, that (1) periodic payments be "received subsequent" to the decree, (2) in discharge of a legal obligation "because of the marital or family relationship," and (3) "imposed upon or incurred by such husband under such decree or under a written instrument incident to such divorce or separation." This understandable effort to link payments, which were entitled to the new treatment accorded alimony, to divorce or separate maintenance proved very troublesome.

Faced with payments made pursuant to separation agreements executed at a time when one or both the parties did not contemplate or anticipate a divorce but which survived a subsequent divorce, the Government adopted a strict interpretation and insisted that, in the absence of some reference to the agreement in the decree or in some writing executed more or less contemporaneously with the decree, payments made subsequent to the divorce were not made "incident to such divorce." [32] This set the courts the task of ascertaining the state of mind of a couple at the time of separation under circumstances which usually encouraged the husband to insist that both pessimistically foresaw divorce and the wife, more optimistically, to recall that neither believed the separation was permanent. The manifest futility of such a search, as well as the unseemliness of a sovereign insisting that the availability of benefits

32. Treas. Reg. 111, § 29.22 (k) -1, Example 3 (1943), as amended by T.D. 5364, 1944 C.B. 86; T.D. 5645, 1948–2 C.B. 14; T.D. 5841, 1951–1 C.B. 11; T.D. 5932, 1952–2 C.B. 76. The manner in which the agreement could be made "incident to" was as follows: "If, however, the decree were modified so as to refer to the antenuptial agreement, or if, at the time of the divorce, reference had been made to the antenuptial agreement in the court's decree or in a written instrument incident to the divorce, section 22 (k) would require the inclusion of the payments received by W after the decree in her income for taxable years beginning after December 31, 1941."

of a "reform" in the tax law turn on a showing of what approached "collusion" to obtain a divorce, quickly led the courts to reject this strict interpretation.[33] In its stead the courts have focused upon the survival of the obligation to support following divorce and the existence of a written instrument evidencing this obligation.[34]

Another source of difficulty caused by the linkage fashioned by Congress arose when decrees or written instruments incident to such decrees were amended subsequent to divorce by either court action or a written agreement by the parties. Are all such amendments either decrees or written instruments "incident to such divorce or separation"? If not, do any such amendments fall within the required characterization? The answer was not difficult where an earlier appropriately linked decree is amended by court order. Clearly periodic payments pursuant to such amendments are as much alimony as are the payments under the original decree.[35]

Amendments of written instruments "incident to such divorce or separation" by later written instruments posed

33. Lerner v. Comm'r, 195 F.2d 296 (2d Cir. 1952); Feinberg v. Comm'r, 198 F.2d 260 (3d Cir. 1952); Comm'r v. Miller, 199 F.2d 597 (9th Cir. 1952). The Tax Court originally supported the Government's position, Joseph J. Lerner, 15 T.C. 379 (1950), but later came into line with the circuit courts. Helen Stewart Cramer, 36 T.C. 1136, 1141–42 (1961). The Government has also abandoned the strict interpretation. *Cf.* Rev. Rul. 60–141, 1960–1 C.B. 33.

34. In Holt v. Comm'r, 226 F.2d 757, 758 (2d Cir. 1955), Judge Medina forcefully stated: "Thus where a legal obligation to support survives the dissolution of the marital relationship and such obligation is evidenced by the terms of a written agreement, as is the case now before us, the wife must pay the income taxes on the amounts received by her for support and maintenance. . . . It is, accordingly, immaterial whether the husband and the wife or either of them intend the agreement shall be 'incident to the divorce.'" It is possible for a predivorce settlement agreement to preclude survival of a legal obligation to support. See Rev. Rul. 60–142, 1960–1 C.B. 34. This issue of survival is reminiscent of the comparable problem under the pre–1942 law in connection with alimony trusts. See pp. 267–68 *supra*.

35. *Cf.* Gale v. Comm'r, 191 F.2d 79 (2d Cir. 1951).

a more difficult problem. If the statutory language required the amendments to be "incident to the decree of divorce," those occurring years after the divorce very well might fail to be reached by even an extended interpretation of an admittedly elastic phrase. While in some instances this elasticity brought payments pursuant to such amendments within the statute,[36] most courts have read the statute as meaning that the written instrument need only be incident to the "status" of divorce or separation.[37] The Government has accepted this view,[38] providing payments pursuant to amendatory agreements are "because of the family or marital relationship in recognition of the general obligation of support." [39]

Thus, what began as an effort on the part of Government to insist upon a very direct and, at times, formalistic relationship between the divorce or separate maintenance and the written instrument has become insistence that the purpose of the payments be that ordinarily served by alimony. In keeping with this insistence, it remains true under section 71 (a) (1) that, in the absence of a decree of divorce or separate maintenance, payments pursuant to a written instrument following separation in fact are not taxable to the recipient spouse.[40]

36. *Cf.* Mahana v. United States, 88 F. Supp. 285 (Ct. Cl. 1950), *cert. denied*, 339 U.S. 978, *rehearing denied*, 340 U.S. 847 (1950); Smith v. Comm'r., 192 F.2d 841 (2d Cir. 1951).

37. Heath v. Comm'r, 265 F.2d 662 (2d Cir. 1959); Hollander v. Comm'r, 248 F.2d 523 (9th Cir. 1957); Newton v. Pedrick, 212 F.2d 357, 360–62 (2d Cir. 1954).

38. Treas. Reg. § 1.71–1 (b)(i) (1957) provides: "Such periodic payments [those described in § 71 (a) of the 1954 Code] must be made in discharge of legal obligation imposed upon or incurred by the husband because of the marital or family relationship under a court order or decree divorcing or legally separating the husband and wife or a written instrument incident to such divorce status or legal separation status."

39. Rev. Rul. 60–140, 1960–1 C.B. 31.

40. Smith v. Comm'r, 168 F.2d 446 (2d Cir. 1948); Daine v. Comm'r, 168 F.2d 449 (2d Cir. 1948).

b. *Under Section 71 (a) (2) and (3) of the 1954 Code*

Most of these "linkage" problems, however, have been reduced in significance by sections 71 (a) (2) and (3) enacted by the 1954 Code and made feasible by the adoption in 1948 of income-splitting between spouses. Under section 71 (a) (2) periodic payments by a husband separrated [41] from his wife to such wife pursuant to a written separation agreement (whether or not legally enforceable) because of the marital or family relationship and received subsequent to the execution of such writing are taxable to the wife, provided, first, the husband and wife file separate returns and, second, the agreement was executed after August 16, 1954, the date of enactment of the 1954 Code.[42] Thus, when these provisions are met, it is no longer necessary for the instrument to be "incident to" divorce or separate maintenance, or that a decree of divorce or separate maintenance exists. Postnuptial, predivorce separation agreements are now governed by the terms of section 71 both before and after a decree of divorce or separate maintenance.[43]

Congress in 1954 also extended section 71 treatment to another type of periodic payment which was a source of

41. Legal separation is not required, only separation in fact.

42. Treas. Reg. § 1.71–1 (b)(2)(ii) (1957) now provides as follows: "For purposes of section 71 (a)(2), any written separation agreement executed on or before August 16, 1954, which is altered or modified in writing by the parties in any material respect after that date will be treated as an agreement executed after August 16, 1954 with respect to payments made after the date of alteration or modification." This enables those living under earlier agreements to obtain the consequences of section 71 (a)(2) should they desire to do so. Also, see Rev. Rul. 56–418, 1956–2 C.B. 27.

43. Treas. Reg. § 1.71–1 (b)(2)(i) (1957) provides: "Moreover, if the wife is divorced or legally separated subsequent to the written separation agreement, payments made under such agreement continue to fall within the provisions of section 71 (a)(2)."

difficulty under the 1942 legislation, viz., payments made by a husband pursuant to a decree other than one of divorce or separate maintenance [44] requiring payments for the wife's support and maintenance. Embraced within this category is alimony *pendente lite* and alimony under interlocutory decrees of divorce.[45] Similar to the terms of the Code relating to payments under separation agreements, section 71 (a) (3) requires that (1) the husband and wife be separated, (2) separate returns be filed, and (3) the payments be received subsequent to August 16, 1954. In addition the subsection requires that the decree be one entered after March 1, 1954, and that the payments thereunder be for the support and maintenance of the wife. The effective dates set forth in subsections 71 (a) (2) and (3) represent an effort to avoid altering the tax consequences of arrangements worked out on tax assumptions different from those provided therein.[46]

Presumably, the problems relating to the validity of the decree, although on a reduced scale, exist here as they do under subsection 71 (a) (1).[47] Moreover, both the advan-

44. Prior to the 1954 changes, it was necessary to distinguish between decrees for separate maintenance or divorce and decrees which merely provided for support and maintenance of the wife. *Cf.* n. 19 *supra* and Rev. Rul. 59–248, 1959–2 C.B. 31. This necessity remains with respect to decrees other than divorce and separate maintenance entered prior to March 1, 1954, and not altered or modified since that date.

45. Treas. Reg. § 1.71–1 (b)(3)(ii) (1957); Florence Korman, 36 T.C. 654 (1961), *aff'd per curiam*, 298 F.2d 444 (2d Cir. 1962). For the treatment accorded these payments under the 1942 Act, see Riddell v. Guggenheim, 281 F.2d 836, 842 (9th Cir. 1960); Comm'r v. Evans, 211 F.2d 378 (10th Cir. 1954). See n. 22 *supra*.

46. S. REP. No. 1622, 83d Cong., 2d Sess., 171 (1954). As in the case with respect to payments under support agreements, parties governed by decrees entered before March 1, 1954, may avail themselves of subsection 71 (a)(3) by having the decree altered or modified subsequent to that date. Treas. Reg. § 1.71–1 (b)(3)(ii) (1957). See n. 42 *supra*. A refusal by the court to alter or modify subsequent to March 1, 1954, is not such an alteration or modification, Rev. Rul. 59–248, 1959–2 C.B. 31.

47. *Cf.* Harry L. Clark, 40 T.C. 57 (1963) (dictum suggests "decree"

tages and disadvantages of *Borax* are relevant in this context.

5. *The Requirements (1) That Payments Be Made "Because of the Marital or Family Relationship" and (2) Periodicity*

Putting aside these linkage problems and the judicial and legislative response which they generated, Congress has relied upon two essential characteristics to distinguish alimony payments from other transactions. The first is that the payments be "periodic" and the second, that they be made "because of the marital or family relationship." While the meaning of the former is developed at some length in section 71 (c) , neither this enlargement nor the second characteristic has relieved the courts of the necessity to examine the factual setting of the divorce or separation to determine whether the payments in question are alimony within the meaning of the Code or an adjustment of property rights failing to conform to one or both of these characteristics.

Periodic payments constituting the discharge of a bona fide debt [48] or a purchase-price obligation [49] owing by the husband to the wife obviously are not made because of the family or marital relationship. This remains true even though the decree or written instrument requires such

---

within meaning of § 71 (a) (3) , refers to one by a court of civil jurisdiction rather than an ecclesiastical court). The regulations, however, speak of payments "under any type of court order or decree . . . entered after March 1, 1954, requiring the husband to make payments for her support or maintenance." Treas. Reg. § 1.71–1 (b)(3)(i) (1957) .

48. Thorsness v. United States, 260 F.2d 341 (7th Cir. 1958) ; Treas. Reg. § 1.71–1 (b)(4) (1957) .

49. Frank J. Du Bane, 10 T.C. 992, 995 (1948) . Presumably, such payments should constitute a part of the basis of the property acquired. *But cf.* United States v. Gilmore, 372 U.S. 39 (1963) ; Illinois Nat'l Bank v. United States, 273 U.S. 231 (7th Cir. 1959) .

payments. However, the animosities attending the dissolution of a marriage make inevitable ambiguous decrees, written instruments, or other arrangements. Moreover, the delicacy of the negotiations leading to divorce and the tax stakes involved often make recollections of the parties both uncertain and unreliable.[50] These circumstances contribute significantly to an already difficult task of distinguishing various types of property settlements from alimony.

In struggling with this task, certain useful principles and bench marks have been established. For example, it is uniformly recognized that the characterization given a settlement by either the parties or the local law applicable thereto is not controlling.[51] Parol evidence is usually, if not always, admissible to aid the court in its effort.[52] Nonetheless, the language of the decree or written instrument, as well as those aspects of local law which appear helpful,[53] are considered in affixing the proper tax label to the payments.

The technique ordinarily employed is to determine

50. The following extract from Helen L. Hilgemeier, 42 T.C. 496, 502 (1964), illustrates this: "Petitioner testified that it was her understanding from her attorney that she would not be required to pay tax on the $2000 and Edward testified that it was his understanding from his accountant that he could exclude the $2000 from his income. Edward's attorney testified that he could not remember precisely the discussions as to the tax effect which would result from the alimony payments."

51. Taylor v. Campbell, 335 F.2d 841 (5th Cir. 1964); Bardwell v. Comm'r, 318 F.2d 786 (10th Cir. 1963); Solterman v. United States, 272 F.2d 387 (9th Cir. 1959); Ann Hairston Ryker, 33 T.C. 924 (1960). Sometimes, parties may describe what otherwise appears to be alimony as a property settlement to eliminate future court supervision. See Bardwell v. Comm'r, *supra,* when in the Tax Court. 38 T.C. 84, 91 (1962).

52. Scofield v. Greer, 185 F.2d 551 (5th Cir. 1950). Frequently, it is said that the parol evidence rule does not apply because the Government was not a party to the instrument. For an analysis of the proper role of the parol evidence rule in tax litigation, see Sneed, *Some Reflections About The Impact of Federal Taxation On American Private Law,* 12 BUFFALO L. REV. 241, 242–46 (1963).

53. *Cf.* Julia Nathan, 19 T.C. 865, 872 (1953).

whether certain characteristics usually possessed by alimony payments are present. Thus, an indefinite duration [54] of the required payments, the terminability of the obligation to make payments on the death of one or the other spouse,[55] the similarity, in terms of amount and frequency of payment, of the postdivorce payments to predivorce payments made after separation,[56] the absence of any credible showing of property rights the adjustment of which could be the basis of the payments,[57] the apparent settlement of all property rights by provisions other than those being considered,[58] and the absence of any stated principal sum being discharged,[59] all point toward periodic payments made "because of the marital or family relationship." Conversely, the opposite of these characteristics suggest an adjustment of property rights.[60]

Admission to the fold of payments made "because of the marital or family relationship," however, does not bestow section 71 treatment unless the payments are "periodic." Moreover, as indicated earlier, periodicity is limited by excluding from its scope instalment payments discharging a part of an obligation the principal sum of which is specified in the appropriate instrument and which is payable within a period of ten years or less. As an original

54. Helen L. Hilgemeier, 42 T.C. 496, 501 (1964); Julia Nathan, 19 T.C. 865, 872 (1953).

55. Bardwell v. Comm'r, 318 F.2d 788, 789 (1963); Scofield v. Greer, 185 F.2d 551 (5th Cir. 1955); Ann Hairston Ryker, 33 T.C. 917, 930 (1960); Julia Nathan, 19 T.C. 865, 872 (1953).

56. Julia Nathan, 19 T.C. 865, 872 (1953).

57. *Id.* at 871.

58. Taylor v. Campbell, 335 F.2d 841, 845 (5th Cir. 1964); Bardwell v. Comm'r, 318 F.2d 786, 790 (10th Cir. 1963).

59. Ann Hairston Ryker, 33 T.C. 924, 929 (1960).

60. Campbell v. Lake, 220 F.2d 341 (5th Cir. 1955). The problem of distinguishing property settlements from payments entitled to § 71 treatment is particularly difficult in community property states.

matter it is not readily apparent why this limitation on the meaning of "periodic payments" exists. The committee reports shed no light.[61] Perhaps the thought was that an arbitrary ten-year line would significantly reduce the necessity to distinguish between payments made because of the marital or family relationship and all others, the reasoning being that those payable in ten years or less are much more likely to be property settlements than those payable over a longer period. In any event, alimony unconditionally payable in a lump sum[62] or in instal-

61. See H.R. Rep. No. 2333, 77th Cong., 2d Sess. 71–74 (1942) ; S. Rep. No. 1631, 77th Cong., 2d Sess. 83–87 (1942).

62. The courts have used the "lump sum" characterization to remove from § 71 treatment various types of transactions. Thus, a lump-sum purchase of an insurance policy on the life of the husband and its irrevocable assignment to the wife was not a periodic payment. Samuel Morrison, 15 T.C.M. 740 (1956). Similarly, a right by the wife to occupy rent-free a home was considered a "single right to occupy until her death or remarriage" and hence not "periodic." Pappenheimer v. Allen, 164 F.2d 428 (5th Cir. 1947) ; James Parks Bradley, 30 T.C. 701 (1958). This result is probably a distortion of the requirement of periodicity induced because of the failure to tax imputed income derived from ownership of property. See chap. v. Medical and dental expenses (which the uncharitable might designate as "fixing up" expenses) incurred by the husband for the benefit of the wife also sometimes fail to meet the requirement of periodicity. F. Ewing Glasgow, 21 T.C. 211 (1953) (A). However, such expenses are governed by § 71 if (1) no principal sum is specified in the decree, or (2) if specified, is either payable over more than a ten-year period or is subject to contingencies of death of either spouse, remarriage of the wife, or change in the economic status of either spouse. Rev. Rul. 62–106, 1962–2 C.B. 21. Similar treatment appears accorded payments of principal and interest in respect to an indebtedness secured by property owned by the wife, real estate taxes, and utility bills incurred by the wife. Rev. Rul. 62–39, 1962–2 C.B. 17. To the extent "periodic," such payments are covered by § 71. Presumably, other segregated expenses of the wife will receive similar treatment.

In one area, however, the courts have expanded the "periodic" characterization to include lump-sum payments. The general rule is that the husband may deduct and the wife must include in the year of receipt any lump-sum settlement representing arrearages in periodic alimony. Mavity v. Comm'r, 65–1 U.S.T.C. ¶ 9272 (2d Cir. 1965) ; Holahan v. Comm'r, 222 F.2d 82 (2d Cir. 1958) ; Grant v. Comm'r, 209 F.2d 430 (2d Cir. 1953) ; Virginia B. Adriance Davis, 41 T.C. 815 (1964) ; Margaret O. White, 24 T.C. 452 (1955). The Service's position is to treat the payments in the same manner as the periodic payments would have been treated if paid when due. Rev. Rul. 55–457, 1955–2 C.B. 527. Difficulty may arise, however, if

ments over a period not more than ten years is denied section 71 treatment.[63]

At one time considerable doubt existed about the proper classification of payments for a period of ten years or less pursuant to obligations subject to termination upon the occurrence of certain contingencies, such as death of the wife or a substantial change in the economic condition of the husband. Initially, the Government, supported by the Tax Court, considered them instalment payments of a principal sum not entitled to section 71 treatment.[64] The circuit courts differed,[65] and at present both the regulations and the Tax Court recognize that the existence of such contingencies removes the payments from the category of instalment payments of a principal sum.[66] It is doubtful, however, that mere omission of state-

---

the settlement contract also relieves the ex-husband of his obligation to make future payments. In Grant v. Comm'r, a leading case, the ex-husband had only to pay up the arrearages to receive a release. The court there considered the payment of the arrearages the "nub" of the contract and required the ex-wife to include the total sum in her income. In a more recent case, Elinda W. Parker, 20 T.C.M. 597 (1961), the ex-husband paid his wife an amount in excess of the due arrearages for his release—a $2,200 settlement instead of merely the $1,940 arrearages. The court, applying the Cohan rule, treated $1,400 as the amount representing arrearages includable in the wife's income and $800 as the amount paid for the release.

63. William M. Haag, 17 T.C. 55 (1951). This is true even though the lump-sum or instalment payments are accompanied by payments which are plainly entitled to § 71 treatment. Ralph Norton, 16 T.C. 1216 (1951). Also see Jean Cattier, 17 T.C. 1461 (1952).

64. J. B. Steinel, 10 T.C. 409 (1948). The court said: "We are of the opinion that the word 'obligation' is used in section 22 (k) [1939 Code] in its general sense and includes obligations subject to contingencies where those contingencies have not arisen and have not avoided the obligation during the taxable years." *Id.* at 42.

65. Prewett v. Comm'r, 221 F.2d 250 (9th Cir. 1955); Davidson v. Comm'r, 219 F.2d 147 (9th Cir. 1955); Smith's Estate v. Comm'r, 208 F.2d 349 (3d Cir. 1953); Baker v. Comm'r, 205 F.2d 369 (2d Cir. 1953).

66. See Treas. Reg. § 1.71–1 (d)(3)(i) (1957); Helen Stewart Cramer, 36 T.C. 1136 (1961). The consequence is that payments subject to such contingencies are periodic payments without regard to their expected duration. Thus, payments to extend over more than ten years subject to

ment in the decree or instrument of a principal sum will bestow "periodic" character upon payments not otherwise so qualified.[67] This narrowing of the scope of alimony payments not taxable to the wife probably has increased the pressure of litigation and dispute on the distinction between payments made because of the "family or marital relationship" and property settlements.

6. *The Necessity of Receipt by the Wife*

The highly charged emotional atmosphere enveloping this area has also produced quite a bit of litigation over whether certain payments otherwise qualified for treatment as alimony have been "received" by the wife within the meaning of that statutory term. The regulations merely state that the wife must include section 71 (a) payments when received and that she is to be regarded for this purpose as a cash basis taxpayer.[68] As a consequence, cash or property constructively received is includable in the wife's income.[69] Thus, amounts set apart for her so that she may draw upon them at any time are constructively received. Moreover, when property has been so set apart, the wife has received alimony to the extent of the fair market value of the property.[70]

Despite these fairly obvious principles, their application has been difficult in several areas. Foremost of these has been that of insurance premiums paid by the husband as

---

such contingencies are not subject to the 10 per cent limitation imposed by § 71 (c)(2) of the 1954 Code. Rev. Rul. 59–45, 1959–1. C.B. 666; Rev. Rul. 60–250, 1960–2 C.B. 435; Treas. Reg. § 1.71–1 (d)(4) (1957) .

67. *But see* Myers v. Comm'r, 212 F.2d 448 (9th Cir. 1954) .

68. Treas. Reg. § 1.71–1 (b)(5) (1957) .

69. On the meaning of constructive receipt, see Treas. Reg. § 1.451–2 (1957) , as amended by T.D. 6723, 1964–1 C.B. 73.

70. *Cf*. chap. v, pp. 81–84, *supra*.

required by the terms of the decree or written instrument. The arrangements which can be hammered out with respect to insurance are almost infinite. Correspondingly, the extent of economic benefit which can be derived by the wife from these arrangements is quite variable. Practicality suggests that the task of valuing this benefit in each individual case be avoided and that rules somewhat arbitrary in character be designed which in most instances will classify the entire premium as alimony or not.

To a significant degree this has occurred. Thus, when insurance policies on the life of the husband are used only to secure his obligation to make alimony payments to his wife, any premiums required to be paid with respect thereto by the husband are not taxable to the wife under section 71.[71] No effort is made to measure the true economic benefit of such payments to the wife. On the other hand, when policies are irrevocably assigned to the wife, subsequent premiums paid by the husband are fully taxable to the wife. That his obligation to make such payments terminated upon her death or remarriage and that the agreement provided for cash alimony in addition to the insurance provisions does not change the result.[72]

In situations lying between these two poles, the tendency has been to eschew the nice calculation of the value of economic benefits to the wife and to make taxation of premiums to her turn on whether she has obtained "non-contingent substantial proprietary rights in the proceeds of the policies."[73]

71. Baker v. Comm'r, 205 F.2d 369 (2d Cir. 1953); Blumenthal v. Comm'r, 183 F.2d 15 (2d Cir. 1950).

72. Hyde v. Comm'r, 301 F.2d 279 (2d Cir. 1962); I.T. 4001, 1950-1 C.B. 27.

73. Piel v. Comm'r, 340 F.2d 887 (2d Cir. 1965) (husband and wife divided between themselves certain incidents of the policies); Weil v.

In a very similar manner the benefits derived by a wife as a result of the husband's payment of principal and interest on an indebtedness, insurance, and real estate taxes with respect to a residence owned by them as tenants by the entirety are disregarded, and the entire amount may not be regarded as includable in her income under section 71.[74] The contingent interest of the husband in the entire property insulates the wife from tax on the benefits which she receives. However, where the tenancy is in common, the wife is taxable on her proportionate part of such payments.[75] Only administrative convenience can sanction this twisting of the term "received."

7. *Payments for Support of Minor Children of Husband*

Before turning to income attributable to property transferred by husband to wife, the formerly troublesome area of child support should be mentioned. As pointed out

---

Comm'r, 240 F.2d 584 (2d Cir. 1957) (policies in possession of beneficiary wife but not assigned to her, and husband could not before her death or remarriage change benefits of policy); Segilmann v. Comm'r, 207 F.2d 489 (7th Cir. 1953) (policy placed in trust to provide income for wife and children after husband's death under which husband also had some vested and contingent interests). The Tax Court sometimes appears more willing to impose tax on the wife. See Estate of Boies C. Hart, 11 T.C. 16 (1948). *But see* Florence H. Griffith 35 T.C. 882 (1961). On the treatment of insurance proceeds, see § 101 (e), Int. Rev. Code of 1954; Jones, *Life Insurance As an Element until Death or Divorce Do Us Part: Marital Deduction and Divorce and Separation Settlements,* N.Y.U. 22d INST. ON FED. TAX. 1268 (1964).

74. See Rev. Rul. 58–52, 1958–1 C.B. 29; Rev. Rul. 62–38, 1962–1 C.B. 15. The Tax Court is divided on this matter. Neely B. Taylor, Jr., 45 T.C. 120 (1965). Judge Simpson would accept the insurance-policy analogy and tax the wife only when the value of the benefit can be "definitely determined." *Id.* at 127. On the other hand, Judge Tannenwald would tax the wife when the facts establish that the payments by the husband extinguish his right of contribution against the wife or discharge pro tanto a personal obligation of the wife. *Id.* at 123.

75. Rev. Rul. 62–39, 1962–1 C.B. 17.

earlier, the Revenue Act of 1942 did not require inclusion in the wife's income of payments which the decree or instrument "fix" as payable for support of minor children of the husband. Again, the committee reports reveal no statement of the purpose of this provision. Perhaps it was thought its "natural justice" would be apparent to each beholder. If so, it must be said that this "justice" did not prevent many disputes when the decree or written instrument did not explicitly state what portion of the payments were intended for child support. For a good many years some courts conceived their task to be that of examining the decree or written instrument as a whole to determine if any portion of the payments was fixed as payable for the support of minor children.[76] This view proved to be a misconception when the Supreme Court in *Commissioner* v. *Lester*[77] held that only sums "specifically earmarked in the agreement as payable for the support of children"[78] were not deductible by the husband. In the absence of specific designation the payments were taxable to the wife without regard to the "sufficiently clear purpose" of the parties or "variant legal obligations"[79] which local law might impose upon the recipient wife with respect to all or any part of such payments. As the Court observed, the result contributes significantly to the power of the husband and wife to fix with certainty tax liability for payments intended for support of minor children.

76. *Cf.* Mandel v. Comm'r, 185 F.2d 50 (7th Cir. 1950); Truman W. Morsman, 27 T.C. 520 (1956).

77. 366 U.S. 299 (1960).

78. *Id.* at 304. The Court relied heavily upon the legislative history of the 1942 Revenue Act, particularly S. REP. No. 1631, 77th Cong., 2d Sess., 86 (1942). On the effect of a *nunc pro tunc* order fixing payments for support of children, see Gloria P. Johnson, 45 T.C. 530 (1966). Compare Michel M. Segal, 36 T.C. 148 (1961).

79. 366 U.S. at 304–5.

8. *Income Attributable to Property Transferred from Husband to Wife*

While the 1942 legislation eliminated the uncertainties surrounding the alimony trusts, the statutory structure for doing so is somewhat complex. In brief, under what is now section 72 it is provided that when property is transferred, in trust or otherwise, under the circumstances described therein, periodic payments attributable to such property are taxable to the wife and excluded from the income of the husband.[80] It matters not whether these periodic payments are paid from income of the property; even when paid from corpus, the recipient wife is taxable.[81] When so paid, there is, of course, nothing to be excluded from the husband's gross income.

There remain situations in which trusts are created under circumstances other than those described in section 71 (a) . For example, even under the current less stringent interpretation of the extent to which there must be a link between divorce or separate maintenance and the transaction on which the payments are founded, a trust created long before any separation, decree of divorce, or separate maintenance, or written instrument, may afford a means by which the wife can be supported following divorce. When this is done, it can not be said that distributions by the trust constitute periodic payments attributable to property transferred in trust "in discharge of a legal obli-

80. Int. Rev. Code of 1954, §§ 71 (a) , (d) .

81. S. Rep. No. 1631, 77th Cong., 2d Sess. 84 (1942) ; Treas. Reg. § 1.71–1 (c)(3) (1957) . This principle of disregard of the source of periodic payments received by the wife is applied generally. Thus, payments governed by § 71 (a) from capital of the husband are taxable to the wife. Treas. Reg. § 1.71–1 (c)(2) (1957) . See A. R. G. Welsh Trust, 16 T.C. 1398 (1951) , *aff'd sub nom.* Girard Trust Corn Exch. Bank v. Comm'r, 194 F.2d 708 (3d Cir. 1952) .

gation imposed upon or incurred by the husband because of the marital or family relationship under a decree of separate maintenance or under a written instrument incident to such divorce status or legal separation status." [82]

Nonetheless, under what is now section 682 "the amount of the income" of any such trust (1) which a wife, who is divorced, legally separated, or separated from her husband under a written separation agreement, is entitled to receive, and (2) which would otherwise be taxable to the husband is included in the gross income of the wife.[83] Observe, however, that the wife is treated as a beneficiary of the trust and is only taxable to the extent of "income," as determined under the usual rules governing the taxability of trust beneficiaries.[84] Corpus distributions, under

---

82. Treas. Reg. § 1.71–1 (c)(1)(i) (1957).

83. Section 171, Int. Rev. Code 1939; § 682, Int. Rev. Code 1954. S. REP. No. 1631, 77th Cong., 2d Sess., 85 (1942) explains the provision this way: "Supplement E is amended by adding a new section, section 171. Section 171 (a) states the rule applicable to trust income after a decree of divorce or separate maintenance in the case of trusts created prior to divorce or separation *and to which the provisions of section 22 (k) are not applicable.*" (Italics added). Note how this provision solved certain alimony trust problems existing before 1942 by eliminating the importance of any "continuing" obligation of support in determining who should be taxed on the trust income. The present regulations make clear that § 682 applies only when § 71 does not. Treas. Reg. § 1.682 (a)–1 (a) (2) (1957).

84. Treas. Reg. § 1.682 (a)–1 (a) (2) (1957). *Cf.* Anita Quinby Stewart, 9 T.C. 195 (1947) (divorced wife receiving payments pursuant to a separation agreement from a trust established by husband's father for benefit of husband entitled to proportionate part of benefit of tax-exempt income received and distributed by trust). Normally, of course, the character of funds while in the hands of the husband does carry over to the wife. See n. 73 *supra;* Muriel Dodge Neeman, 26 T.C. 864 (1956) , *aff'd per curiam,* 255 F.2d 841 (2d Cir. 1958). The status of the recipient wife, however, may override the mandate of § 71. See Rev. Rul. 62–187, 1962–2 C.B. 27 (basic allowance for quarters received by wife of serviceman pursuant to a decree of support retains non-taxable character) ; Rev. Rul. 56–585, 1956–2 C.B. 166 (alimony received by wife, a citizen and resident of Puerto Rico, excludable under § 933 of 1954 Code) .

these provisions, are no more taxable to the wife than where distributed to other beneficiaries. Finally, trust income under these circumstances which is fixed as payable for the support of minor children is not taxable to the wife. Presumably the *Lester* case also controls the meaning of the term "fix" in this setting. Fortunately, the difference in coverage of sections 71 and 682 seldom appears to be troublesome, perhaps because most settlements using trusts make provision for keeping the corpus intact.

9. *Postscript*

In retrospect, the appeal of full contractual freedom remains strong. Such a step, however, would not be without its problems. Presumably under such a system the distinction between property settlements and payments because of the marital or family relationship would continue with contractual freedom limited to the latter type of payment. Also, assumption of the tax burden by the husband should result in a return to *Gould* v. *Gould,* not a deduction by the husband and the payment by him of that tax the wife would have paid had the payments been considered her income. The requirement of periodicity could be retained, modified, or eliminated in describing those payments to which freedom to fix the consequences exists. It would be necessary to require, as the Supreme Court did in *Lester,* that the tax consequences be specifically designated. The issue of whether contractual freedom extends to each type of alimony payment, or only to the aggregate amounts, as well as what law governs the validity of the contract, would have to be faced. One can certainly be forgiven if, when faced with these issues, he expresses a preference for old and familiar problems, be they ever so complex and wasteful of human energy.

XVIII. Tax-exempt Interest and Income of Governmental Units

1. History and the Constitutional Immunity

THE EXCLUSION from gross income of interest on state and local bonds has a long and often recounted [1] history marked with discord and passion. It is enmeshed in a course of constitutional litigation commencing with *McCulloch* v. *Maryland.*[2] Out of this decision, it will be recalled, grew the doctrine of implied reciprocal immunity enunciated in *Collector* v. *Day.*[3] In *Pollock* v. *Farmers Loan & Trust Co.*[4] the Court, in striking down the 1894 income tax as unconstitutional, held that Congress lacked the power to impose a tax on income derived from municipal bonds.[5] It was reasoned that the tax "would operate on the power to borrow before it is exercised . . ." and was "a tax on the power of the States and their instrumentalities to borrow money. . . ." [6] Although the Court divided

1. *E.g.,* Kirby, *State and Local Bond Interest* in *Tax Revision Compendium, House Committee on Ways and Means,* 86th Cong., 1st Sess. pt. 1 at 679, 680–83 (1959) ; S. REP. No. 2140, *Taxation of Governmental Securities and Salaries, Views of the Minority,* 76th Cong., 3d Sess., pt. 2. at 22–43 (1940) .

2. 17 U.S. (4 Wheat.) 316 (1819) .

3. 78 U.S. (11 Wall.) 113 (1870) .

4. 157 U.S. 429 (1895) .

5. *Id.* at 583–86.

6. *Id.* at 586.

sharply on the direct tax issue,[7] all eight Justices sitting on the original hearing agreed with this view. The characterization "direct" or "indirect" was not thought to be controlling so far as the tax on income from municipal bonds was concerned.[8]

Ratification of the sixteenth amendment was accompanied by fears expressed by many, most notably Governor Hughes of New York, that its words "from whatever source derived" were sufficiently broad to permit the taxation of income from state and municipal bonds. Proponents of the amendment insisted these fears were groundless, Senator Borah doing so from the floor of the Senate [9] and Senator Root by way of a letter to a New York State senator.[10] Their view of the matter was given added weight by Congress when interest on state and municipal securities was excluded from gross income under the income tax of 1913.[11] The exclusion, despite vigorous efforts from time to time to eliminate it, has remained in the law to this day.[12]

Congress also excluded from tax "any income derived from any public utility or from the exercise of any essen-

7. *Cf.* chap. vii, *supra.* For an interesting summary of the numerous speculations about how the Justices voted in both the hearings of *Pollock,* see PAUL, TAXATION IN THE UNITED STATES, 55–61 (1954). Another brief summary appears in BITTKER, FEDERAL INCOME ESTATE AND GIFT TAXATION, 7–8 (3d ed. 1964). The vote on rehearing was 5–4 with Justices Harlan, Brown, Jackson, and White dissenting.

8. *Cf.* Pollock v. Farmers' Loan & Trust Co., 158 U.S. 601, 618 (1895) (rehearing).

9. 44 CONG. REC. 1694–95 (1910).

10. 44 CONG. REC. 2539 (1910).

11. Tariff Act of 1913, § II.B, 38 Stat. 166. Representative Cordell Hull said: "It was not the desire of those who have been taking the most active interest in this measure to inject any more constitutional questions or controversies into the bill, especially for the sake of only a few thousand dollars in taxes." 63 CONG. REC. 1262 (1913).

12. Int. Rev. Code of 1954, § 103 (a).

tial governmental function accruing to any State, Territory, or the District of Columbia, or any political subdivision of a State, Territory, or the District of Columbia. . . ." [13] This too endures in the present code.[14] No effort was made either to exclude or include "the income of a State or municipality resulting from its own direct participation in industry." [15] The Government has construed this silence as evidence of Congressional intent not to subject such income to tax,[16] but has not conceded that a power to do so is lacking.[17] The only inroad on this statutory immunity which exists today is section 511 (a) (2) (B) of the Code, which subjects the business income of state colleges and universities to the corporation income tax.

Without regard to whether the fears of Governor Hughes and others that the sixteenth amendment overturned that portion of *Pollock* relating to interest from municipal securities are justified,[18] it is clear that the doc-

13. Tariff Act of 1913, ch. 16, § II.G (a) , 38 Stat. 172.

14. Int. Rev. Code of 1954, § 115 (a) .

15. G.C.M. 14407, XIV–1 C.B. 103, 105 (1935) (profits realized by state from operation of liquor stores not subject to income tax under Revenue Act of 1934 containing same relevant provisions as 1913 Tariff Act). On congressional power to impose an excise tax on agents of states acting as liquor dealers, see South Carolina v. United States, 199 U.S. 437 (1905). Also see New York v. United States, 326 U.S. 572 (1946); Allen v. Regents of the University System of Georgia, 304 U.S. 439 (1938).

16. G.C.M. 14407, XIV–1 C.B. 103 (1935). In reaching this result, the Commissioner concluded that a state is not a "corporation" within the meaning of the tax. The Government has not always required explicitness in taxing statutes as a condition to an imposition of a tax on activities carried on by states. See Mr. Justice Rutledge's concurring opinion in New York v. United States, 326 U.S. 572, 588 (1946).

17. An earlier concession made in G.C.M. 13745, XIII–2 C.B. 76 (1934), was eliminated by G.C.M. 14407, XIV–1 C.B. 103 (1935).

18. T. R. Powell's views on this were, as usual, blunt and succinct: "There is the gravest of doubts, however, whether as a matter of plain political honesty, the phrase 'from whatever source derived' should be taken to have sanctioned a one-sided modification of the scope of intergovernmental immunities." *The Remnant of Intergovernmental Tax Immunities,* 58 HARV. L. REV. 757, 805 (1945).

trine of governmental immunities has undergone great changes since that decision. Thus, in *New York ex rel. Cohn* v. *Graves* [19] it was held that the State of New York could require its residents to include rents derived from real estate outside New York in computing their state income tax. The salary of an employee of a state agency was made subject to the federal income tax in *Helvering* v. *Gerhardt*,[20] while one year later in *Graves* v. *New York ex rel. O'Keefe* [21] a state was found to have power to apply its income tax to the salaries of employees of federal instrumentalities. Additional state power was found in *Alabama* v. *King and Boozer*,[22] which held that state sales taxes might be applied to sales of material to a contractor whose contract with the Federal Government required it to reimburse the contractor for the cost of his materials including state sales taxes. Federal power was found to be sufficient to impose a non-discriminating tax on admissions to an athletic exhibition conducted by a state university,[23] the sale of mineral waters by the State of New York,[24] as well as an admissions tax on admissions to a bathing beach operated by a local park district of Illinois.[25]

The result of these decisions is that in the area of intergovernmental immunities the present focus is upon their

19. 300 U.S. 308 (1937).

20. 304 U.S. 405 (1938).

21. 306 U.S. 466 (1939). Collector v. Day, 78 U.S. (11 Wall.) 113 (1870) was overruled.

22. 314 U.S. 1 (1941).

23. Allen v. Regents of the University System of Georgia, 304 U.S. 439 (1938).

24. New York v. United States, 326 U.S. 572 (1946).

25. Wilmette Park Dist. v. Campbell, 338 U.S. 411 (1949).

limitations.[26] The one-time favored line between immune and vulnerable activities, consisting of the distinction between "historically recognized governmental functions of a State, and business engaged in by a State of a kind which theretofore has been pursued by private enterprise," [27] has been put aside as not providing a satisfactory guide in a century of expanding governmental activities. The primary test appears to be whether the specific burden or interference is one which is "actual and substantial," as opposed to speculative and conjectural, and which unduly interferes with a state's performance of its functions as a sovereign government.[28]

These and other decisions [29] have led many to contend that there exists no constitutional impediment to subjecting the interest received in respect to state and municipal securities to the federal income tax.[30] In addition, they argue that since the basic premise of *Pollock,* that a tax on income is a tax on its source, has been rejected,[31] its hold-

26. Mr. Justice Frankfurter in New York v. United States, 326 U.S. 572, 581 (1946) put it this way: "In the older cases, the emphasis was on immunity from taxation. The whole tendency of recent cases reveals a shift in emphasis to that of limitation upon immunity."

27. New York v. United States, 326 U.S. 572, 579 (1946).

28. *Cf.* United States v. Washington Toll Bridge Authority, 307 F.2d 330 (1962), *cert. denied,* 372 U.S. 911 (1963).

29. *E.g.,* Plummer v. Coler, 178 U.S. 115 (1900) (New York inheritance tax could be imposed upon a bequest of United States securities); Greneir v. Llewellyn, 285 U.S. 384 (1922) (Federal estate tax can be imposed on an estate including municipal bonds); Willcuts v. Bunn, 282 U.S. 216 (1931) (Federal income tax can be applied to profit made on resale of municipal bonds).

30. For a compilation of these authorities, see Kirby, *State and Local Bond Interest* in *Tax Revision Compendium, House Committee on Ways and Means,* 86th Cong., 1st Sess. pt. 1, at 679, 682 (1959).

31. In Graves v. New York *ex rel.* O'Keefe the court said: "The theory, which once won a qualified approval, that a tax on income is legally or economically a tax on its source, is no longer tenable. . . ." 306 U.S. 466, 480 (1939).

ing as to interest derived from municipal bonds is no longer valid. Nonetheless, others contend that, at least in this respect, *Pollock* survives.[32] In their behalf it can be said that rejection of *Pollock*'s identification of income with its source does not preclude holding that a tax on interest of municipal bonds unduly interferes with the performance of state governmental functions. Moreover, it is possible to read those decisions of the Court which have circumscribed and limited the scope of immunity enjoyed by municipal bond interest [33] as implicitly recognizing its constitutional basis.[34]

In any event, despite repeated efforts to have the exemption removed from the statute so that the constitutional issue could be tested directly,[35] Congress has stood firm.

32. *Cf. Hearings on the Revenue Revision of 1951 before the House Ways and Means Committee,* 82d Cong., 1st Sess. 915–18, 922–30 (1951).

33. The reference is to Willcuts v. Bunn, n. 29 *supra;* Denman v. Slayton, 282 U.S. 514 (1931) (denial of deduction for interest on indebtedness incurred to purchase or carry tax-exempt bonds constitutionally valid); United States v. Atlas Life Ins. Co., 381 U.S. 233 (1965).

34. Lowndes, *Current Constitutional Problems In Federal Taxation,* 4 VAND. L. REV. 469, 481 (1951). For another approach to the relevance of these and similar decisions to immunity of municipal bond interest, see T. R. Powell, *The Remnant of Intergovernmental Immunities,* 58 HARV. L. REV. 757 (1945). Implied recognition also exists in the recent Court decision in United States v. Atlas Life Ins. Co., 381 U.S. 233 (1965). One issue was the constitutional validity of that part of The Life Insurance Company Income Tax Act of 1959 which required a portion of the company's tax-exempt interest to be apportioned to policyholder reserves in computing the taxable investment income in the company. Increments to the policyholder reserves were not part of taxable investment income. It was argued by the taxpayer company that such an allocation forced it to surrender the tax benefit of that portion of the tax-exempt interest which was assigned to the policyholder reserves. It followed, argued the company, that this infringed the constitutional and statutory immunity of tax-exempt interest. The Court found that neither was infringed. In doing so, however, it did not assert that interest derived from State or municipal bonds was entitled to no constitutional immunity, a position which would have narrowed the issue to one of interpreting the 1959 Act; rather, the Court held that the case fell within the principle of Denman v. Slayton, n. 33 *supra,* which, as interpreted, is that tax laws may charge exempt income "with a fair share of the burdens properly allocable to it."

35. A brief history of these efforts, the most recent serious one of which was in 1951, is set forth in Kirby, *State and Local Bond Interest* in *Tax*

This stalwart performance provides some wry consolation to those who have urged that removal of the constitutional immunity would not imperil state and local government because Congress, being chosen from the states, could be depended upon to resist undue encroachment by federal power. Except to the extent the effort to tax the business income of state colleges and universities previously mentioned represents some faltering, this unyielding posture on the part of Congress banishes most questions concerning the vitality of *Pollock*'s one unanimous holding to the realm of speculation.

2. *Application of the Macrocriteria*

The revenue loss, while difficult to estimate accurately, attributable to exclusion of interest received in respect to state and local bonds appears to be very substantial.[36] On the basis of 1964 figures, a loss of between $1 and $1.2 billion appears not unlikely.[37] Adequacy thus requires

---

Revision Compendium, House Committee on Ways and Means, 86th Cong., 1st Sess. pt. 1, at 679, 680–81 (1959).

36. Kirby, *ibid.,* estimated on the basis of 1958 figures that the loss was "in the vicinity of some $600 million." Pechman estimated on the basis of 1957 figures that $300 million in revenue was lost because of tax-exempt interest received by individuals. *What Would a Comprehensive Individual Income Tax Yield?* in *Tax Revision Compendium, House Committee on Ways and Means,* 86th Cong., 1st Sess. pt. 1, at 251, 279 (1959). Hellmuth, *id.* at 283, 289, estimated that in 1956 corporations received $528 million in tax-exempt interest. At a rate of 50 per cent, this represents an additional loss of $264 million in revenue. However, estimates which ignore both the change in interest rates of both municipal and corporate bonds likely to follow removal of the immunity and any altered pattern of holdings by individuals and corporations are probably inaccurate. *Cf.* Maxwell's estimate for 1955, which appears in the same volume, and which to a degree makes such allowances. His figure is a loss within the range of $550–$680 million. *Id.* at 712.

37. There are several rather crude ways in which this guess can be substantiated. The first is to compare the total amount of state and local securities outstanding and held by individuals and private corporations in 1958 with that existing in 1964. The extent to which this amount has increased when expressed as a percentage and applied to the revenue loss estimates for 1958 set forth in n. 36 *supra* will yield an estimate of 1964 losses. The following table sets forth this estimate:

that this omission from the tax base be carefully examined in the light of other criteria. Practicality also lends no aid and comfort to the exclusion. Not only does the scope of tax-exempt interest pose difficulties,[38] but policing the de-

Year	Total Amount Outstanding	Percentage Increase over 1958	Revenue Loss
1958	48.9	. .	.6
1964	91.3	.87	1.1

The amounts outstanding are derived from Annual Report of the Secretary of the Treasury on the State of Finances, 590 (1964).

A somewhat more refined estimate can be obtained by (1) dividing the total amount outstanding in 1964 between individual and corporate holdings, (2) assuming an interest rate of 3.28 per cent on state and local securities, (3) approximating the amount of interest received by these two classes of owners, and (4) applying to such approximate amounts a rate of tax of 35 per cent for individuals and 45 per cent for corporations. The results of these steps are as follows:

(In Billions of Dollars)

Type of Owner	Amount Outstanding *	Amount of Interest at 3.28% †	Tax Rate	Estimated Loss of Revenue
Individuals.......	33.5	1.1	35%	.38
Corporations ‡....	49.8	1.6	45%	.72
Tax-exempt Organizations.....	8.0	.26		
Total..........	91.3	2.96		1.1

* SECRETARY OF THE TREASURY, ANNUAL REP. ON THE STATE OF FINANCES, 590 (1964).

† May, 1965, interest rate for state and local bonds (not significantly different from rates prevailing in May, 1964), FED. RES. BULL. 852 (June, 1965).

‡ Includes commercial banks, insurance companies, mutual savings banks.

These estimates ignore any changes in interest rates, distribution of holdings, or rate of growth in amount of such securities should the exemption be removed. Also ignored is the fact that a removal of the exemption may operate only prospectively.

38. See pp. 306–10 *supra*.

nial of a deduction for interest on an indebtedness incurred or continued to purchase or carry obligations whose interest is tax-exempt also generates enforcement problems.[39]

Equity obviously condemns the exclusion. The source of income is irrelevant under the terms of this criterion. Spokesmen against the exclusion have long made this deviation a focal point of their attack.[40]

Because of graduated rates it is not possible to assert that in all instances the market will depress the rate of interest yielded by state and local bonds to a degree sufficient to eliminate any tax advantage attributable to the exclusion. Higher-bracket taxpayers obtain a greater advantage than do their less fortunate fellows.[41] Tables in

39. *Cf.* Bishop v. Comm'r, 342 F.2d 757 (6th Cir. 1965), where issue was whether an indebtedness was "continued" in order to purchase or carry obligations producing tax-exempt interest. The case at least stands for the proposition that one cannot avoid the proscription of § 265, Int. Rev. Code 1954 by (1) borrowing funds to purchase non-exempt obligations, (2) their sale at a profit not followed by payment of the debt incurred for their purchase price, and (3) the investment of the sales proceeds in tax-exempt obligations. What should be the result where cash is used to purchase tax-exempt obligations followed shortly by borrowing to purchase non-exempt obligations which are used as collateral to secure the loan? Simons condemned the statutory denial as useless. "While the law clearly prohibits this device of evasion [direct borrowing to purchase tax-exempt securities], the prohibition is entirely ineffective. Congress may rest comfortable in the notion that it has dealt with the problem; actually, it has only laid down an ambiguous and unenforceable rule; for application of the rule requires determination of purpose or intention." PERSONAL TAXABLE INCOME, 179, (1938).

40. *E.g.*, Kirby, *State and Local Bond Interest* in *Tax Revision Compendium, House Committee on Ways and Means,* 86th Cong., 1st Sess. pt. 1, at 679, 683–85 (1959); Statement of John W. Snyder, Secretary of the Treasury, *Hearings on the Revenue Revision of 1951 before the House Ways and Means Committee,* 82d Cong., 1st Sess. 4, 13–14 (1951); Statement of Randolph E. Paul, Special Tax Adviser to Secretary of the Treasury, *Hearings on the Revenue Revision of 1942 before the House Ways and Means Committee,* 77th Cong., 2d Sess. Vol. 3, 3079–84 (1942); S. REP. No. 2140, 76th Cong., 3d Sess. pt. 1, 6, 7 (1940).

41. "If all income were taxed proportionately, and all holders were taxable, then exemption of income from certain bonds would bring about increase in their price equal to the value of the exemption to each buyer.

Moody's Municipal & Government Manual [42] bring this home to the interested investor. Thus, a taxpayer whose marginal rate is 50 per cent will find a 3.3 per cent yield by tax-exempt securities equivalent to a pre-tax yield from taxable securities of 6.6 per cent, while a taxpayer with a marginal rate of 25 per cent will find an identical tax-exempt yield equivalent only to a pre-tax yield of 4.4 per cent from taxable securities. [43] The rate of tax-exempt interest would have to drop to 2.2 per cent before its value to a 50 per cent taxpayer would fall to the level of 4.4 per cent from taxable securities. Thus, when the interest rate on tax-exempts stabilizes at 3.09 and 4.44 per cent for Aaa corporate bonds—the levels prevailing in May 1965 [44]—the 50 per cent taxpayer will continue to find the tax-exempts a better buy, but the 25 per cent taxpayer will not. [45]

Free Market Compatibility also does not support the exclusion. As the foregoing inter-taxpayer comparisons should make clear, the exclusion, when joined with graduated rates, can significantly influence individual investment decisions. Elimination of graduation, while retain-

---

The Government would not be a loser since the lower yield at which it issued the tax exempts would be equivalent to the taxes it agreed to forego. But when income is taxed progressively, the value of exemption becomes worth more to buyers according to the size of their taxable income, and this graduated value will not be fully reflected in the price of an issue." Maxwell, *Exclusion from Income of Interest on State and Local Government Obligations* in *Tax Revision Compendium, House Committee on Ways and Means,* 86th Cong., 1st Sess. pt. 1, 701, 706 (1959) .

42. *E.g.,* Special Features Section at a14, a15, a16 (February, 1965) .

43. These figures are fairly obvious, but they can be checked in Moody's Municipal & Government Manual, a15 (February 1965) .

44. Fed. Res. Bull. 852 (June 1965) .

45. The after-tax yield of the Aaa corporate bond to the 50 per cent taxpayer is 2.22 per cent. 3.09 per cent is obviously preferable, *ceteris paribus.* To a 25 per cent taxpayer the *A* and *a* corporate bond will yield an after-tax return of 3.33 per cent, a return in excess of that of equivalent tax-exempts.

ing the exclusion, would restore neutrality in the market place between taxable and tax-exempt securities,[46] but there would remain a greater allocation of total resources to state and local governments than would be the case were there no exclusion.[47]

While Stability has little to offer here, besides the obvious point that inclusion of all interest will broaden the tax base,[48] Reduced Economic Inequality speaks loudly. Tax-exempt interest, without regard to its other possible beneficiaries, directly benefits the rich; and what is more, the richer the taxpayer, the greater the benefit. It is hard to imagine a provision more deficient when measured by this criterion. Its effect in this respect is to increase economic inequality, not to reduce it.

Justification, if at all possible, must be found within the broad confines of the criterion of Political Order. Although estimates vary somewhat in accordance with the bias of the investigator, a spokesman not too friendly toward the exemption stated in 1959 that interest costs to state and local governments would increase three-fourths to one percentage point were the exemption eliminated.[49] The case for the exemption rests upon the undesirability

46. *Cf.* n. 40 *supra*.

47. That is, there would remain a revenue loss by the Federal Government which would approximate in amount the interest savings to State and local governments made possible by the exemption. See Kirby, *State and Local Bond Interest* in *Tax Revision Compendium, House Committee on Ways and Means*, 86th Cong., 1st Sess. pt. 1, at 679, 688 (1959). These interest savings result in a greater allocation of resources to such governments than would exist in their absence.

48. It is conjectural how much elimination of the exemption would improve "built-in flexibility" inasmuch as the responsiveness of tax-exempt interest to changes in the level of economic activity is not great. However, aggregate demand perhaps may be increased, albeit under some circumstances this may not be desirable, by relieving bond holders with a relatively low marginal propensity to consume of part of their interest income and giving it to others with a higher marginal propensity.

49. See Kirby, *State and Local Bond Interest* in *Tax Revision Compendium, House Committee on Ways and Means*, 86th Cong., 1st Sess. pt. 1, at

of this increase and the contribution which immunity of state and local bond interest from the taxation by the Federal Government makes to federalism.[50] Proponents argue that an increase in interest costs would require heavier reliance by states and municipalities on property and sales taxes, or result in reduced outlays, or both.[51] Moreover, they point out that another not unlikely consequence is intensified pressure for additional direct aid by

---

679, 687 (1959). This estimate roughly corresponded to the then differential in yield between high-grade municipals and comparable corporate bonds. As of May 29, 1965, the differential between *A* and *a* tax-exempts and *A* and *a* corporates was 1.35 per cent. FED. RES. BULL. 852 (June 1965). An earlier Treasury study estimated the additional interest cost at between one-quarter and five-eighths of 1 per cent. *Hearings on the Revenue Revision before the House Ways and Means Committee,* 77th Cong., 2d Sess. Vol. 3, 3083 (1942). *Accord, Hearings on Proposed Legislation Relative to Tax-Exempt Securities before the House Committee on Ways and Means,* 76th Cong., 1st Sess. 47 (1939). Spokesmen more friendly to the exemption have usually estimated the "cost" of removal of the exemption at a somewhat higher figure, Statement by Professor F. R. Fairchild, *Hearings on the Revenue Revision before the House Ways and Means Committee,* 77th Cong., 2d Sess. Vol. 2, 1518 (1942).

Ott estimates the increased interest cost as a 1.10–2.02 percentage point rise. Rejecting the typical method of determining the yield differential between tax-exempt and taxable securities by reference to the yields on outstanding long-term corporate and municipal bonds of comparable quality as given in Moody's series, Ott relies on the opinions of capital market experts. From these, he concludes that the removal of the exemption will have two basic effects: (1) a general rise in interest costs of 1.01–1.84 percentage points (the minimum figure equals the differential between *public* corporate new issue and municipal yields; the maximum figure equals the differential between yields on *private* corporate placements and yields on municipals of comparable quality); (2) a further increase caused by the "flattening," of the municipal bond yield curve (due to the weakening of support by banks in short-dated obligations and the increased investment at the long end by life insurance companies and pension funds). The compounding of these two effects gives the 1.19–2.02 estimate. Ott, *Federal Tax Reform: The Exemption of State-Local Bond Interest,* PROCEEDINGS OF THE FIFTY-FIFTH NAT'L TAX ASS'N 70, 71–74 (1963). For a more detailed explanation, see OTT & MELTZER, FEDERAL TAX TREATMENT OF STATE AND LOCAL SECURITIES 50–61 (1963).

50. McGee, *Exemption of Interest on State and Municipal Bonds* in *Tax Revision Compendium, House Committee on Ways and Means,* 86th Cong., 1st Sess. pt. 1, at 737 *et seq.* (1959).

51. *Id.* at 735–55.

the Federal Government. No proponent denies that the exemption provides very substantial indirect help to state and local government, but all emphatically insist its present form is preferable to more direct assistance.[52]

The opposition to the exclusion usually counters by pointing out that because the revenue loss suffered by the Federal Government exceeds the value of the benefits received by state and local governments,[53] the "subsidy" to these instrumentalities is inefficient and wasteful. This "waste," it is pointed out, goes into the pockets of the wealthy and contributes little to the welfare of state and local government. A federalism which demands for its sustenance such a disregard of Reduced Economic Inequality is, it is suggested, not worth preserving. Particularly is this true when direct aid by the Federal Government is too common to merit either concern or notice. That this rebuttal amounts to asserting that the end of Reduced Economic Inequality makes desirable some impairment of federalism is seldom explicitly recognized.

52. See Sneed, *The Criteria of Federal Income Tax Policy*, 17 STAN. L. REV. 567 (1965) for a summary of the reasons which indirect assistance through the structure of the income tax is thought to be preferable by some.

53. The difference between the extent of the revenue loss to the Federal Government and the interest savings made possible by the exemption is largely attributable to rate progression. Kirby, *State and Local Bond Interest* in *Tax Revision Compendium, House Committee on Ways and Means*, 86th Cong., 1st Sess. pt. 1, at 679, 688 (1959). As previously indicated, pp. 301–2 *supra*, interest rates on municipal securities level out at a point which provides an after-tax rate of return to the wealthy taxpayer in excess of that obtained by the less wealthy. This "excess" benefit to the wealthy is thus not directly reflected in reduced interest rates available to state and local governments. However, to the extent such benefit draws additional funds into the municipal bond market, the interest rate is lowered. It has been pointed out that the differential in rates between corporate and municipal bonds is attributable, not only to the exclusion, but also to rate progression, level of rates, and the volumes of state and local issues. Maxwell, *Exclusion From Income of Interest on State and Local Government Obligations* in *Tax Revision Compendium, House Committee on Ways and Means*, 86th Cong., 1st Sess. pt. 1, at 701, 708 (1959).

Thus, the lines are drawn. A tangible economic benefit to state and local government and a political belief are arrayed against Practicality, Equity, Free Market Compatibility, and Reduced Economic Inequality. The power of Political Order as a macrocriterion is nowhere better demonstrated.

3. Scope of Exclusions

Notwithstanding the statutory language which only excludes interest "on the obligations of a State . . . , or any political subdivision" thereof, the Treasury and the courts have given the language a generous interpretation. Thus, as early as 1921 the regulations construed the exclusion to embrace securities issued "on behalf of" a state or a political subdivision thereof.[54] Moreover, in 1914 the term "political subdivision" was given a "broad and comprehensive" meaning which embraced divisions that exercised, although not all, at least some of the functions of a state for a public purpose.[55] The present regulations are written in the same spirit.[56] Thus, divisions lacking the power of taxation may constitute a "political subdivision." [57] In addition, the exclusion of interest established by the Code is

54. T.D. 3146, 23 Treas. Dec. Int. Rev. 352, 377 (1921). This language now appears in Treas. Reg. § 1.103–1 (1956).

55. 30 Ops. Att'y Gen. 252, 253 (1914), quoted and interpreted in Comm'r v. Shamberg's Estate, 144 F.2d 998, 1004 (2d Cir. 1944).

56. The term "political subdivision," for purposes of this section, denotes any division of the State, Territory, or possession of the United States which is a municipal corporation, or to which has been delegated the right to exercise part of the sovereign power of the State, Territory, or possession of the United States. As thus defined, a political subdivision of a State, Territory, or possession of the United States may or may not, for the purposes of this section, include special assessment districts so created, such as road, water, sewer, gas, light, reclamation, drainage, irrigation, levee, school, harbor, port improvement, and similar districts and divisions of a State, Territory, or possession of the United States." Treas. Reg. § 1.103–1 (1956).

57. Comm'r v. Shamberg's Estate, 144 F.2d 998, 1005 (2d Cir. 1944).

not drawn to correspond to any constitutional limitations on the power of Congress.[58]

In keeping with this expansive interpretation, interest on the obligations of the Port of New York Authority,[59] the Triborough Bridge Authority,[60] the Massachusetts Turnpike Authority,[61] the Mackinac Bridge Authority,[62] and, to mention only one more, the New York State Housing Finance Agency [63] have been considered tax-exempts. The exclusion of interest also reaches that paid with respect to special assessment certificates which evidence assessments against specific property and which are payable only from special funds.[64]

Perhaps, interpretational generosity reached a high-water mark in the ruling that interest on the obligations of certain industrial development corporations was within the sacred circle.[65] Usually, these are revenue bonds of private "non-profit" organizations sold to permit the construction of an industrial facility which is to be leased to private concerns for thirty or forty years, after which it belongs to a designated political subdivision. Although it has been argued that these "non-profit" organizations are not "political subdivisions" and that their obligations are not issued "on behalf of" any such subdivision,[66] the Serv-

58. *Id.* at 1003.

59. *Ibid.*

60. Comm'r v. White, 144 F.2d 1019 (2d Cir. 1944).

61. Rev. Rul. 57–308, 1957–2 C.B. 94.

62. Rev. Rul. 55–75, 1955–1 C.B. 238.

63. Rev. Rul. 60–248, 1960–2 C.B. 35.

64. Treas. Reg. § 1.103–1 (1956). A contrary position once prevailed. *Cf.* G.C.M. 16861, XV–2 C.B. 179 (1936).

65. See Spiegel, *Financing Private Ventures With Tax-Exempt Bonds: A Developing "Truckhole" in the Tax Law,* 17 STAN. L. REV. 224 (1965).

66. *Id.* at 230–32.

ice holds the obligations within the "on behalf of" language when certain quite not-too-restrictive requirements are met.[67]

There are, however, limits on the interest exclusion. Thus, instalment payments of a condemnation award providing interest have been held not to generate tax-exempt interest;[68] but an ordinary written contract of purchase and sale between a governmental unit and a private individual which provides for deferred payments with interest will have this effect.[69] In addition, gain on the sale of a municipal obligation,[70] premiums received on redemption,[71] and penalties on default[72] do not constitute

67. Rev. Rul. 63–20, 1963–1 C.B. 24. These requirements are: "(1) the corporation must engage in activities which are essentially public in nature; (2) the corporation must be one which is not organized for profit (except to the extent of retiring indebtedness); (3) the corporate income must not inure to any private person; (4) the state or a political subdivision thereof must have a beneficial interest in the corporation while the indebtedness remains outstanding and it must obtain full legal title to the property of the corporation with respect to which the indebtedness was incurred upon the retirement of such indebtedness; and (5) the corporation must have been approved by the state or a political subdivision thereof, either of which must also have approved the specific obligations issued by the corporation." The Treasury indicated in June 1966 that restrictions in this area were being studied.

68. Halley v. United States, 124 F.2d 909 (6th Cir. 1942) (debt must be incurred under borrowing power not under power of eminent domain); U.S. Trust Co. of New York, 65 F.2d 577 (2d Cir. 1933) (taxation of interest on condemnation award will not impair borrowing power of States and their subdivisions).

69. Kings County Dev. Co. v. Comm'r, 93 F.2d 33 (9th Cir. 1937), *cert. denied,* 304 U.S. 559. Rev. Rul. 60–179, 1960–1 C.B. 37. However, a binding "obligation" to pay must exist. Newlin Mach. Corp., 28 T.C. 837 (1957) (A). While prior to the enactment of §483 it was clear that these written agreements must explicitly provide for interest payments, see I.T. 2674, XI1–1 C.B. 96 (1933), it is probable that this is no longer necessary.

70. Willcuts v. Bunn, 282 U.S. 216 (1931).

71. District Bond Co., 1 T.C. 837 (1943) (premium not compensation for use of money and, hence, not interest).

72. Susanna Bixby Bryant, 2 T.C. 789 (1943).

tax-exempt interest; on the other hand, original issue discount does constitute such interest.[73]

As indicated earlier, Congress has not sought to tax the income of state and local governments except to the extent section 511 (a) (2) (B) of the 1954 Code purports to subject the business income of state colleges and universities to the corporation tax.[74] Moreover, there is excluded income derived from a public utility accruing to a state or political subdivision.[75] In view of this, the fairly elaborate language of subsections 115 (b) and (c), whose predecessors first appeared in 1918 and 1928 respectively, is puzzling when first examined. However, its general purpose is not difficult to grasp. The effort is to bring within the exclusion, by means of permitting a refund of taxes previously paid, certain proceeds attributable to the operation of utilities or bridges by private instrumentalities which "accrue directly to or for the use of" a state or political subdivision. In short, it extends the exclusion a bit, but only a bit, beyond the limits fixed by Congressional silence and subsection 115 (a).[76] However, this dispensation is limited to certain contracts entered into before September 8, 1916, in the case of subsection 115 (b), and May 29, 1938, in that of subsection 115 (c). And even

73. G.C.M. 10452, X–1 C.B. 18 (1932); I.T. 2629, X–1 C.B. 20 (1932). "Market discount," the discount at which bonds previously issued at par are sold and purchased, is not interest but capital gain.

74. See p. 295 *supra*.

75. "Accruing" has been interpreted to mean "to come into existence as an enforceable claim; to vest as a right; as, a cause of action has *accrued* when the right to sue has become vested." Omaha Pub. Power Dist. v. O'Maulley, 232 F.2d 805 (8th Cir. 1956); Bear Gulch Water Co. v. Comm'r, 116 F.2d 975 (9th Cir. 1941.)

76. *Cf.* Philadelphia Rapid Transit Co. v. United States, 8 F. Supp. 152 (E.D. Pa. 1934).

in the case of such contracts, a direct accrual to or for the use of the governmental instrumentality is required.[77] Interpretive generosity is not apparent in this area.

77. *Cf.* City of Burlington v. United States, 148 F.2d 867 (8th Cir. 1945). For an instance where the requirements of these provisions appear to have been met, see City of Galveston v. United States, 10 F. Supp. 810 (Ct. Cl. 1935), *cert. denied*, 297 U.S. 712 (1936). The courts appear quite willing to find no appropriate accrual when there stands between the governmental unit and the utility legal entities whose existence can not be disregarded on the grounds of sham. *Cf.* Town of Fairhaven v. United States 142 F. Supp. 590 (Ct. Cl. 1956).

XIX. Cancellation of Indebtedness

IT IS NEVER EASY to locate appropriately in discussions of gross income the problems arising from the cancellation of indebtedness. The difficulty is caused primarily by the unsatisfactory state of theoretic analysis of the transaction and, secondarily, by the confusion which characterizes both the results and language of the relevant cases. In this discussion it has been decided to place these problems at the conclusion of the treatment of statutory modifications and refinements because, first, there is partial statutory treatment of the area [1] and, second, the complexities are better understood with the perspective provided by all that has gone before. Nonetheless, the cancellation-of-indebtedness area does not fit neatly here or elsewhere; it is unique and resists stubbornly the skill of the taxonomist.

1. Two Approaches to the Cancellation-of-Indebtedness Transaction

With this acknowledgment of hesitancy and uncertainty out of the way, what passes as the base rule in the area should be stated. It is that the cancellation of a debt, in whole or in part, may result in the realization of income.[2]

1. Int. Rev. Code of 1954, §§ 108, 1017.
2. Treas. Reg. § 1.61–12 (a) (1957).

Whether it does depends on numerous subordinate rules; but it is fairly clear that if A borrows $1,000 from B and, while A's assets exceed his liabilities, B agrees to cancel A's debt in exchange for the present payment of $900 by A, that A has income of $100, providing the discharge cannot be characterized as a gift.[3] The result is proper because A's net worth from a balance sheet standpoint has been increased by $100 and, under the facts as stated, there is now available to A $100 in "assets previously offset"[4] by a now extinguished debt of $100. It is not inaccurate to insist that A has received an "accession to wealth" in the amount of $100 which should be taxed as income.

There is another way to view the transaction, however. It begins by recalling that A's promise to repay the $1,000 constitutes an investment by him in the loan proceeds.[5] It continues by pointing out that A may use these proceeds for current consumption or to acquire other assets or benefits which may be used in either gain-directed or personal activities. The current consumption of borrowed funds or their use to obtain current benefits is a form of "living on capital," the capital consisting of the future productive capacity of A. On the other hand, A's *use* of the funds to acquire other assets is neither "living on capital" nor an *additional* investment of $1,000. A's total investment re-

3. The proper starting point in the long procession of decisions relating to this area is United States v. Kirby Lumber Co., 284 U.S. 1 (1931), where Mr. Justice Holmes, in delivering the opinion of the Court, stated a purchase in the open market of bonds issued by the taxpayer at a price less than the issue price, which was par, resulted in income. A more recent decision, Comm'r v. Jacobson, 336 U.S. 28 (1949), involves facts closer to those stated in the text than does *Kirby* and reaches the same result.

4. The Court in *Kirby*, n. 3 *supra*, said: "As a result of its dealings it made available $137, 521.30 assets previously offset by the obligation of bonds now extinct." 248 U.S. at 2.

5. Chap. ii, p. 19 *supra*.

mains $1,000 and does not become $2,000. Put slightly differently, A's only investment remains a commitment of his future productive capacity to the extent of $1,000. A's purchase of assets with borrowed funds, therefore, merely constitutes a *transformation* of A's original investment.

Because it is clear that both A's promise to pay $1,000 and his payment of that sum cannot both be treated as investments, the decision to treat A's promise as an investment requires that his payment not be so treated. It follows that A's payment *legitimates* his only investment—his promise to pay B $1,000 in the future. Put another way, A's commitment of his future productive capacity is honored when he pays his debt to B. However, should A pay B only $900 in discharge of the entire $1,000 debt, a portion of A's investment is not *legitimated*. Where A has consumed the entire loan proceeds, the result of the discharge by the payment of only $900 is that he has enjoyed consumption in the amount of $100 for which he has not been required to pay. On the other hand, where A used the loan proceeds to acquire other assets or benefits, the cost thereof should now be corrected to reflect the fact that it has been legitimated only to the extent of $900. This would require either a downward adjustment of the basis of the acquired assets to the extent of $100 or recognition of gain of $100 if the expenditure resulted in a deductible expense.

It follows under this view of the cancellation-of-indebtedness transaction that, to the extent A used the loan proceeds to satisfy personal wants, it is necessary to regard $100 as income. However, to the extent that assets acquired with the loan proceeds have generated business or investment deductions (computed on the assumption that A's investment of $1,000 would be legitimated by full performance of his obligation), it is necessary in theory to regard as income the difference between such deductions so computed and those which would have been proper in light of the necessary $100 reduction in basis or deductible expenditures. Only in this way can there be proper compensation for the understatement of income in the periods prior to discharge. Finally, the logic of this view makes a single reduction of basis without recognition of gain appropriate when, and only when, (1) there has been neither personal consumption nor a previous understatement of income and (2) the assets acquired by use of the loan proceeds have not been transferred and can be identified,[6] should the basis of the acquired assets be reduced and gain not recognized. To insist upon recognition of gain in these circumstances on the ground of a "balance sheet improvement" is to ignore the linkage between the borrower's promise to pay the debt and the basis of the acquired assets.

Obviously, these conditions for non-recognition often do not exist, and, more important, it is frequently extremely difficult to ascertain whether they exist or not. Thus, both Practicality and Equity, albeit the latter to a smaller degree, suggest that, even under this more elaborate view, it be assumed as a general rule that debt forgiveness is income. In this way nice distinctions and laborious complications involving several tax years are usually

6. In Helvering v. American Chicle Co., 291 U.S. 426 (1933), the argument was made that where bonds assumed in an acquisition of assets were purchased for less than their par value, there should be no recognition of gain but rather a reduction in the purchase price of the assets. The Court rejected the position and found gain. In doing so, however, the Court pointed out that it was not shown what had become of the acquired assets or whether they still existed. Presumably, such facts were considered to be relevant. The decision supports, and is not inconsistent with, the approach set forth in the text.

avoided. Only when the taxpayer can show (1) that there has been neither personal consumption of the loan proceeds nor an understatement of income and (2) that the assets acquired, if any, by the use of the loan proceeds have not been transferred and can be identified, should gain not be recognized.

The critic, puzzled by the labyrinth through which he has just been led, may assert that the simple "accession to wealth" approach with which the discussion began is but an elliptical form of the more complex one just described. Perhaps so, but this ellipsis, if such it be, induces analysis and reasoning different from that which follows from the more complete analysis. The focus under the "accession to wealth" approach becomes the extent to which the taxpayer has experienced an increase in net worth and not whether the taxpayer has succeeded in demonstrating that a basis adjustment is appropriate.

Moreover, it is easy to demonstrate that the idea of an "increase in net worth" is also complex. For example, measurement of the accession to the debtor's wealth is not easy when the obligation discharged is one which he disputed in good faith. Where the debtor pays an amount not less than what, if anything, he admits is due, and the creditor, although claiming more is due, agrees to accept the amount paid in full discharge, it is not easy to assert that the debtor has received an increment to wealth. Whether there has occurred a balance sheet improvement depends upon the amount of the liability discharged for balance sheet purposes, and this is precisely what the dispute was about. It is reasonable in such a case to regard the debtor as realizing no gain, either at the time of the discharge or later, even though subsequent events demonstrate that the debtor obtained a "bargain." Existing decisions tend to support this view.[7]

The complexity is reduced somewhat when the discharge is of a liability contingent upon circumstances which are unknown at the time. Again the value of the thing received by the debtor from the creditor, the discharge, cannot be said unequivocally to be greater than what the debtor has given therefor. The second circuit once put it this way: "If A covenants under seal to pay B half of next year's business profits and later pays B $1000 for release of the covenant, it is obviously impossible to tell immediately whether the transaction was profitable or the reverse. . . . Moreover, the release of A's covenant could not possibly free capital assets from a pre-existing liability (as in the *Kirby* case) for the covenant created no charge upon his capital assets."[8]

Under the second and more elaborate approach, it is also possible to contend that in none of these cases is recognition of income necessary. For example, settlement of a disputed liability by payment of a sum not less than what the debtor admits is owing merely determines the extent of the debtor's investment in the first instance. The *legitimation* of consumption, a previous expense deduction, or investment by the inclusion of some amount in income in many instances would be either unnecessary or

7. Fidelity & Columbia Trust Co. v. Lucas, 11 F. Supp. 537 (W.D. Ky. 1935), *aff'd on another issue*, 89 F.2d 945 (6th Cir. 1937) (compromise of a claim of dower disputed by estate results in no gain to estate although estate in compromise recognized that claimant was wife of decedent and paid less than the value of dower) ; N. Sobel, Inc., 40 B.T.A. 1263 (1939) (NA) (compromise of note given as purchase price of bank shares by payment of less than its face results in no income where taxpayer in good faith contested his liability on the notes and ownership of shares by seeking rescission). *Cf.* Ruben v. Comm'r, 97 F.2d 926 (8th Cir. 1938) ; David L. Zips, 38 T.C. 620, 632 (1962) (dissenting opinion).

8. Corporacion de Ventas de Salitre y Yoda de Chili v. Comm'r, 130 F.2d 141, 144 (2d Cir. 1942) (L. Hand, J. dissenting).

impractical. Much the same can be said where an original contingent liability is discharged, or where a primary obligation is reduced to a secondary one, providing in the latter case the further elimination of the secondary liability is not permitted to occur without close scrutiny to ascertain whether recognition of gain is necessary.

In truth, the difference between the two approaches lies not in the simplicity of the first and the complexity of the second, but in the superior rationality of the second. Under it a holding in the cancellation-of-debt case can be evaluated more critically and, as will be seen, a means is provided by which certain apparently erratic cases can be understood even if not approved.

2. Some Puzzling Cancellation-of-Indebtedness Situations

a. Where Cancelled Debt May Exceed Value of Consideration Received by Debtor at Debt's Creation

The asserted superiority of the second approach can be put promptly to test by focusing on an unusual, but analytically revealing, situation which occurs when the debtor receives from the creditor at the time of the debt's creation consideration (1) having either no ascertainable value or a value less than the face of the debt, or (2) which directly benefits a third party.

Simply put, the issue can be framed by asking whether the discharge of a debt of $100, incurred to obtain $50 in cash without stated interest, in exchange for repayment of $50 results in gain. Even more simply put, does the discharge of a debt of $100 result in gain where no funds were received at its creation and none paid to obtain the discharge? Viewed from the standpoint of the second approach, the answer is fairly clear. In neither case is a finding of gain necessary because in each the repayment (zero in the latter case) matches the extent to which there could have been any consumption, deductible expenditure, or investment by the debtor of the loan proceeds. One who receives loan proceeds of $50 can invest from that source only that amount or less. When he repays that amount every possible cent of expenditure made from the loan proceeds is now backed by an investment in the form of cash. Hence, no gain under this analysis need exist in either case, even though in both there has been a balance sheet improvement. The point is, of course, that this balance sheet improvement is merely the rectification of a balance sheet impairment which occurred when the loan was made. Neither impairment nor improvement should have tax consequences under these circumstances. In both, the debt forgiveness may be considered a return of capital which the promise to pay represented.

This analysis, albeit unusual, is not fanciful inasmuch as it accords with the results of several cases and provides an explanation better than that usually employed by the courts. In *Fashion Park, Inc.,*[9] for example, debentures, having the stated face value of $50 issued as the result of transactions which fixed the amount received on issuance at $5.00, were discharged through their acquisition by the debtor for a price greater than $5.00 and less than $50. No gain resulted from this transaction. The court viewed the test to be "whether there has been in fact an increase in the taxpayer's assets by reason of the transaction."[10] In a narrow sense this test is met in every debt-forgiveness case

9. 21 T.C. 600 (1954).
10. *Id.* at 606.

because the discharge never increases assets qua assets. It is net worth, if anything, which is increased. But the court intended a broader test, one which focused attention on the entire transaction in the manner that Mr. Justice Butler employed when, in sweeping aside the assertion that the discharge of a debt with depreciated currency resulted in income, he observed that there was no gain because "The result of the whole transaction was a loss." [11] This wide-lens approach is not too helpful, however, because the nub of the problem is not the necessity for viewing the transaction as a whole, but rather the manner in which the whole transaction should be viewed.

Fashion Park, Inc. had its progenitors. In *Commissioner v. Rail Joint Co.*[12] debentures issued as dividends against an upward reappraisal of assets were discharged by the payment of less than their face value. No gain resulted. The court moved close to the mark in observing that the determination of the presence of gain requires an examination of what is received at the time of issuance as well as what was paid upon discharge. In addition, it appears settled that the reacquisition of bonds at a discount by the obligor results in gain only to the extent the issue price, where this is less than par, exceeds the cost of reacquisition.[13]

11. Bowes v. Kerbaugh-Empire Co., 271 U.S. 170, 175.

12. 61 F.2d 751 (2d Cir. 1932).

13. Kramon Dev. Co., 3 T.C. 342 (1944); Norfolk So. R.R., 25 B.T.A. 925 (1932). The statement in the text does not account for the consequence of having amortized a portion of the discount prior to reacquisition. How should this affect the gain on reacquisition? It is said that the amount of gain realized upon reacquisition of bonds is the difference between the face amount, *increased* by any premium not previously reported as income or *decreased* by any amount of discount not previously deducted, and the reacquisition price. The recognition of gain to the extent of previously deducted discount is simply an adjustment for interest which, although previously deducted, was never in fact paid.

The alternative to an inflexible balance-sheet-improve-ment approach offered here admittedly encounters addi-tional difficulties, however, when the consideration received consists of benefits other than money and tangible property or when the consideration moves to one other than the obligor. A somewhat simple, but melodramatic, example will serve to illustrate these difficulties. Assume a father is concerned about the welfare of his daughter because of attentions being directed toward her by a particular young man. This concerned father promises to pay the young man the sum of $1,000 if he will cease such attentions and re-move himself from the daughter's life. The young man does so. Later, because of circumstances other than the father's insolvency (which for the moment the imagina-tion may be relied upon to supply), the debt is settled by a payment of $500.

The alternative analysis suggests that the concerned fa-ther has gain of $500 provided it can be said that he has enjoyed, or will enjoy in the future, through consumption a benefit having a fair market value of $1,000. On the other hand, the result may be otherwise if benefits to the daughter are considered as consumption by her and not the father, or if the benefit to the father is considered as being reduced by one-half by reason of the discharge, or if the value of the entire benefit received by the father is taken to be only $500 rather than $1,000. The reasons for this are fairly clear. It can be asserted that the consump-tion by one other than the debtor should not be taxed to him upon discharge unless making available that con-sumption satisfies the debtor's obligation to support the consumer. Moreover, there is no good reason why the original price set by the terms of the debt should be con-sidered in all cases as the final determination of the fair market value of what the debtor consumes. Finally, it can be argued that gain should not result from cancellation of indebtedness which involves a reduction in future consumption. Gain does not result, for example, from a discharge of a binding commitment to purchase at an exorbitant price during the next month twenty sumptuous meals at a particular exclusive restaurant.

The "concerned father" case provides helpful insight when the facts of *Bradford* v. *Commissioner* [14] are considered. A wife gave her own note in the amount of $205,000 in exchange for the payee bank substituting this note for a like amount of indebtedness owed by the husband. Later the bank forgave $50,000 of this debt. The reason the wife entered the transaction was to enable the husband to avoid impairment of his position on the New York Stock Exchange. It was held the discharge resulted in no gain because "the taxpayer was in fact poorer by virtue of the entire transaction." While it is clear that inclusion in income of the amount discharged is not necessary to correct previous erroneous assumptions as to basis of assets acquired with the loan proceeds, it is by no means clear the extent to which prior or subsequent consumption attributable to the wife should be gathered into income. The problem is insoluble.[15] This leaves only an "all or nothing" solution. Adequacy and Reduced Economic Inequality, pursued rigorously, might tip the scale toward "all," while uncertainty about the direction of Equity's pointer can justify the court's result.

14. 233 F.2d 935 (6th Cir. 1956).

15. On whether the facts constitute a gift by the wife to the husband, see Eleanor A. Bradford, 34 T.C. 1059 (1960) (no gift). If there is a gift, does the compensatory approach require that it be treated as consumption by the donor with the discharge as gain to compensate therefor? See pp. 311–17 *infra*.

b. *Reduction of Purchase Price*

The superiority of the second approach is also indicated in analyzing the "reduction of purchase price" cases. The facts of *Hirsch* v. *Commissioner* [16] convey the problem. The taxpayer acquired property for $29,000, paying cash of $10,000 and assuming a mortgage indebtedness of $19,000. Additional payments of $4,000 were made on the mortgage debt. The property, however, depreciated in value. At a time when it was worth only $8,000 the taxpayer and the mortgagee [17] agreed to discharge the balance of the debt in exchange for the payment of $8,000. Property worth $8,000 was thus acquired by the taxpayer free of liens by the payment of $22,000. No gain resulted because the effect was merely a reduction of cost. [18]

The difficulty with *Hirsch* is not that it failed to tax the balance sheet improvement but that it reached its result without any discussion of the character and use of the property in question. It will be recalled that the Supreme Court in *Helvering* v. *American Chicle Co.*, [19] when faced with the argument that the discharge of a portion of a debt assumed in the acquisition of the assets constituted a price adjustment, pointed out that the argument could not be accepted when the nature, present status, and exist-

16. 115 F.2d 656 (7th Cir. 1940).

17. This mortgagee was not the original one. When the assumed mortgage came due, the taxpayer "borrowed the same amount from another and satisfied the first mortgage." This was held not to distinguish this case from a true reduction-of-purchase-price case. 115 F.2d 656, 658.

18. For other cases reaching the same result, see Helvering v. A. L. Killian Co., 128 F.2d 433 (8th Cir. 1942); Hextell v. Huston, 28 F. Supp. 521 (S.D. Ia. 1939) (reduction of purchase price resulted in offsetting gain or discharge against loss on decline in value of purchased property); Gehring Publishing Co., 1 T.C. 345 (1942).

19. 291 U.S. 426 (1933).

ence of the acquired assets were unknown.[20] This recognition of the importance of the history of the acquired assets was ignored in *Hirsch*. This was its fundamental error.

The courts have created a number of exceptions to *Hirsch*. It is said, for example, that when the fair market value of the acquired property exceeds the purchase-money debt, immediately prior to discharge, gain upon discharge is recognized.[21] It would be better to recognize that, without regard to the relationship of the purchase-money debt and the value of the property, gain is recognized in all instances where the taxpayer fails to show that no consumption or understatement of income has occurred prior to discharge.[22] The same can be said of the exception which restricts *Hirsch* to situations involving "face-to-face negotiations between the debtor and the seller-creditor in regard to the purchase price." [23]

On the other hand, an early case, *B. F. Avery & Sons,*

20. *Id.* at 430. "We know nothing concerning the nature of the assets acquired from the Sen Sen Company, have no means of ascertaining what has become of them, or whether any of them exist. Nothing indicates whether respondent lost or gained by the transaction."

21. L. D. Coddon & Bros. Inc., 37 B.T.A. 393 (1938). "From an examination of these cases the present state of authority seems to be that where a solvent debtor is under direct obligation to make payments for physical property purchased by him or by his assignor, which is still held by him, and satisfies this obligation by paying less than the amount called for by the obligation, the property continuing to be of value sufficient to pay the indebtedness, the transaction will result in taxable income to the debtor in the amount paid by him for its satisfaction." *Id.* at 398–99. *Cf.* Comm'r v. Coastwise Transp. Corp., 71 F.2d 104 (1st Cir. 1934).

22. In L. D. Coddon & Bros., Inc., 37 B.T.A. 393, 396 (1938), the Board in its findings of fact stated that depreciation had been taken on the basis of a value in excess of the "reduced price."

23. Eustice, *Cancellation of Indebtedness and the Federal Income Tax: A Problem of Creeping Confusion*, 14 TAX L. REV. 225, 246 (1959). See Fifth Avenue–Fourteenth Street Corp. v. Comm'r, 147 F.2d 453, 457 (2d Cir. 1944), where the *Hirsch* approach was considered "irrational," but its existence and the exceptions recognized.

Inc.,[24] sometimes cited as representing another exception to *Hirsch* to the effect that it has no application where the purchased property was sold prior to discharge, does correctly emphasize the essence of the second approach. It points out that the original purchase price generated income tax computations which now require that the reduction of purchase price be included in income.[25]

24. 26 B.T.A. 1393 (1932).

25. It is worthwhile to quote from this opinion at length. At pages 1399–1400 the opinion reads: "We are satisfied that the petitioner was put to considerable expense on account of the defects in machines and equipment purchased, and we feel reasonably sure that the additional expense to which it was put exceeded the amount of the canceled notes. It has deducted in past years most, if not all, of these expenditures from income through cost of goods sold, ordinary and necessary expenses and other means. Deductions for depreciation and loss, the latter allowed for the year before us, have permitted the petitioner to offset the entire cost of the manufacturing machinery against income. These deductions were based upon the assumption that the company would actually pay the costs accrued as liabilities.

"The cost of this machinery and the cost of goods manufactured for the petitioner by the International Harvester Company, as originally agreed upon, were accrued on the petitioner's books in an open account. At a time when this account showed a large amount owing from the petitioner to the International Harvester Company, the petitioner gave its notes for the balance due. This transaction had no significance from an income standpoint. Later, some of the notes, having a total face value of $300,000, were canceled by the International Harvester Company. The cancellation took place in the taxable year before us. If all of the petitioner's transactions with the International Harvester Company had taken place in one year, the adjustment necessitated by the note cancellation probably would have been accomplished by eliminating the basis for depreciation and loss on the manufacturing machinery and reducing inventory and cost of goods sold. *Cf.* Des Moines Improvement Co., 7 B.T.A. 279 (1927). The effect of this would have been to increase net income for that year and perhaps for some later years. The total increase in net income would have amounted to $300,000.

"But the various transactions did not take place in one year. Instead, they were spread out over ten years. Income or loss of the first nine years has been computed on an accrual basis on facts known in those years, as was proper. In the tenth year it was known for the first time that $300,000 theretofore accrued as cost liability and offset against income would not have to be paid. It is not proper or possible to go back over prior years and adjust income in the light of this new development. *Cf.* Burnet v. Sanford & Brooks Co., 282 U.S. 359 (1931); Highland Milk Condensing Co. v. Phillips, 34 F.2d 777 (3d Cir. 1929); Cleveland Woolen Mills, 8 B.T.A. 49 (1927); Helvetia Milk Condensing Co., 5 B.T.A. 271 (1926). Does the fact that the cancellation occurred in the tenth year after almost all of the

Finally, it is said that *Hirsch* is inapplicable to the discharge of debt incurred subsequent to the purchase of property which serves to secure the debt.[26] Once more, a rigid balance-sheet-improvement analysis provides less help to understanding than does an analysis which draws attention to the necessity of connecting the acquisition of loan proceeds with the use to which they are put.[27]

The fact is that when these "reduction of purchase price" cases are approached from the standpoint of a "net worth increase," it appears as if gain from the discharge of the purchase price obligation is being reduced by what may be an unrealized loss on the purchased property.[28] Any such result deserves no support and quite logically leads to complete rejection of *Hirsch*. A rejection based on this ground is erroneous, however. The *Hirsch* result is wrong when the purchaser-debtor is unable to show that the original purchase price has not generated tax-reducing deductions in prior taxable periods. When he can demonstrate that no such deductions existed and that no personal consumption occurred which requires legitimation, the *Hirsch* result is appropriate.

The same analysis should be employed in evaluating

---

cost had been offset against income, and after it was too late to change the tax situation for prior years, deprive the cancellation of income tax significance?"

26. Edward W. Edwards, 19 T.C. 275 (1952) (Government sought to reduce basis of property pledged to secure debt which was discharged) .

27. The result in Edward W. Edwards, 19 T.C. 275 (1952) , which denied a basis adjustment, is questionable, however. The loans secured by the stock were obtained to secure funds to pay the purchase price. However, the possibility that the stock could have been withdrawn from the pledge and sold with a cost basis determined by the original purchase price influenced the court to distinguish Hirsch v. Comm'r, 115 F.2d 656 (7th Cir. 1940) . A case similar on its facts to *Edwards* which applied the adjustment-of-purchase-price theory is Charles L. Nutter, 7 T.C. 480 (1946) .

28. See Eustice, *op. cit.* n. 23 *supra*, at 225, 245.

those cases which hold that no gain results from a discharge of a debt on which the taxpayer is not personally liable but which is secured by a lien against his property.[29] Where the indebtedness constitutes a portion of the basis of the property, there is no reason to treat this situation differently from that where the taxpayer is personally liable. In both, the debt and its discharge for a sum less than the principal amount make possible the understatement of income during the periods prior to the discharge.[30] And in both, the taxpayer should be permitted to adjust basis and escape gain only when he can show that this did not occur.[31] Where creation of the indebtedness has not affected the basis of the property (as when incurred subsequent to the acquisition of the property), it generally will be extremely difficult for the debtor to show that recognition of gain is not necessary. Under such circumstances legitimation of personal consumption or investment will usually be necessary.

When these no-personal-liability cases are approached from the standpoint of a net worth increase, difficult and misleading questions must be asked. Should a discharge,

29. Hotel Astoria, Inc., 42 B.T.A. 759 (1940) ; P. J. Hiatt, 35 B.T.A. 292 (1937) ; Fulton Gold Corp., 31 B.T.A. 519 (1934) .

30. In Blackstone Theater Co., 12 T.C. 801 (1949) , it was held that following the discharge of a lien debt which was not a personal liability of the taxpayer, there should be no retroactive recognition of gain to account for excess depreciation taken during the years prior to the discharge. The court did not pass on the issue whether the purchase by such liens for less than their face resulted in gain in the year of purchase. The compensatory analysis indicated that gain should be recognized.

31. Fulton Gold Corp., 31 B.T.A. 519 (1934) , which permitted an adjustment of basis following the discharge of a lien debt against improved real estate is undoubtedly incorrectly decided. In Hotel Astoria, Inc. 42 B.T.A. 759 (1940) , the basis of the property subject to the lien debt apparently did not reflect the debt. It is possible under these circumstances that no gain should result from the discharge. Perhaps the same could be said where the property was farm land, as in P. J. Hiatt, 35 B.T.A. 292 (1937) .

for example, which merely brings the debt in line with the current value of the property result in gain because the achievement of an equity having a value greater than zero is made more easily attainable? Or is there gain only to the extent that the discharge increases the positive value of the taxpayer's equity? Such questions deflect attention from the essential inquiry, viz., the extent to which recognition of gain is necessary to legitimate previous consumption and/or suppositions regarding deductible expenditures or the basis of assets acquired with the loan funds.

c. The Insolvency Cases

The mischief caused by the net worth approach is also illustrated in cases in which the debtor is insolvent at the time of the debt cancellation. Both the case law and current regulations take the position that no income results from cancellation of an indebtedness by virtue of an agreement among creditors not consummated under any provision of the Bankruptcy Act "if immediately thereafter the taxpayer's liabilities exceed the value of his assets." [32] Case law goes further and finds no income when the debtor remains insolvent following the discharge, even though only one creditor participated in the transaction.[33] When the discharge makes the debtor solvent, income is realized to the extent that the assets become "clear and free of any claims of the creditors," i.e., to the extent the discharge renders him solvent.[34]

---

32. See Treas. Reg. § 1.61–12 (1957), as amended by T.D. 6653, 1963–1 C.B. 15; Astoria Marine Constr. Co., 12 T.C. 798 (1949).

33. *Cf.* Texas Gas Distrib. Co., 3 T.C. 57 (1944).

34. Lakeland Grocery Co., 36 B.T.A. 289 (1937); Conestoga Transp. Co., 17 T.C. 506 (1951) (NA). *But cf.* Dallas Transfer & Terminal Warehouse Co. v. Comm'r, 70 F.2d 95 (5th Cir. 1934) (no income although debtor probably solvent following discharge).

Thus, the net worth approach is molded to eliminate any reduction in the extent to which capital is impaired as an improvement in net worth by insisting that any such improvement depends upon the existence of assets not offset by liabilities. This shaping of the meaning of net worth improvement is not a response to the inner logic of the net-worth-improvement theory but is rather an effort to co-ordinate the income tax results with the aims of the Bankruptcy Act.[35] In fact, the net-worth-improvement theory, as applied, serves only to obscure the extent to which the Government cancels its rightful claims in an effort to give the debtor a "fresh start." That this is the heart of the matter is clear when it is remembered that the debtor may have reduced his previous tax bills by reason of either deductible expenditures or assumptions relating to the basis of assets acquired with the proceeds of the loans, and that a holding—following cancellation—of no gain amounts to relinquishment of the Government's right of reimbursement. This forgiveness of taxes is undoubtedly justified, but one must have an affection for deviousness to prefer the "explanation" presently employed to the more straightforward one here suggested.

The Government's generosity has limits even with respect to insolvents, however. Thus, the insolvent individual remains taxable on his salary,[36] and all taxpayers are taxable on the gains resulting from the sale of assets when not associated with debt cancellation, even though insolvent at the time of sale.[37]

35. The regulations provide: "Income is not realized by a taxpayer by virtue of the discharge, under section 14 of the Bankruptcy Act (11 U.S.C. 32), of his indebtedness as the result of an adjudication in bankruptcy. . . ." Treas. Reg. § 1.61–12 (B) (1957).

36. Parkford v. Comm'r, 133 F.2d 249 (9th Cir.), *cert. denied,* 319 U.S. 741 (1943).

37. Home Builders Lumber Co. v. Comm'r, 165 F.2d 1009 (5th Cir.

d. *The Gift Cases*

No doubt influenced by the precarious financial position of many taxpayers during the depression years, in 1943 the Supreme Court in *Helvering* v. *American Dental Co.*[38] threatened to eliminate gain from debt cancellation from gross income. Its technique for doing so was an expansion of the gift exclusion to include those instances in which there was "a release [by the creditor] of something to the debtor for nothing." [39] A "receipt of financial advantages" [40] was enough to warrant immunity as a gift, even though no "donative intent" on the part of the creditor existed. Although Congress in both the Bankruptcy Act and the 1939 Code had carved out certain exclusions for gains from debt cancellation, the Court's expansive generosity in *American Dental Co.* was somewhat startling.

During the approximately six years that followed, there were generally ineffective efforts made by the Government to classify cancellation transactions as instances in which

1948). There are some quite complex problems which arise when property is transferred in exchange for cancellation of a debt. Essentially they turn on the extent to which any gain from the cancellation is to retain its ordinary income character or be either eliminated or transmuted into capital gain. The key to preservation of the cancellation gain's ordinary character is to treat the transaction as if the debtor-transferor never receives as an "amount realized" on the exchange more than the fair market value of the property transferred. Thus, where the debt is $100, the fair market value $80 and the adjusted basis $70, the gain on the exchange of the property would be $10 rather than $30. Gain from cancellation of indebtedness would be $20. Where the fair market value is $60, there would be a loss of $10 and ordinary income from cancellation of indebtedness of $40 rather than a single gain of $30. The case law does not require that the components of the transaction be treated separately. R. O'Dell & Sons Co., v. Comm'r, 169 F.2d 247 (3d Cir. 1948); Lutz & Schramm Co., 1 T.C. 682 (1943). See Surrey & Warren, Federal Income Taxation 843, 849 (1960 ed.).

38. 318 U.S. 322 (1943).

39. *Id.* at 331.

40. *Id.* at 330.

the release was for "something" rather than "nothing." [41] In 1949 the Court had second thoughts. Faced with a situation in which the taxpayer could not demonstrate that legitimation of consumption, assumed investment, or previous deductions were not necessary, the Court restricted the "release for nothing" analysis by making it inapplicable when the creditor intended to, and did, get "all that he could for all that he had." [42] Moreover, the Court indicated that gift characterization would rarely exist in transactions in the ordinary course of business. This virtually terminated the debtor's opportunity to escape tax on the grounds of the gift exclusion.[43] Assuming that the thesis of this chapter is correct, at present a solvent taxpayer can escape tax on cancellation of his indebtedness only when he can demonstrate that legitimation is not necessary or that he is entitled to the provisions of the Code which permit exclusion.[44] To these the discussion now turns.

3. *The Statutory Provisions*

As already indicated, the Bankruptcy Act contains provisions excluding gain from the discharge or reduction of debts pursuant to a Chapter X reorganization, a Chapter XIII "wage earner's plan, or an "arrangement" or "real

---

41. *Cf.* Liberty Mirror Works, 3 T.C. 1018 (1944). See also Shellabarger Grain Products Co. v. Comm'r, 146 F.2d 177 (7th Cir. 1944).

42. Comm'r v. Jacobson, 336 U.S. 28, 50 (1949).

43. *Cf.* Denman Tire & Rubber Co. v. Comm'r, 192 F.2d 261 (6th Cir. 1951); Capitol Coal Corp. v Comm'r, 250 F.2d 361 (2d Cir. 1957).

44. The textual statement ignores the possibility that the cancellation may constitute a contribution of capital when the shareholder creditor forgives the debt of his corporation. See Treas. Reg. § 1.61–12 (a). The contribution-of-capital area is somewhat unique and has been dealt with elsewhere. See Sneed, *The Criteria of Federal Income Tax Policy,* 17 STAN. L. REV. 567, 604–13 (1965).

property arrangement" confirmed under Chapters XI or XII.[45] Somewhat consistent with the theory advanced throughout this discussion, the price exacted for exclusion is an adjustment of the basis of the debtors' assets,[46] except as limited by sections 372, 373, 374, and 1018 of the Code. In this case the exceptions practically eliminate the general rule.

Of more general importance, however, are the provisions of sections 108 and 1017 of the Code. Their history is quite interesting. The Revenue Act of 1939 provided that the income from the discharge of certain corporate securities would be excluded from gross income provided it was established that at the time of the discharge the taxpayer corporation "was in an unsound financial condition" and that the taxpayer consented to basis adjustments which the Commissioner would prescribe.[47] In addition, the provision was to lapse at the close of 1942. There is evidence that the primary beneficiaries of the legislation were to be railroads.[48] The Revenue Act of 1942 not only extended the provisions for three more years but more significantly, as it turned out, eliminated the requirements that the taxpayer establish his unsound financial condition and that the discharged securities be in existence on June 1, 1939.[49] In this manner what began as a provision limited

45. Bankruptcy Act, §§ 268–70, 11 U.S.C. §§ 668–70 (1964). Treas. Reg. § 1.61–12 (b).

46. Bankruptcy Act, § 270, 11 U.S.C. § 670 (1964). Treas. Reg. § 1.1016–7 (1960).

47. Revenue Act of 1939, § 215 (a), 53 Stat. 875. The provisions became §§ 22 (b) and 113 (b)(3) of the 1939 Code.

48. S. Rep. No. 648, 76th Cong., 1st Sess. 5 (1939); S. Rep. No. 1631, 77th Cong., 2d Sess. 77 (1942).

49. Revenue Act of 1942, § 114 (a), 56 Stat. 811. Railroads were dealt with explicitly in § 114 (b). These became Int. Rev. Code of 1939, §§ 22 (b) (9) and (10).

both as to time and to beneficiaries became more general in scope although still limited temporally.[50] Thereafter, the life of these provisions was repeatedly extended until made permanent by the Revenue Act of 1951.[51] In 1954 the House attempted to write into what became the 1954 Code a comprehensive treatment of the discharge-of-indebtedness area, a part of which was an expansion of the now permanent and amended 1939 legislation which broadened its coverage to all debts of corporations, whether or not represented by a security, and those of individuals incurred or assumed in connection with property used in his trade or business.[52] The Senate rejected the comprehensive treatment but retained the broadened version of the 1939 legislation.[53] This view prevailed, and constitutes the heart of section 108 of the present Code. There are few better examples of the permanency of "temporary" tax provisions.

The basis adjustments required by the regulations under section 1017 nicely illustrate the appropriateness of considering debt cancellation a revision of the amount invested by the debtor. Thus, the income from discharge is first applied against property (other than ordinary income-producing assets such as inventory and accounts receivable) the acquisition of which gave rise to the debt, then against property subject to a lien, then all other property, and, finally, against inventory notes and ac-

50. The Senate Report is quite specific about the intention to make the provision available to all corporations.

51. The extensions occurred in 1945, 1949, and 1950. The Revenue Act of 1951 deleted the sentence which would have made § 22 (b)(9) of the Code inapplicable to discharges after December 31, 1951.

52. H.R. REP. No. 1337, 83d Cong., 2d Sess. 12, A35 (1954).

53. S. REP. No. 1622, 83d Cong., 2d Sess. 13, 14 (1954).

counts receivable.[54] In making the just described second and third tier adjustments, a fairly speedy recovery of the "postponed" income is assured by requiring that depreciable property be preferred over property not subject to this allowance.[55]

The relative ease with which basis adjustments may be worked out forces the question whether sections 108 and 1017 should be expanded to cover all debt discharge cases. The difficulty in doing so, of course, is that recognition of present gain is often necessary to legitimate previous consumption or suppositions as to deductible expenses or basis of assets. Non-recognition at the price of basis adjustment only further delays the final reckoning and, in some cases, may defer it permanently. The theoretical merit of these two sections is that their mechanics draws attention to the relationship between debt forgiveness and the investment by a taxpayer at the time of the debt's creation. This merit can be enjoyed without their further expansion; moreover, if understood properly, it can be the foundation for increased comprehension of the entire debt-forgiveness area. To this end this chapter has been written.

54. Treas. Reg. §§ 1.1017–1 (a) (1), (2), (3), (4) (1960).
55. Treas. Reg. § 1.1017–1 (b)(7) (1960).

Index

Accident and health insurance, 229–39; defined, 207 n. 11; employer contributions not taxable to employee, proceeds attributable to, 233–34; history of tax treatment of, 229–33; matured endowment life insurance as, 236; overhead expenses during prolonged disability, 236; permanent loss of member or body function, 233; self-insured plans, 233–34; wage continuation payments, 233, 237–38; workmen's compensation, 235

Alimony, 265–92; characteristics of, for tax purposes (link between payments and divorce or separate maintenance, 275–81; payments to be made because of family or marital relationship, 281–86; periodicity, 281–86; receipt by wife, 286–88; validity of decree of divorce or separate maintenance, 271–75); child support, 288–89, 292; history of tax treatment of, 265–68; Revenue Act of 1942, 268–71; treatment of (alimony trusts, 266–68; amendments to underlying written instrument or decree, 277–78; income attributable to property transferred to wife, 290–92)

Allocation of receipts between income and return of capital, 29–37; see also Return of capital

Annuity, 215–25; allocation of payments between income and return of capital, 33–34; as allowance for personal injury or sickness, 231–32; definition of, 219–21; definition of investment in, 221; definition of expected return from, 222; distinguished from life insurance, 206 n. 4; dividends and interest under, 218; history of tax treatment of, 215–18; option to take lump sum, 223 n. 37

Awards, 157–60, 168

Basis, 16–23; of corporation or partnership in property contributed by shareholder or partner, 23 n. 28; of property acquired by gift, bequest, devise or inheritance, 180–86; of trustee in property contributed by trustor, 23 n. 28; part gift, part sale transaction, 174–76; substituted, 23 n. 28; see also Return of capital

Bequests, 131–38; "constructive realization," 137–38; definition of, 176–80; property transferred between spouses and members of same generation, 134

Bonds, government; see Government bonds

Cancellation of indebtedness; see Discharge from indebtedness